SAGE was founded in 1965 by Sara Miller McCune to support the dissemination of usable knowledge by publishing innovative and high-quality research and teaching content. Today, we publish over 900 journals, including those of more than 400 learned societies, more than 800 new books per year, and a growing range of library products including archives, data, case studies, reports, and video. SAGE remains majority-owned by our founder, and after Sara's lifetime will become owned by a charitable trust that secures our continued independence.

Los Angeles | London | New Delhi | Singapore | Washington DC | Melbourne

INDO-AMERICAN BILATERAL RELATIONS

INDO-AMERICAN BILATERAL RELATIONS

Politico-Strategic Partnership and the Power Dynamics

RAJESH KUMAR

Los Angeles | London | New Delhi
Singapore | Washington DC | Melbourne

First published in 2021 by

SAGE Publications India Pvt Ltd
B1/I-1 Mohan Cooperative Industrial Area
Mathura Road, New Delhi 110 044, India
www.sagepub.in

SAGE Publications Inc
2455 Teller Road
Thousand Oaks, California 91320, USA

SAGE Publications Ltd
1 Oliver's Yard, 55 City Road
London EC1Y 1SP, United Kingdom

SAGE Publications Asia-Pacific Pte Ltd
18 Cross Street #10-10/11/12
China Square Central
Singapore 048423

Published by Vivek Mehra for SAGE Publications India Pvt Ltd. Typeset in 10.5/13 pt Berkeley by AG Infographics, Delhi.

Library of Congress Control Number: 2020949365

ISBN: 978-93-5388-678-3 (PB)

SAGE Team: Amrita Dutta, Neena Ganjoo and Kanika Mathur

Dedicated to
my mother—Late Srimati Uma Devi

Thank you for choosing a SAGE product!
If you have any comment, observation or feedback,
I would like to personally hear from you.

Please write to me at **contactceo@sagepub.in**

Vivek Mehra, Managing Director and CEO, SAGE India.

Bulk Sales

SAGE India offers special discounts
for purchase of books in bulk.
We also make available special imprints
and excerpts from our books on demand.

For orders and enquiries, write to us at

Marketing Department
SAGE Publications India Pvt Ltd
B1/I-1, Mohan Cooperative Industrial Area
Mathura Road, Post Bag 7
New Delhi 110044, India

E-mail us at **marketing@sagepub.in**

Subscribe to our mailing list
Write to **marketing@sagepub.in**

This book is also available as an e-book.

CONTENTS

PREFACE

India and the USA have had different perceptions on politico-strategic, nuclear, defence, economic, trade and commercial issues at the global, regional and bilateral levels. Their relations since India's independence in 1947 have been a major factor in India's foreign policy calculations. Indo-US relations have never remained constant in the last 73 years. The relationship, from 1947 to 2020, has often been marked by instability and fluctuations. Nevertheless, in the past three decades, there has been a significant measure of stability in it. It has seen neither violent conflict nor virtual alliance in its wavering course. Today, in 2020, it has reached its peak. The two countries will be celebrating the 75th anniversary of their diplomatic relationship in 2022.

As their individual national interests have been basic to the structure and functioning of the foreign policy of either country, the two have been clashing over a number of issues having global, regional or bilateral significance. Till the beginning of the new millennium, their relations largely reflected a pattern of misunderstandings, miscalculations and missed opportunities. In the recent decades, India became a priority area for the USA only when developments in the South Asian subcontinent directly affected its global or regional policies, such as in 1962 and 1971, which witnessed the growing involvement of China, and the Soviet invasion of Afghanistan in late December 1979. Towards the end of the Cold War and with the emergence of a unipolar world in the 1990s, there was a convergence of Indian and US interests over the US–Iraq war in 1991. Further, the USA becoming the torchbearer of globalization and India becoming one of the big emerging markets for the USA in the late 1990s were significant for bringing them closer to each other.

In the last few decades, historic changes have been witnessed in their approach towards each other. In the past, the USA's relations with India were guided by its global or regional policies and were rarely bilateral, whereas India resented that the USA had subordinated their bilateral relations and interests to regional, extra-regional and global considerations. In 2020, one can see a complete turnaround in Indo-US politico-strategic relations, as the USA remains committed to cover the extra mile in helping India emerge as a global power. The foundations for this turnaround were laid during the landmark visit of PM Rajiv Gandhi to the USA in May 1985, which helped both countries in experiencing an enhanced level of security, economic, scientific, technological and defence cooperation. All these years, the two countries have struggled hard in managing their differences over various political, security and other strategic issues. The issues of Kashmir, the Treaty on the Non-Proliferation of Nuclear Weapons (NPT), Comprehensive Nuclear-Test-Ban Treaty (CTBT), India's nuclear explosions in May 1998, nuclear non-proliferation concerns and their linkages with dual-use-technology transfer and strict export controls led by international regimes dominated their relationship and consumed much energy and resources on the part of both countries.

The hallmark of the 21st-century Indo-US relations has been the complete transformation in their bilateral politico-strategic relations in the aftermath of the 9/11 attack against the USA in 2001. As on date, the two countries are cooperating with each other in fighting the war against global terrorism in a joint and coordinated manner. The visit of the then PM A. B. Vajpayee to the USA in 2004 led to the declaration of India and the USA being 'natural allies'. Another milestone in Indo-US relations was achieved during the July 2005 visit of PM Manmohan Singh to the USA, which resulted in the formalization of the historic 'Indo-US nuclear deal' between the two countries. It reflected the institutionalization of their high-level politico-strategic relationship. The 2006 visit of US President Bush to India once again showed the USA's commitment to and keenness in helping India become a major power in the South Asian region. The historic Indo-US Civil Nuclear

Agreement, 2008, brought a paradigm shift in their bilateral strategic cooperation. It helped both countries in enhancing their defence and technological cooperation to the highest level.

The momentum gained during PM Manmohan Singh's and President Bush's tenures is also being sustained under Narendra Modi's consecutive tenures since May 2014 as the PM of India. The two visits of US President Barack Obama to India, five-plus visits of Indian PM Narendra Modi to the USA and the recent visit of US President Donald Trump to India in February 2020 are sufficient to prove the historic turnaround in the Indo-US strategic partnership at the end of the second decade of the 21st century. Their engagements, under PM Modi, have witnessed a new dynamism, as the USA has become the largest trading partner of India, besides engaging with India's flagship programmes, such as 'Make in India', 'Digital India', 'Smart Cities', 'Clean India' and 'Skill India'.

It was the outcome of the new dynamism in their bilateral relations that their annual bilateral trade in 2019 crossed the mark of US$145 billion and that the sale of US defence equipment and weapons systems to India, which was almost zero till 2008, crossed the mark of US$18 billion in 2020. Their bilateral defence and strategic cooperation has moved beyond the stage of mere conduct of annual joint military exercises to the stage of joint development and production of defence projects. The present book attempts to make a comprehensive and analytical study of their engagements through the frameworks of the Next Steps in Strategic Partnership (NSSP), the Logistics Exchange Memorandum of Agreement (LEMOA), the Major Defence Partner status of India, the 2+2 dialogue, the Quad and the evolving hedging system. The factors that have led to the quantum jump in these areas are mapped out.

This work, 'Indo-American Bilateral Relations: Politico-Strategic Partnership and the Power Dynamics', assumes importance, as it covers the history of almost 75 years of Indo-US politico-strategic cooperation. The author has also incorporated the outcomes of the recent visit of President Donald Trump to India in February 2020 and the challenges and prospects of Indo-US cooperation in fighting the menace of the novel coronavirus disease (COVID-19), a new enemy to humankind.

Thus, the present book goes the extra mile in providing a comprehensive analysis of the historic transformation in Indo-US politico-strategic cooperation at the end of the second decade of the 21st century.

The present book is based on the assumption that India's perception of its role as a regional power stands transformed in the USA's global strategic formulations, thus making their defence, strategic and technological cooperation a reality. The USA's global goals in the 21st century are witnessing greater convergence with India's security perspectives. Despite the improvement in their relations, the political and strategic interests of the USA form the raison d'être for closer US–Pakistan relations, though the USA may claim that Indo-US relations are de-hyphenated from US–Pakistan relations in the 21st century. This book analyses the truth of this de-hyphenation.

The book makes a historical analytical enquiry based on primary and secondary documents. Government of India's parliamentary debate records and the annual reports of the Ministry of External Affairs, Ministry of Defence and Ministry of Foreign Affairs have been extensively used. The collected works of Jawaharlal Nehru, Indira Gandhi, Rajiv Gandhi and P. V. Narasimha Rao have also been consulted. US congressional records, hearings and many other official documents have also been used. Secondary sources, such as books, national and international journals and Indian and US newspapers, have been extensively used. Interviews of Indian Members of Parliament and government officials and experts have also been used in this book. It also uses web resources of different think tanks exhaustively.

The book consists of eight chapters, and the important contents of each chapter are outlined further.

The first chapter begins with the definitions and concepts of security and foreign policy. Titled 'The Historical Background (1947–1984)', it deals with the historical background of Indo-US relations since India's independence through the period under review. It deals with global issues such as Cold War politics and non-alignment, the differences between the two countries over the Korean crisis, India–China war in 1962, India–Pakistan war in 1965 and 1971, and India's nuclear explosion in 1974 and the deterioration in Indo-US relations with the beginning of the new Cold War in 1979.

The second chapter, 'Politico-Security Dynamics: 1985, A New Beginning', deals with two decades of Indo-US relations, from 1985 till the end of the Cold War and during the emergence of a unipolar world order in the 1990s. The chapter analyses PM Rajiv Gandhi's visit to the USA and the signing of a Memorandum of Understanding (MOU) in 1985 that ushered in a new chapter in their relations. It analyses the trends in the Indo-US relations in the context of US arms transfers to Pakistan and security situation emerging as a result of increased internal disturbances in India and also looks at the US policy of accommodating India's pre-eminence in the region, especially India's role in Sri Lanka and the Maldives in 1987 and 1988, respectively. It takes a closer look at the developments of the post-Cold War period, such as the disintegration of the former Soviet Union and its implications for Indo-US relations. The limited prospect for their defence cooperation during the 1991 Iraq–Kuwait crisis, the divergent approaches of the two countries towards terrorism in Kashmir in the 1990s and their joint war against global terrorism after the 9/11 incident are also analysed.

The third chapter, 'Nuclear Cooperation: Past and Present', analyses the factors shaping India's response to the nuclearization of the South Asian region by highlighting the threats posed to its national security towards the end of the 20th century and in the early years of the 21st century. India's response to the USA's global and regional pressures on it with regard to the NPT and CTBT during the Cold War and in the post-Cold War period is analysed. The freeze in their relationship after India's May 1998 nuclear explosions, the circumstances leading to the finalization of the 'Indo-US nuclear deal of 2005–2006' and the differences arising over the issue of its implementation are also discussed.

The fourth chapter, 'Energy Security Dynamics', analyses the factors that led to the normalization of Indo-US nuclear cooperation in the aftermath of the May 1998 nuclear explosions by India and Pakistan. It analyses the transition from their limited nuclear cooperation near the end of the 20th century to the signing of the Civil Nuclear Cooperation/Agreement in 2005/2008.

The fifth chapter, 'Defence Ties: Trajectories in the 21st Century', analyses India's growing strategic importance in the South Asian region, making it imperative for India and the USA to have long-term defence and strategic cooperation in the 21st century.

The sixth chapter, 'Transfer of Technology', discusses the transfers of 'dual-use' technology with regard to theory, practice and trends. It also looks into the imperatives for India's policy of diversifying its sources of high technologies in the absence of the erstwhile Soviet Union and the factors impeding the flow of US technology to India during and till the end of the Cold War. At the end of the second decade of the 21st century, the two countries have entered a mature stage of their joint technology incubation, joint development of technologies and co-production of defence technologies.

The seventh chapter, 'Indo-US Strategic Partnership: The Contemporary Era', focuses on the institutionalization of Indo-US strategic cooperation as visualized under 'Kicklighter's proposal', the institutionalization of the NSSP and the holding of the annual USA–India 2+2 dialogue. It highlights Indo-US engagements under the LEMOA, the Major Defence Partner status given to India, the Quad and the evolving hedging system. It also analyses the US sales of major weapons systems worth more than US$18 billion to India till 2020.

The concluding eighth chapter, 'The Road Map Ahead: Indo-US Relations at 75 and Beyond', highlights the new directions in their relationship. It gives suggestions to their policymakers for fine-tuning their relationship according to the needs and necessities of the 21st century post-COVID-19 global order.

ACKNOWLEDGEMENTS

I am indebted to all those scholars and authors whose works enlightened my ideas and broadened my vision for this work, and the extent of my debt is indicated in the footnotes. I owe particular debts of gratitude to Dr Nancy Jetly, Professor (Retd) and Former Chairperson, Centre for South, Central, South East Asia and West Pacific Studies, School of International Studies (SIS), Jawaharlal Nehru University, New Delhi. I owe lifelong obligations to her for her untiring efforts in enlightening me and sharpening my ideas.

I remain grateful to my friends Professor Sanjay Bhardwaj (JNU), Professor Sharad K. Soni (JNU), Dr Sanjeev Kumar (ICWA), Dr Saurabh (JNU), Professor Satish Kumar (CUH) and Professor Sanjeev Kumar (DU) for giving me their valuable inputs whenever I approached them. I must place on record my sincerest gratitude for Professor Amita Singh, Professor Suman Sharma, Professor Rabindranath Bhattacharya, Professor Huong (Singapore), Professor Lalitha Fernando (Sri Lanka) and Professor Sanjeev Mahajan for giving their blessings by associating me academically with the Network of Asia Pacific Schools and Institutes of Public Administration and Governance (NAPSIPAG), Colombo, Sri Lanka. They have been a great source of inspiration to me.

It is my honour to gratefully acknowledge the help, guidance and interview given to me by Professor Muchkund Dubey, former foreign secretary of the country. My heartfelt thanks are also due to Dr Ifteekkar Zaman and Major General (Retd) Dipankar Banerjee, Directors of Regional Centre for Strategic Studies (RCSS), Colombo, for providing me the opportunity to have serious interactions with the USA, Chinese, South Asian and Western scholars during a Summer Workshop in Shanghai, China, and RCSS Alumni Conference in Colombo, Sri Lanka.

I also take the opportunity to express my deepest gratitude to all the distinguished faculty members of the Department of Political Science, Guru Nanak Dev University, Amritsar, without whose guidance and encouragement I would never have reached this level. I thank all of them for being my teachers and mentors on the campus. I also owe lifelong gratitude to Professor S. P. Singh, former vice chancellor, and Professor (Dr) Jaspal Singh Sandhu, incumbent vice chancellor of Guru Nanak Dev University, Amritsar, for reposing their complete faith in me. I remain beholden to all of them.

Above all, I owe a special debt to my parents, brothers Rakesh and Manish and sister Pinki for their unstinted support. I pray to God to make the departed soul of my mother, Late Smt. Uma Devi, rest in peace. She left all of us on 29 October 2019 and could not see the publication of this volume in 2020. I would be failing in my duty if I miss out on acknowledging the support and cooperation I got from my wife Devika and son Vashu Narayan for the pains they took in providing me congenial conditions for completing this project. I also owe special debts to my in-laws and respected Late Shri N. K. Pandeya, dada jee, who constantly supported me in my all endeavours. I also acknowledge the help extended and research inputs given to me from time to time by my fellow PhD scholars Sharanpreet Kaur, Navcharan Singh and Renu.

I am extremely thankful to the publisher, SAGE, New Delhi, and its team members led by Ms Amrita Dutta, for agreeing to publish this work, and I remain beholden to them for associating me with the SAGE family on a worldwide basis.

The Historical Background (1947–1984)

International relations are a set of policies and actions between or among nations for the promotion and protection of their national interests on a continuous basis. The nature of actions is expected to either enhance cooperation or result in a conflict between or among nations. Decisions of state actors are likely to be affected by external and domestic factors. In order to have a better understanding of international relations, one must analyse both global and regional factors, besides a host of other tactical and strategic factors. Thus, analysis of the dynamics of a given set of relationships between or among nations, in terms of both the politics of the individual nations and the dynamics of their regional and global relations, is highly complex and challenging in nature.

International relations comprise all aspects of relations between countries and peoples, formal or informal, political or non-political, economic or geopolitical, peaceful or warlike, scientific or cultural, social or legal, besides interactions between state and non-state actors. On the other hand, international politics highlight only formal or political aspects of interaction between or among sovereign states represented by their governments. It is study of participation of governments for pursuing their national interests vis-à-vis each other. To realist thinkers such as Hans J. Morgenthau and Kenneth Thompson, the crux of international politics is a process of adjustment of relationships among nations in favour of a nation or a group of nations by means of power under conditions of either conflict or cooperation.

It is held that the foreign policies of countries are subsets of overall international relations. Countries strive hard for achieving their national goals or interests, which might be in conflict with those of other countries, through their foreign policies and actions. Feliks Gross[1] and Russell Fifield[2] view that the study of international politics is identical to the study of foreign policy. The foreign policy of a country is determined by both internal and external environments. A number of factors are responsible for determining foreign policy making in any country. For James N. Rosenau,[3] the foreign policy of a country is determined by size, geography, economic development, culture and history, power structure, alliances, technology, social structure, public opinion, political accountability, governmental structures and situational factors, both external and internal. A non-Western scholar, J. Bandopadhyaya,[4] takes into account geography, economic development, political tradition, domestic and international environment, military strength and national character as determinants of any country's foreign policymaking.

Foreign policy is thus a major component of international politics and is key to the relational description of international behaviour. It is difficult to understand interstate relations without a comprehension of the foreign policies of different states, which in turn are determined by their national interests. Understanding these concepts would help us in analysing the various stages of Indo-US diplomatic relations, which were largely of an asymmetric nature since their establishment in 1947. The USA was a developed country from the First World group of countries, whereas India was a least developed country from the Third World group of countries after its independence in 1947, which posed a severe challenge to the conduct of their international relations because of differing perceptions about their national interests.

The concept of national interests represents the wide interests of the people of a nation as a whole as against the narrow and limited interests of the rulers, as it was understood traditionally.[5] Charles Lerche

---

[1] Gross, *Foreign Policy Analysis*, 2, 24 and 29.

[2] Fifield, 'The Introductory Course in International Relations', 1190.

[3] Rosenau et al., *World Politics*, 19–27.

[4] Bandopadhyaya, *The Making of India's Foreign Policy*, 2.

[5] Rosenau, 'National Interest', 33–39.

and Abdul A. Said[6] have defined it as 'the general long term, and continuing purpose which the state, the nation, and the government, all see themselves as serving'. Thus, national interest is sum total of goal and objectives which a state seeks to protect or achieve in relation to each other. It can be said that a nation's foreign policy ensures that it conducts foreign relations in a way to maximize its national interests as favourably as possible.

After the Second World War, the concept of national interest became almost synonymous with the concept of national security. 'Security' was seen as some sort of protection of values that had been previously acquired. Walter Lippman has said that a nation is secure to the extent to which it is not in danger of having to sacrifice its core values if it wishes to avoid war and is able, when challenged, to maintain them through victory in such a war.[7] This definition implies that security is a matter of a nation's own power to dissuade an attack and, if need be, to defeat it. Nations, while formulating policies of national security considerations, also take into account, to a certain extent, the security interests of other nations. It is only by doing so that the acquiescence of others to resort to violence can be minimized. Mahender Kumar, an Indian scholar, states that an ideal national security policy is the one that helps in the distribution of values that is satisfactory to all nations and thus helps in minimizing the possibility of aggression. It is thus an approximation between the demands of national security and the concern for others' interests.[8] It is important for a country to take into account internal and external security considerations at the time of formulation of foreign policies. Western countries are known for giving more primacy to the military aspects of national security.

With the emergence of Third World countries at the international stage, the meaning and nature of the term 'security' underwent a change, and a viewpoint emerged that various segments of the international system are interlinked to such an extent that their security

---

[6] Lerche Jr. and Said, *Concepts of International Politics*, 6.

[7] Lippman, *United States Foreign Policy*, 51.

[8] Kumar, *Theoretical Aspects of International Politics*, 16.

and welfare depend upon each other.[9] Mohammed Ayoob[10] differs from the definition of security that dominated the Western literature on international relations during the post World War II. He defines security–insecurity in relation to vulnerabilities, both internal and external, that threaten or have the potential to bring down or weaken state structures, both territorial and institutional, and governing regimes. This definition helps one in understanding security in the case of Third World countries.

While injecting greater flexibility into the concept of security, Caroline Thomas has argued that in the context of the Third World,

> security does not simply refer to the military dimensions as often assumed in Western discussions of the concept, but to the whole range of dimensions of state's existence which are already taken care of in the more developed states, for example, the search for internal security of the state through nation making, the search for secure systems of food, health, money and trade, as well as the search for security through nuclear weapons.[11]

The concept of security includes the protection of territorial integrity, sovereignty and political independence of a country; the identification of national interests; and the promotion and protection of these by using all the resources of the nation. To Barry Buzan,[12] security is an essentially contested concept that encompasses major contradictions between defence and security, between individual and national security, between national and international security and between violent means and peaceful ends. The analysis in the following sections shows the number of occasions when differences over security badly impinged upon Indo-US relations.

One also needs to differentiate between security and strategy. Going by its traditional meaning, 'strategy' concerns only the problems around the raising, arming, equipping, movement, battle and maintenance of

---

[9] Beaton, *The Reform of Power* and the writings of Jervis, 'Co-operation Under the Security Dilemma', 167–214.

[10] Ayoob, *The Third World Security Predicament*, 8–9.

[11] Thomas, *In Search of Security*, 1.

[12] Buzan, *People*, 2–17.

a fighting force in an area of operations. However, in the present era, the strategy of a country, or the 'national strategy', concerns not only the military but the whole gamut of national existence. The national identity, internal endurance, military capacity and, lastly, will and strength as a nation to make sacrifices in order to protect these basic values are part of a country's national strategy or approach.

INDO-US RELATIONS: THE EARLY YEARS

India had strong political reasons to remain attracted towards the USA, as the latter was the oldest democracy of the world. India was treading the path of constitutional democracy, and it was natural for the country to look for cooperation with a country like the USA, as both shared many common democratic values and principles. With the beginning of bi-polar world and unfolding of the Cold War between the USA and the Union of Soviet Socialist Republics (USSR), Indo-US relations started experiencing a strain. The decision of India to pursue the path of non-alignment often resulted in an eruption of differences with US leadership in later years. As a result, Indo-US relations were often been marked by instability and fluctuations. Despite this, there has been a minimum measure of stability in Indo-US relations. Both the countries have been bound by their national interests, which have been basic to the structure and functioning of their foreign policies. They have also clashed over a number of issues having international as well as regional significance during the Cold War years. However, after the end of the Cold War and the arrival of a new world order, Indo-US relations have attained newer heights, and the two countries are set to celebrate 75 years of their diplomatic relationship in 2022.

This chapter provides a detailed discussion on the complexities of Indo-US relations between 1947 and 1984 only. However, further chapters capture the journey of Indo-US relations entering into a new phase after the signing of the memorandum of understanding (MOU) in 1985, by Prime Minister (PM) Rajiv Gandhi and President Reagan, of the historic 'Indo-US Civil Nuclear Cooperation Deal/Agreement in 2005/2008'. They help us in analysing the events that took another three decades and a half in enabling both the democracies to institutionalize

their bilateral relations and take them to the peak in 2020, thereby realizing the goals of being 'natural allies' in letter and spirit.

It is important to mention here that the present book does not
focus on Indo-US economic and trade relations, which have been a
very important component of Indo-US relations in any given period
of time since the independence of India in 1947. Even today, the USA
is the largest trading partner of India, which has been the case since
2017–2018. The initiation of the famous Green Revolution in India in
1970s with the help of USA under PL-480 program has enabled India
today in achieving food-security goals and is largely attributed to help
from the US Administration only. India benefitted immensely from the
USA because of the Science Technology Initiative (STI) agreement in
the 1960s, which enabled India to set up several technical institutions,
like the Indian Institute of Technology (IIT), Kanpur, and other medical, agricultural and scientific laboratories and research organizations
that played a very important role in India's socio-economic development. Several studies have pointed out that even in the worst phases
of Indo-US relations, such as during the Indo-Pak war in 1971 or the
nuclear explosion in 1974, the USA continued to provide much-needed
help to India purely on humanitarian grounds. The shipping of US
wheat to Indians during a famine in India for saving the latter from death
by starvation, under PL-480, is a very good example of Indo-US cooperation. This book largely focuses on the political and strategic issues,
including the Kashmir issue, politico-security dynamics, nuclear cooperation, defence and strategic cooperation and technology transfer, that
have been responsible for shaping Indo-US relations in the last 75 years.

The Independence Years

Historically, India was inspired by the US Declaration of Independence
and aspired for the USA's ideas of progress and democracy. The
USA supported India's freedom movement, as was evident when, in
1941, the US State Department advised Britain to grant a temporary
dominion status to India so that India's wholehearted support could
be gained to carry on in the Second World War effectively.[13] It was

---

[13] Hope, *America and Swaraj.*

India's interactions with the USA during the pre-independence period that resulted in the country being allowed to join the United Nations (UN) as a founding member in 1945. Many provisions in the 'fundamental rights' chapter of the Indian Constitution were inspired by the provisions of the American Constitution.

Subsequently, India's policy towards the USA was indicated in the very first policy statement of Jawaharlal Nehru on 7 September 1946, in which Nehru acknowledged the dominant role that the USA was destined to play in world affairs.[14] During the Second World War, the USA had lent moral support to the Indian struggle for independence. For this, Indian leaders were grateful, and they wanted to see the development of friendly relations with the USA. Nehru visited the USA in 1949, the first visit to a country outside the Commonwealth, after becoming the PM.

However, Nehru's declaration that India would follow the policy of non-alignment and his liking for socialist ideas disillusioned the USA. Henceforth, Nehru was regarded as anti-American and pro-Russian. The USA's attitude on Kashmir gradually turned in favour of Pakistan, and it decided to make Pakistan its military ally in the region. Pakistan later became the vortex of US foreign policy in the South Asian region. The victory of communists in China in 1949 gave further impetus to US efforts to befriend Pakistan. It has taken 70-plus years on the part of both the countries in reversing this prejudice for India, and finally, India and the USA have become 'natural allies' in the 21st century.

India's non-alignment reflected the rejection of excessive military or political association with either superpower, the USA or the Soviet Union. It reflected India's desire to avoid compromising its newly won independence and its belief in non-violence as an alternative to the military-oriented response to the Cold War. There was a realization in India that developmental needs prohibited lavish defence expenditures, and it was hoped that distance from both the blocs would give India an independent international, political and moral role. Non-alignment would also keep the Cold War away from South

[14] Nehru, *India's Foreign Policy*, 3.

Asia, enhancing India's freedom of action in the region.[15] The policy of non-alignment in the post-Cold War period is described as the seeking of 'strategic autonomy' for India in its foreign policy matters.

INDO-US RELATIONS: THE 1950s (COLD WAR PERIOD)

India resisted the USA-led world order inimical to Indian national, regional and global preoccupation. The US concerns were of 'containment of communism' and the USSR, whereas India remained preoccupied with the needs of social and economic development, the forging of political and national unity and the maintenance of its dominance over Pakistan.[16] India's views differed vastly from those of the USA, with New Delhi advocating that non-alignment, rather than alliance, was an effective policy to promote peace.[17] Nehru made this clear in his 8 March 1949 address to the Constituent Assembly when he stated, 'Our policy will continue to be not only to keep aloof from power alignments...'.[18] British PM Winston Churchill had officially announced the beginning of the Cold War in his famous speech, stating the 'lowering down of iron curtains' between the two camps, the Eastern Bloc and the Western Bloc, on 5 March 1946.

US experts state that it was only against such a background that the USA resented Nehru's policy of 'neutralism' and the decision to incorporate Pakistan into the system of anti-Soviet and anti-China alliances was given importance in US foreign policy calculations.[19] The Indian position was seen as being antagonistic to the basic objectives of the US foreign policy, that is, the containment of communism and Soviet expansionism. The US leadership was so obsessed with international communism that it regarded India's refusal to collaborate with the Western collective security efforts against the Soviet Union as a form

---

[15] Limaye, *US-Indian Relations*, 3–19.

[16] Ibid., 15.

[17] Ibid., 180.

[18] Nehru, Address to the Constituent Assembly, cited in Kumar, 'Defence in Indo-US Relations', 8.

[19] Gould and Ganguly, *The Hope and the Reality*, 5.

of open hostility undermining the USA's national interests and foreign policy objectives. It suspected India's non-alignment to be an indirect support to the communist bloc.[20]

India's Policy of Non-alignment

The US Secretary of State John Foster Dulles characterized India's policy of non-alignment as immoral. He once declared, 'those who are not with US are against us'.[21] India, on its part, did not approve of the US policy of containing communism, and it condemned the military alliances as endangering international peace and security. It was explicit that most of the differences in Indo-US international relations could be traced to the confusion over the non-alignment issue.[22] Nehru believed that 'the Soviet and Chinese leaders were nationalist's first and communist's second, and not basically aggressive'. Washington, however, looked upon Nehru as a 'political saboteur' with a soft corner for international communism.[23] One could see personality clashes on both sides of the leadership.

From India's perspective, independence and non-alignment were connected closely with the larger question of world peace. Nehru, during his first visit to the USA in 1949, emphasized that 'The preservation of peace forms the central aim of India's foreign policy. It is in the pursuit of this policy that we have chosen the path of non-alignment'.[24] India's non-alignment was thus in pursuance of its desire to emerge as an independent regional power with a certain global role to play. India often disagreed with the US policy of forging worldwide cooperation and alliances against international communism. India, even in year 2020, supports the idea of maintaining complete strategic autonomy in its foreign and security policy and has resisted all US moves of making the country a military ally of the USA, despite enjoying the

[20] Appadorai and Rajan, *India's Foreign Policy and Relations*, 215–216.

[21] Dulles, 'The Cost of Peace', 1000.

[22] Narayanan, *India and America*, 6.

[23] Jain, *India and the United States*, 10–11.

[24] Gopal, *Jawaharlal Nehru*, 377–379.

highest level of strategic cooperation with it. Thus, Indo-US relations suffered on account of misunderstandings, miscalculations and missed opportunities. The US obsession with communist USSR was such that it went ahead and roped Pakistan into two of its military alliances, the Southeast Asia Treaty Organization (SEATO) and Central Treaty Organization (CENTO). As mentioned earlier, the Cold War politics had reached the Indian subcontinent and had been impinging upon Indo-US relations. It was only after the India–China war in 1962 and the Indo-Pak war in 1971 that the USA began to take interest in the subcontinental affairs. Scholars[25] attribute US actions to the crisis in South Asia with the growing involvement of China, the eruption of the Cuban crisis in 1962 and the invasion of Afghanistan in late December 1979.

Throughout the Cold War period, the USA wanted to fit India into its global policies, whereas India opposed the USA's attempts of linking regional and extra-regional issues to its global considerations.[26] India often invoked moral values, norms and ideals in its relationship with the USA, whereas the USA always practised realist policies insofar as its interests in or relationship with India was concerned. India and the USA were at loggerheads over many other foreign policy questions involving regional and global dimensions during the Cold War period, such as the international control of atomic energy; the Kashmir issue; the Palestine and the creation of independent Israel; Indonesia; India–China relations; emergence of communist China; and the Korean crisis in early 1950. The beginning of the Korean crisis, with the involvement of communist China, and the Vietnam crisis placed India and the USA poles apart and created several differences in Indo-US relations.

Korean Crisis and Communist China Concerns

Immediately after the North Korean attack on South Korea, India[27] voted for a US-sponsored resolution in the United Nations Security Council (UNSC), calling for a cessation of the movement across the

---

[25] Palmer, *The United States and India*, 3–4.

[26] Ibid., 25.

[27] Ibid., 21, also see Brands, *India and the United States*, 52–55.

38th parallel and authorizing military assistance to the invasion by a UN force. In January 1951, India changed its stance and voted against a US-sponsored resolution in the UN General Assembly, condemning the Chinese invasion of Korea and calling for the immediate cessation of hostilities by China and its withdrawal from north of the Yalu River.[28] Despite US condemnation of the attack on South Korea inside the UN General Assembly as a conspiracy of communism emanating from the Soviet Union and China, India voted with the Soviet Union against the US-sponsored resolution.[29] This created a wedge between the two countries, given the US antipathy to China and India's efforts to befriend China. The hostility increased because of the growing Sino-Indian friendship in the 1950s and India's refusal to recognize China as an aggressor in the Korean War of 1950.

For the USA, the emergence of China was a victory of world communism, and henceforth, it continuously tried to prevent China from entering the mainstream of international relations.[30] Overlooking US concerns, India gave recognition to Mao's China on 30 December 1949, and it strongly propounded the idea of making China a member of the UNSC.[31] India's recognition of Mao's China and non-recognition of the Formosa government had compounded Indo-US relations to a very large extent. The Government of India maintained that Formosa was part of China and had to be restored to China, whereas the USA refused to recognize China and effectively blocked its entry into the UN.[32] Further, the USA continued pursuing the policy of isolating and containing 'Communist China'.[33]

The US intervention in Vietnam in 1954 in support of the French government placed India opposite to the USA, because of India's foreign policy principles that stood for the liberation of all colonies. India was thus was very reluctant to support the US moves to provide

[28] Kux, *Estranged Democracies*, 80.

[29] Sultan, *Indo-US Relations*, 44.

[30] Freeman Jr., 'The Process of Rapprochement', 1–27.

[31] Appadorai and Rajan, *India's Foreign Policy and Relations*, 217.

[32] Freeman, 'The Process of Rapprochement', 2.

[33] Hasiao and Witunski, *Sino-American Normalization and Its Policy Implications*, 1–2.

military assistance to French occupation of Indochina. By the mid-1950s, India was also apprehensive of SEATO because of Pakistan's membership in that security alliance.[34]

If one looks at things in the 21st century, the USA–India–China dynamics have changed fundamentally. In the aftermath of the 1962 war, India and China had become enemies, whereas Sino-US rapprochement was the norm after the USSR–China war in 1966. As on date, the China factor is a very important basis for closer Indo-US strategic partnership under the Indo-Pacific cooperation. The formation of the USA, Australia, Japan and India–led Quadrilateral Security Dialogue (Quad) to counter 'Rising China' has resulted in a paradigm shift in Indo-US relations in the 21st century. These changes are discussed in detail in subsequent chapters.

Kashmir Issue: The USA's and the United Nations Security Council's Role

Kashmir has remained one of the most contentious issues shaping Indo-US relations over the past several decades. India has held that the USA–USSR rivalry and the Sino-Soviet conflicts often impinged upon the security of the South Asian countries in many ways. Their confrontational policies and actions in South Asia had increased tensions in the region, restricted regional cooperation and destabilized the region. This had altered the balance of power in the region and posed challenges to India playing an important role as a leading power in the region.

Since India's independence, Kashmir, due to its strategic location, has remained a source of disagreement between the two neighbours India and Pakistan. Ever since the maharaja of Kashmir agreed to Kashmir's accession to India[35] and signed the Instrument of Accession on 26 October 1947, Pakistan's strategy has been to secure foreign intercession to change the power equation in the subcontinent as well as to undo Kashmir's accession to India.[36] Soon after the declaration of

---

[34] Mohite, *Indo-US Relations*, 79–80.

[35] Menon, *The Story of the Integration of the Indian States*, 119.

[36] Dutt, *India's Foreign Policy*, 23–24.

accession, the Pakistan government declared in 1947 that the accession was a 'fraud perpetrated on the people of Kashmir by its cowardly ruler with the aggressive help of the Government of India'.[37] In late 1947, the dispute over Kashmir flared into warfare between the new nations within the subcontinent. The Kashmir issue got internationalized after India raised the question of Kashmir in the UNSC in early 1948.

India, which lacked experience in the conduct of diplomacy in the UNSC, was quite unhappy with the position taken by the USA on the issue of Kashmir.[38] India maintained that Pakistan, being an aggressor in Kashmir, must be asked to vacate the territory it had illegally occupied.[39] The USA, instead of condemning Pakistan's aggression, pressurized India, in the UN, to hold a plebiscite, even before Pakistan had pulled its forces out of the occupied territory. From 1948 to 1953, the USA, inspired by Cold War considerations, cast doubts on the validity of Kashmir's accession to India and brought resolutions in favour of Pakistan in the UNSC, diverting attention from the basic question of Pakistani aggression in Kashmir. India was made to fall back on the Soviet Union veto[40] or the threat of that veto in the UNSC to prevent the adoption of the most patently hostile resolutions against India.

The USA, in 1953, also flirted with the idea of an independent Jammu and Kashmir, hobnobbing with Sheikh Abdullah, the then PM of Kashmir. It was amply clear that the USA's position on the Kashmir issue was largely determined by its Cold War strategy without going into the merits of the case. The main concern of the USA in the 1950s was the containment of communism, and as Pakistan was on the front line of the 'ring deterrence', it increased the USA's interest in the Indo-Pak dispute over Kashmir.[41]

---

[37] These views were expressed by the Prime Minister Liaquat Ali Khan of Pakistan in a broadcast on 4 November 1947 and see *The Dawn* (Karachi), 5 November 1947 cited in Bindra, *Indo-Pakistan Relations*, 24.

[38] Palmer, *The United States and India*, 20.

[39] Appadorai and Rajan, *India's Foreign Policy and Relations*, 219.

[40] Dutt, *India's Foreign Policy*, 9.

[41] Sultan, *Indo-US Relations*, 84–87.

India and Pakistan tried to solve the Kashmir dispute between 1953 and 1956, through negotiations and discussions, but US military aid to Pakistan in 1954 changed the whole context of the Kashmir issue and brought about a sharp deterioration in Indo-US relations. On Nehru's objection, the small US contingent in the UN observers' group was withdrawn. Thus, the Kashmir issue continued to be considered in US Cold War policies because of Pakistan's strategic location in Western and Eastern Asia, which could be crucial in the event of a war with the USSR and China.[42] Pakistan received large economic and military aid that only improved its military capacity and intensified Indo-Pak tensions.[43]

Nehru also made efforts to solve the Kashmir matter domestically, and as a result of his efforts, the Constituent Assembly of Jammu and Kashmir ratified the accession to India in 1954. Since then, India has held that the accession of Kashmir is complete in law and that, in fact, Pakistan has no locus standi in Kashmir.[44] The USA criticized the move of the Constituent Assembly of Jammu and Kashmir ratifying the accession to India. India was hurt by the unsympathetic and hostile US attitude towards its position on the Kashmir issue, affirming that the USA–Pakistan agreement had changed the entire complexion of the Indo-Pak conflict and that withdrawal of troops from Kashmir and holding of a plebiscite had become impossible.[45]

The issue of plebiscite continues to haunt India even today, as Pakistan keeps raising this issue intermittently in the UN without realizing that the UN had dropped plebiscite from its agenda since India and Pakistan fought wars in 1965 and 1971. Thereafter, the Kashmir issue has been recognized as a bilateral matter under the Shimla Agreement of 1972, and India does not accept mediation by any third party on the issue. The Kashmir issue has led to the eruption of tensions on the borders several times, besides the new era of proxy war in Kashmir in the 1980s, the Kargil crisis in 1999 and the latest abrogation of Article

[42] Bindra, *Indo-Pak Relations*, 32–33.

[43] Dixit, 'India', 25–26.

[44] Bindra, *Indo-Pak Relations*, 26–29.

[45] Chopra, *Pentagon's Shadow over India*, 70.

370 ending the 'special status of Kashmir' in the Indian Constitution on 5 August 2019 by the Modi government in India. The complexities of Kashmir arisen in the last three decades are discussed in later chapters.

Pakistan's membership in USA-led military alliances made Nehru react vehemently.[46] Nehru was of the view that the military pact between Pakistan and the USA had changed the whole balance in the region and that the USA was arming Pakistan as per its pressure tactics for compelling India to change its policy of non-alignment.[47] Nehru warned that the US arms to Pakistan would bring the Cold War to the region.[48] A US scholar, Dennis Kux, confirmed that Nehru cast apprehensions about bringing the Cold War into the subcontinent, whereas Washington shrugged off New Delhi's concern over military assistance to Pakistan, saying that given India's military superiority over Pakistan, military aid to the latter posed no 'reasonable' threat to India.[49]

A number of other scholars argued that Pakistan's membership of SEATO and CENTO had made it easier for Pakistan to raise the Kashmir issue repeatedly at international forums. Intertwining of the Kashmir issue with Cold War politics compelled India to move closer to the Soviet Union, whose support had become necessary in the UNSC for countering the US pressures on Kashmir resolutions.[50] Experts also opined that open US aid to Pakistan was an open intervention in South Asian affairs that paved the way for subsequent superpower rivalry in the region. They saw the USA as a 'hegemonic global power' that aimed at containing 'all actual or aspirant independent centers of power like India'.[51]

[46] Ibid.

[47] Nehru, *Letters to the Chief Ministers*, 442.

[48] Ibid., 454.

[49] Kux, *Estranged Democracies*, 105. For details, see Mahapatra, *Indo-US Relations into the 21st Century*, 93–96, also see, Dixit, 'India, Pakistan and the Great Powers', 25–26.

[50] Kux, *Estranged Democracies*, 111, also see, Mahapatra, *Indo-US Relations into the 21st Century*, 93–96; Palmer, *The United States and India*, 120–123; and Dixit, 'India', 25–26.

[51] Nayar, *Super Power Dominance and Military Aid*. Also see, Nayar, 'Regional Power in a Multi Polar World', 147–172.

As argued earlier, the USA tried to bring India into US policies against its communist adversaries, the Soviet Union and China. Its containment policy led the USA to seek defence links with both India and Pakistan, because of their strategic locations. India rejected the USA's offer due to its non-alignment policy and the USA's controversial stand on the issue of Kashmir. The decision was also governed by its belief in non-violence as an alternative to the military-oriented response to the Cold War and its realization that accepting the USA's offer would affect its development and curb its role in international relations. The USA's controversial stand on Kashmir persisted till the end of the Cold War period in 1991. It was the post-Cold War period, characterized as the 'new world order', that prepared sufficient grounds for bringing a transformation in Indo-US relations, which is discussed in Chapters 4 and 6.

US Arms Transfer to Pakistan as SEATO and CENTO Member

The US arms transfer during the Cold War period remained a critical component of US policy towards South Asia, which only added to the instability in the Asian subcontinent. To balance Pakistan receiving US arms, Indian scholar Venkatramani[52] states that India also tried to obtain 1,000 jeeps and 12 B-25 and 31 B-25 bombers from the Pentagon in May 1948. However, none of the Indian proposals ever materialized. At one point of time, the USA also placed an 'informal embargo' on military sales to India, because of India's conflict with Pakistan over the Kashmir question. The US president said that given the possibility of war between India and Pakistan over Kashmir, it would not be in the US interest to authorize the sale or transfer of combat materials to either Pakistan or India.[53]

India's non-alignment policy regarding defence ties and divergent security and strategic concerns hampered USA–Indian defence coopera-tion in the 1950s.[54] The USA–Pakistan security alliance relationship,

[52] Venkatramani, 'An Elusive Military Relationship', 67–68.

[53] Ibid, 70.

[54] Limaye, *US-Indian Relations*, 180; also see Palmer, *The United States and India*, 183–191.

in large measure, prevented the normalization of Indo-Pak relations, which remained a very important factor in strengthening Pakistan militarily vis-à-vis India.[55] Some experts were also of the view that the USA, by providing military aid to Pakistan, 'sabotaged' the bilateral negotiations on Kashmir held between India and Pakistan in 1953, which otherwise could have brought about a settlement of the Kashmir issue.[56] It took around 50 years for the USA to agree with India's stand on Kashmir and adopt a tougher stand against Pakistan over its support to a proxy war in Kashmir.

The USA–Pakistan military relations got a boost in the aftermath of the 1959 CENTO agreement that guaranteed the alliance partners that in the case of an attack, the USA would 'take appropriate action, including use of armed forces'.[57] A major concern existed regarding whether the US arms aid to Pakistan was to prevent Red China from exercising influence over Pakistan or if it was meant for saving Pakistan from Indian fears, rather than from any perceived threat from the Soviet Union or China.[58] The military aid to Pakistan remained a major obstacle in Indo-US relations, with it amounting to some $1.5 billion during the period 1954–1965. Over the next 10 years, it was reduced significantly, because of embargoes imposed by the USA on arms aid to either India or Pakistan in 1965 and 1971, with infrequent and limited relaxations. However, between 1976 and 1980, it once again amounted to $220 million.[59]

India strongly opposed such assistance to Pakistan by the USA, as it felt that such an action would upset the natural balance of power in the subcontinent and would bring the Cold War into the region, forcing India to divert human and physical resources needed for basic development purposes to unproductive programmes of security and defence.[60] Experts were of the view that the cost of the USA's

---

[55] Yadava, 'India's Reaction to US Military Aid to Pakistan', 80.

[56] Ibid, 81–83.

[57] Chakravarty, 'Indo-US Perspective', 61.

[58] Sultan, *Indo-US Relations*, 72–73.

[59] Palmer, *The United States and India*, 125–126.

[60] Brines, *The Indo-Pakistani Conflict*, 104.

blundering decision, which had only a marginal military advantage, was very heavy in political and diplomatic terms to all the three parties involved—the USA, Pakistan and India.[61] India's opposition to the USA–Pakistan alliance was that it placed a burden on the Indian economy. The US military aid to Pakistan had only emboldened Pakistan to launch aggression against India and make blatant use of US-supplied Sabre jets, B-57 bombers and Patton tanks freely in the 1965 and 1971 Indo-Pak wars.[62] The US arms assistance to Pakistan later became one of the important reasons for India to seek closer cooperation with the Soviet Union. Once India started receiving arms assistance from the Soviet Union, Indo-US relations became even more complex.

Consequently, in the mid-1960s and early 1970s, politics of the region had changed completely, as the influence of both the superpowers in the South Asian region had increased considerably, besides causing a split in the communist bloc itself. The US arms transfer to Pakistan continued to act as a major bone of contention in Indo-US relations. It was only after the end of the Cold War in 1991 that a significant departure could be seen in the US arms transfer policy towards Pakistan because of the latter's nuclear programme. It would be interesting to read in Chapter 7 that the historic turnaround in Indo-US relations in the 21st century has made India one of the largest beneficiaries of US arms transfer in 2020.

INDO-US RELATIONS: THE 1960s

Indo-US Defence Cooperation: After the India–China War of 1962

As discussed earlier, many differences existed between India and the USA on the latter's role in South Asia. India's main charge against the USA was that the latter's political and strategic policies were directly in conflict with India's own policy of keeping the region free from

---

[61] Harrison, 'India', 10 cited in Sultan, *Indo-US Relations*, 75.

[62] Yadava, *US-Pakistan Relations*, 44.

any of the external powers' influence. US arms given to Pakistan also unleashed an arms race in the subcontinent at the cost of the much-needed economic development. The USA–Pakistan military nexus also had its own impact on Indo-US relations because it emboldened Pakistan to not settle the Kashmir issue with India.

However, an important change ensued in US policy in the early 1960s. Unlike Dulles's denunciation of non-alignment as 'immoral', the Kennedy administration recognized the importance of non-alignment as the third force in the emergence of a 'pluralistic international system'.[63] India's role in the Cold War period was perceived with greater understanding, and India was viewed as a natural leader of the new group of nations in Asia and Africa.

The 1962 Sino-Indian border conflict brought a perceptible change in Indo-US relations. On India's request, the USA, along with its allies, promptly rushed with emergency military assistance and diplomatic support. However, Pakistan objected that provision of arms to India would pose a serious threat to it. Despite US pressure, India granted no concessions in Kashmir to Pakistan, because of which only a fraction of the promised US arms assistance was delivered to India.[64] It became clear that the 1962 Sino-Indian war had caused only a short-term shift in the US policy towards India. The USA's commitment to Pakistan remained basically unchanged and was sufficient to place a check on any serious Indo-US defence cooperation. S. P. Limaye[65] considered that US military help to India in the aftermath of the 1962 war with China was also a means for the USA to contain China in Asia. It was in consonance with the USA's overall Cold War strategic objectives for the region.

The US military help to India in October 1962 comprised of special clothing for high-altitude warfare, developed from the Korean experience and the sharing of results of the US army's research on fatalities

[63] Crabb Jr., *The Doctrine of American Foreign Policy*, 144, cited in Mohite, *Indo-US Relations*, 33.

[64] Thomas, *The Great Power Triangle and Asian Security*, 67.

[65] Limaye, *US-Indian Relations*, 181.

from trauma suffered in fighting in extremely cold conditions and high altitudes. However, India showed no interest.[66] In 1960–1961, a delegation of the US company Lockheed came to India with a proposal to set up a plant to manufacture F-104 fighter aircraft and other Lockheed products. However, it did not find any positive response from India. After the Chinese invasion of 1962, India's request to the USA included fighter aircraft, and air force pilots, until Indian pilots could be trained. Before President Kennedy could take a decision, China declared a unilateral ceasefire on 22 November 1962.

Although the US Ambassador Bowles observed that the Sino-Soviet split and Sino-Indian war had 'created an unparalleled opportunity for change in our Asian policies',[67] in effect nothing changed. Thus, there were cases of missed opportunities in Indo-US relations. It must be mentioned here that after a gap of almost six decades, Lockheed Martin has entered into a tie-up with Tata Advanced Systems for the production of F-16 wings in India for export, as part of the 'Make in India' initiative, emphasizing stronger defence ties with India under changed circumstances. Details on this are provided in Chapter 7.

In November 1963, the Indian Air Force (IAF) and the United States Air Force (USAF) did, however, hold a joint air exercise, 'Shiksha'—the first and only air exercise held between the two sides till now. Shiksha, in fact, turned out to be a limited air exercise comprising four air forces, including the Royal Air Force and the Royal Australian Air Force. This exercise was thus a symbolic measure of solidarity to a country that had not even participated in the Sino-Indian war save for military supply missions.[68]

In February 1964, the US president approved the 5-year $500 million programme for India. India was told to draw up its own defence plan and set its own priorities, rather than the USA doing it for India. However, there remained US concerns that such assistance should not hurt India's economic development programme through the latter

---

[66] Ray, 'Time to Shed Diplomacy by Harangue'.

[67] Schaffer, *Chester Bowles*, 239–274. Also see, Kux, *Estranged Democracies*, 215.

[68] Schaffer, *Chester Bowles*, 244. Also see, Kumar, 'Defence in Indo-US Relations', 20 and Palmer, *The United States and India*, 191.

spending too much on defence and that India should not seek equipment from the USA that would create fresh trouble with Pakistan.[69]

The US military aid was programmed to equip India with six mountain divisions (a total of 10 were raised), better communications, transportation and air defence capabilities and provide assistance to Indian defence industries. The US administration did not, however, agree to the supply of three squadrons of the F-104 Starfighter supersonic aircraft. Thus, differences had formed even before an accord was reached.[70] This only further fuelled Indian suspicions that the US support was contingent on the objective of containing China while ensuring that Pakistani sensitivities remained protected.[71] Two other possible reasons for the differences were the USA's insistence on dollar payment for the aircraft and Washington's reluctance to permit co-production of F-104s, as it would have involved granting licences to Indian public sector companies to manufacture items produced by US private corporations.[72] Besides, there were other reasons too; for instance, the sale of any form of offensive military equipment would have affected the security of Pakistan.[73]

Despite India allowing the Central Intelligence Agency (CIA) to place secret nuclear-powered sensor devices in the Himalayas capable of collecting data on Chinese nuclear tests, direct US arms transfers to India were not of a sufficient size and could not make any impact on the Indian military establishment. US arms aid to Pakistan, on the other hand, tended to involve the entire subcontinent in the Cold War, alter the normal balance of power in South Asia and force India to devote more attention and resources than it otherwise would have to military preparations and planning.[74] Disenchanted with the

---

[69] Kux, *Estranged Democracies*, 229.

[70] Kux, *Estranged Democracies*, 229. Also see, Palmer, *The United States and India*, 187 and Schaffer, *Chester Bowles*, 260–263.

[71] Limaye, *US-Indian Relations*, 182 and also see, Schaffer, *Chester* Bowles, 261.

[72] Limaye, *US-Indian Relations*, 181.

[73] Lt Col John A. Caputo (USAF), *The Indo-Soviet Relationship and How It Affects US Military Assistance to India*, 19 cited in Limaye, *US-Indian Relations*, 182.

[74] Palmer, *The United States and India*, 206 and Schaffer, *Chester Bowles*, 256.

USA, India turned to the Soviet Union, which by then had resumed a more neutral stand on the Sino-Indian dispute and had offered to begin supplies of MiG-21 fighter aircraft. Thus, in September 1964, 3 months after India and the USA reached a military aid accord, Defence Minister Chavan signed an agreement with Moscow for the import of 45 MiG-21 interceptors.[75] On 11 September 1964, Chavan signed an accord with Moscow under which the Soviet Union agreed to provide 45 MIG-21 and to set up factories in India to assemble another 400 MiGs.[76]

The 1962 war did provide an opportunity for the strengthening of the Indo-US defence cooperation, which remained completely unrealized because of the perceived differences of India and the USA over regional and global security issues. The Indo-US defence cooperation could not be sustained for a longer period, as the USA and Britain had been making another bid to resolve the Kashmir dispute. Surjit Mansingh[77] holds the view that several conditions were placed before India—to hold a series of abortive talks with Pakistan on Kashmir, lower its ceilings on rupee and foreign exchange outlays for defence expenses, delay its decision on the purchase and manufacture of fighter aircraft and, lastly, accept a large supervisory establishment of US personnel—in return for US military help. The then US ambassador[78] in India added that Indo-US political–security relations did not receive much priority and urgency as the US administration focused much of its attention principally on the Soviet challenge in Europe and the Caribbean and the escalating dangers it saw in Southeast Asia. The military assistance programme ended abruptly as the USA suspended all military aid to both India and Pakistan following the outbreak of the Indo-Pak war in September 1965.[79]

The Indo-US defence cooperation since the mid-1960s remained minimal because of two reasons: first, the Indo-Soviet relationship and,

[75] Kumar, 'Defence in Indo-US Relations', 21.

[76] Kavic, *India's Quest for Security*, 198–200 and Schaffer, *Chester Bowles*, 263–264.

[77] Mansingh, *India's Search for Power*, 77.

[78] Schaffer, *Chester Bowles*, 245.

[79] Thomas, *The Great Power Triangle and Asian Security*, 75–77.

second, the US reluctance to transfer to India advanced military technology. Indira Gandhi, who had become PM in 1966, was very critical of the US bombing of North Vietnam, along with the former Soviet Union, and the USA's deeper involvement in the Vietnam crisis.[80] It exposed US limitations towards India after the India–China war in 1962. However, Pakistan moved closer to China and even entered into a border agreement with China on 22 March 1963, ceding hundreds of miles of Indian territory in Kashmir to China.

Much water has flown down since then. The USA is now more than keen to help India in the defence sector through transfer of technology and joint production of weapon systems under the 'Make in India' programme launched by PM Narendra Modi. It is pertinent to mention here that US President Trump visited India in February 2020 and offered similar help to India to build its defence capabilities in the light of threats emerging in and around the Indo-Pacific region. It is sheer coincidence that the US policy towards South Asia has come full circle; from banking on Pakistan during the Cold War period, it is ready to bank on India in the 21st century.

India–Pakistan War of 1965

Pakistan, having lost all hopes of gaining Kashmir through international pressure exerted through a UNSC resolution, started an undeclared war with India by sending infiltrators into the valley in August 1965. On 1 September 1965, Pakistan attacked India with US-supplied Patton tanks across the international border. US-supplied military equipment were used openly by Pakistan despite its repeated assurances in the past that there would not be any such misuse. While New Delhi was outraged that Washington did little to prevent Pakistan from using weapons it had supplied to it, the Pakistanis were upset that despite being an ally, the USA had not only declined to help them against India but had also decided to cut off arms supply to them. For Stephen P. Cohen,[81] the arms embargo against both India and Pakistan

---

[80] Kamath, 'Security Considerations in Indo-US Relations', 127.

[81] Cohen, 'South Asia and United States Military Policy', 113 cited in Limaye, *US-Indian Relations*, 184.

marked the beginning of a new US policy. As the US president was preoccupied with the Vietnam conflict, he was unwilling to intervene on behalf of one or the other country and permitted the US State Department to make a final determination of US policy.

India openly criticized the US military aid to Pakistan that the latter used blatantly, including the Patton tanks, F-86 Sabre jets and the F-104 supersonic fighter aircraft. It was a complete reversal of US President Eisenhower's assurance to India in 1954 that the military equipment supplied to Pakistan would not be used against India.[82] Despite the US administration's neutrality during the 1965 war, in India's view, the USA failed to take any action against Pakistan for using US-supplied weapons against India. For Pakistan, no help came from the USA, which it had counted on as an ally. Overall, it was the USA's larger geopolitical interest, especially its involvement in the Vietnam crisis, which was the important reason for it not coming to the help of either country.[83] H. W. Brands added that the reason for USA maintaining neutrality during the 1965 Indo-Pak war was its increased involvement in the Vietnam crisis.[84] It was therefore not averse to letting the Soviet Union take a proactive role in South Asia. The Soviet Union, which had been making efforts to balance its relations with India and Pakistan, invited the leaders of both countries, and the Tashkent Declaration was formalized on 10 January 1966.[85]

The Soviet Union's action was an attempt on its part to wean Pakistan away from China, whereas the US act of resuming supply of spares for military equipment to Pakistan was also in the direction of not allowing Pakistan to move closer to China. It was also the result of Sino-Soviet split and an attempt to keep the US out of picture and

[82] Mohite, *Indo-US Relations*, 32–33 and Sultan, *Indo-US Relations*, 95.

[83] Mohite, *Indo-US Relations*, 115 and for similar views see, Schaffer, *Chester Bowles*, 269.

[84] Brands, *India and the United States*, 112–113.

[85] 'India–Pakistan', *Kessinger's Contemporary Archives*, 21187. Also see Kaushik, *Soviet Relations with India and Pakistan*. For Tashkent Declaration see, Singh, *Indo-Pak Relations*.

build relations with both the countries.[86] However, things changed. Nixon had won the presidential election on the assurance that he would get the USA out of the Vietnam conflict, for which his administration was ready to move closer to China. As Pakistan had moved closer to China after the 1962 war, it was ready to play the useful bridge for Sino-US rapprochement in the US strategy of mending with China. Thus, Pakistan emerged as the 'most allied ally' of the USA due to its readiness to play the mediator's role.[87] Indo-US relations continued to remain caught in the US-led 'zero-sum game' with India's South Asian neighbours.

INDO-US RELATIONS: THE 1970s

The two superpowers, the USA and the USSR, were obliged to adhere to the outcomes of the détente that had come into being in the aftermath of the 1962 Cuban Missile Crisis. Several arms control measures, such as the Anti-Ballistic Missile Treaty and the 1972 Strategic Arms Limitation Talk Agreement (SALT-I), were concluded between the two superpowers. Sino-US rapprochement was also under operation. Many important disarmament treaties, such as the Outer Space Treaty, the Seabed Arms Control Treaty and the Non-Proliferation Treaty (NPT) of 1968, were formalized under the UN's roof. The NPT resulted in the breaking out of a complete deadlock between India and the USA, which continued to impinge upon their bilateral relations for the next five decades to come.

India–Pakistan War of 1971 and Indo-Soviet Treaty of Peace and Security, 1971

The developments in the early 1970s, such as the emergence of the Bangladesh crisis and Pakistan's mediating role in Sino-US rapprochement, had changed the security dynamics of the South

---

[86] Dixit, 'India', 41 and Government of India, Ministry of External Affairs, *Annual Report 1967–1968*, 11.

[87] Dixit, 'India', 25–29. For detailed analysis of US involvement in Vietnam and its effort to mend relations with China, See Brands, *India and the United States*, 115–139 and *New York Times*, 13 April 1967.

Asian region. As China had developed serious differences with the Soviet Union, it was moving towards a reconciliation with the USA. Globally, communist camps had experienced a vertical split. The USSR and China had turned into severe enemies of each other. Thus, the developments of the early 1970s were going to make the balance of power pentagonal, as the USSR and India moved closer to each other and the USA moved closer to China and Pakistan. It was the turn of serious disruptions erupting between the two democracies of the world, India and the USA, because of the US pursuance of gunboat diplomacy against India during the India–Pakistan war in 1971. S. D. Muni[88] added that the USA, which remained neutral during the 1965 India–Pakistan war, did an about-turn in 1971 and openly sided with Pakistan, at the cost of its relations with India, which led to the emergence of Bangladesh.

While there was a triangular balance of power between the USA, the USSR and China at the global level, in the South Asian region, India and the Soviet Union were on one side, and the USA, Pakistan and China represented the other side.[89] Thus, the Bangladesh war in 1971 had serious implications for Indo-US relations. The USA thought that any success for the Soviet Union-backed India in the Bangladesh conflict would mean a victory for the Soviet Union. In the interest of containing Soviet power, India must therefore be opposed.[90]

In the light of the developments of the early 1970s, the USA agreed to sell Islamabad, as an exception to the continuing restrictions on US military aid to the subcontinent, a $40 million package of weapons.[91] Marking a departure from the USA's earlier stand of displeasure at the growing Islamabad–Beijing ties, Nixon unhesitatingly sought President Yahya Khan's help to convey to the Chinese leadership his interest in opening to China.[92]

[88] Muni, 'Indo-US Relations', 13.

[89] Kamath, 'Security Considerations in Indo-US Relations', 127.

[90] Ibid., 128.

[91] Brands, India and the United States, 130.

[92] Ibid., 124.

India responded to such US actions by formalizing Indo-Soviet relations and signing the 1971 Indo-Soviet Treaty of Friendship and Peace.[93] On 2 December 1971, Washington announced the suspension of military sales worth $70 million to India, and in pursuit of its support for Pakistan, the USA ordered the sailing of USS Enterprise into the Bay of Bengal as part of its gunboat diplomacy.[94] Despite India being burdened with millions of Bangladeshi refugees, the USA supported the West Pakistan regime and continued with its arms supply. India demanded that the USA stop the supply of such aid until Pakistan stops its military action in East Pakistan.[95] In order to seek US support on the emerging refugee crisis, PM Indira Gandhi visited the USA and tried her best to convince the US president to use his proximity with the Pakistani leadership to end the emerging humanitarian crisis, but all in vain. India's point of view was also made clear by diplomat T. N. Kaul, that India did not want a military conflict with Pakistan, as it would be suicidal for both countries and the only gainers would be outside powers.[96]

In the backdrop of the 1971 crisis, India entered into the Indo-Soviet Treaty of Friendship and Cooperation[97] on 9 August 1971.[98] Criticism of the Indo-Soviet treaty by US media started shortly, which described it as Moscow leading 'a major foreign policy coup'. The Indian government castigated Washington for abetting 'genocide', and the Indian media declared, 'The Nixon Administration has chosen to pursue a policy of deliberate cynicism in the face of a massive human tragedy'.[99] India got furious with the USA once war broke out on 3 December 1971, as the USA labelled India as the 'aggressor' at

---

[93] Kamath, 'Security Considerations in Indo-US Relations', 128; Mohite, *Indo-US Relations*, 81; Brands, *India and the United States*, 129; and Bindra, *Indo-Pak Relations*, 140.

[94] Dutt, *India's Foreign Policy*, 102–110.

[95] Government of India, *Annual Report 1971–72*, 75.

[96] Kaul, *The Kissinger Years*, 37.

[97] For details of Indo-Soviet treaty see, Bindra, *Indo-Pak Relations*, 254–258.

[98] Ohajunwa, *India-US Security Relations*, 66.

[99] Palmer, *The United States and India*, 48–50, cited in Brands, *India and the United States*, 133.

the UN, thereby vindicating allegations by experts, after the USA's stand and its subsequent resolutions in the UN, that it was aiming at the containment of India.[100] The US administration responded by cancelling the licences of all US arms sale to India and declared, 'India bears the responsibility for the hostilities that have ensued'. It introduced a resolution in the UNSC on 5 December 1971 demanding the withdrawal of Indian forces from East Pakistan.[101] The USSR saved India from embarrassment by casting its veto that was in line with the formalization of its friendship and security treaty with India, which was definitely going to impinge upon future Indo-US relations. On the 1971 crisis, Henry Kissinger[102] admitted that the US response to the events in East Pakistan in 1971 was largely inspired by the secret opening to China. It was a big setback for the USA too, as US credibility was at stake because of the dismemberment of its ally, Pakistan, at the hands of India, a close friend of the Soviet Union.

Another scholar, citing Kissinger, added, 'the Administration converted a regional South-Asian conflict into global showdown between the superpowers'.[103] The developments proved that on most occasions, regional issues got entangled with US global considerations. Undoubtedly, the Bangladesh crisis reflected a direct conflict between the strategic interests of India and the USA. India's regional goals always clashed with the global interests of the USA. For India, it always looked at the USA for delinking of global issues from regional issues besides being treated at par with Pakistan. This dilemma of India continued in future too.

However, Dilip Mohite highlighted another dimension to the 1971 crisis and said,

> US containment policy towards India had got unfolded as it resorted to a tacit alliance with Pakistan and Iran on India's western flank and Pakistan and China on its north-eastern regions, thereby pursuing a strategy of

---

[100] Ohajunwa, *India-US Security Relations*, 66.

[101] Palmer, *The United States and India*, 52–53, cited in Brands, *India and the United States*, 135.

[102] Kissinger, *White House Years*, 846, cited in Mohite, *Indo-US Relations*, 108.

[103] Brands, *India and the United States*, 136.

inter-regional balancing in its determination to contain India. This was aimed to facilitate the American role as the security manager of South-Asia, to enhance the Sino-US rapprochement against the Indo-Soviet ties and to facilitate the operationalization of the US naval base in Diego Garcia.[104]

From the arguments, it is explicit that during the 1971 crisis, both the USA and India were guided by their divergent interests. The USA resorted to favourable balance of power, whereas India's interest was in ensuring regional stability and the country's security. It was clear that the power politics had taken precedence over the humanitarian crisis. Thus, the Bangladesh crisis confirmed that the USA gave topmost priority to its strategic interests, even at the cost of its relations with India. It did not miss the opportunity to exploit the situation arisen out of the Sino-Soviet rift, as well as the Indo-Pakistan conflict, and adopted policies that would embarrass India and the Soviet Union.

During the 1971 war, on the one hand, Pakistan received substantial quantities of military aid from the USA and, on the other hand, the USA stopped the planned $87 million economic assistance to India. The US policy was directed towards not making any contribution to the Indian economy that would have made the Indian government's task to sustain the military efforts easier.[105] As a result of US actions, relations between both countries virtually came to a standstill, especially when President Nixon called upon the UNSC on 12 December 1971 to take emergency action to halt the fighting between India and Pakistan and asserted that 'East Pakistan is virtually occupied by Indian troops'.[106]

India was not going to forget the Nixon administration ordering the US Seventh Fleet into the Bay of Bengal in support of Pakistan. The nuclear-powered carrier USS Enterprise, the largest aircraft carrier of the USA worth about 100 fighters' bomber aircraft on board, reconnaissance aircraft, helicopters and small cargo planes, sailed towards the Bay of Bengal in a show of force.[107] The movement of the naval

---

[104] Mohite, *Indo-US Relations*, 132–133.

[105] Kissinger, *White House Years*, 901, quoted in Palmer, *The United States and India*, 54.

[106] Dutt, *India's Foreign Policy*, 102–103.

[107] Ibid.

ship was intended to provide clean political and military support for Pakistan. US global objectives were clearly paramount to US policies in South Asia.

An important consequence of the 1971 Indo-Pak conflict, however, was that the Indian victory made the USA more conscious of the new reality that India was a major power and could play an important role in South Asia. For the first time, President Nixon acknowledged India as 'South Asia's most powerful country'.[108] There was a growing realization on the USA's side that a powerful India was in the interest of world peace. During his 3-day visit to India in 1974, Kissinger said, 'India's size and position gave it a special role of leadership in South-Asian and in world affairs'.[109] Praising Jawaharlal Nehru's vision and concept of non-alignment, he claimed that the USA now accepted non-alignment, thus reflecting a clear-cut shift in US policy towards India.

India's military success against Pakistan and consequent emergence as the obvious dominant power in the region supported by the Soviet Union established it as a force to reckon within South Asia. 'By the end of Nixon-Ford Kissinger years, Indo-US relations had reached a certain degree of stability', with the parties 'recognising that each was of some importance to the other and had to be taken into some account'.[110] There had been no worthwhile defence relations between New Delhi and Washington for almost 8 years starting from 1965, till March 1973, when India purchased $91 million worth of communications equipment to complete the Peace Indigo air radar defence system installed in the Himalayas.[111]

On the whole, arms transfer to India remained a non-starter throughout the 1970s. The 1979 developments were very important for Indo-US relations, as they were to lead to a revival of politics of security in Indo-US relations as a result of the Cold War coming close to India's north-western borders. USSR's invasion of Afghanistan in

---

[108] Appadorai and Rajan, *India's Foreign Policy and Relations*, 215.

[109] *The Statesman*, 29 October 1974.

[110] Gould and Ganguly, *The Hope and the Reality*, 10.

[111] Limaye, *US–Indian Relations*, 185.

1979 was a landmark event that led to the collapse of 'détente' at both global and regional levels and marked the beginning of the 'new-cold war' phase.

INDO-US RELATIONS: THE 1980s

Afghanistan Invasion in 1979 and the Front-line Status of Pakistan

The invasion of Afghanistan in 1979 by Soviet forces and the US hostage crisis after the Iranian Revolution had made things complex for the US security planners. The newly created USA–Pakistan–China axis had serious security implications for India. The US stakes in the region had increased considerably. The new-cold-war considerations compelled the USA to place all its bets on Pakistan as the frontline state against its war against the USSR. US policymakers would never have visualized that their obsession with getting Afghanistan vacated by the USSR forces with the Pakistan-trained mujahedeen's help would trouble them for several decades to follow. After the end of the Cold War and withdrawal of the USSR forces, Afghanistan was to become the epicentre of global terrorism in the 21st-century world order. It would be Afghanistan that would be attacked by the USA in 2001 in the name of the global war on terrorism (GWOT) in the hunt for Al-Qaeda chief Osama Bin Laden after the 9/11 attack in 2001.

Considering the geostrategic importance of Pakistan in the wake of the Soviet Union occupation of Afghanistan and the loss of Iran, the USA was prepared to maintain a complete silence over Pakistan's nuclear programme. In 1981, President Reagan used his waiver to the Symington Amendment in favour of Pakistan, which was a clear indication to Pakistan that the USA's need to supply arms to Afghan mujahedeen through Pakistan territory outweighed its non-proliferation objectives.[112] This changed attitude of the USA would impinge upon Indo-US nuclear cooperation throughout the 1980s.

---

[112] Vas, 'Pakistan's Security Future', 59.

In mid-1981, after Pakistani President General Zia's refusal to accept the $400-million-worth military aid offered by the Carter administration, the Reagan administration offered a 5-year economic assistance package and supplied $3.2 billion's worth of armour and support equipment, along with F-16 aircraft, to Pakistan.[113] This was a very significant development having serious security implications for India. Pakistan had acquired a special position and had become a 'front-line state' in the US strategic calculations. The development of the USA, Pakistan and China coming together posed a serious threat to India's security, and the region had got enmeshed in the new cold war between the two superpowers.

India wanted the Soviet Union to withdraw its forces from Afghanistan, as they had increased the possibility of superpower confrontation in the region. The Indian leadership[114] strongly objected to the fresh induction of US arms into the region and the introduction of superpower confrontation threatening the peace and security of the region and preventing any normalization of Indo-Pak relations fostered in the spirit of the Shimla Agreement of 1972.

India responded to this new challenge by building a strong defence force and made heavy purchases from the UK, France and Sweden for the modernization of its forces. It even resumed official-level talks with China in 1982 to resolve the boundary question, and all these developments culminated in an important shift in the role of the extra-regional power in the region. Thus, the early 1980s demanded a new Indian approach towards the major powers of the USSR and the USA. It made sense for India to diversify its defence procurements, reduce its dependence upon the USSR and give preference to Western technologies.

India's new approach towards the USA was evident during PM Indira Gandhi's visit to the USA in August 1982, during which she emphasized correcting US misperceptions about India's relations with the Soviet Union. She openly sought US foreign investment and US

---

[113] Thomas, *The Great Power Triangle and Asian Security*, 59 and Brands, *India and the United States*, 167.

[114] *India and Foreign Review* (New Delhi), 1–14 February 1980, 15.

technology transfers so as to augment India's exports, improve India's balance of payments and strengthen the country's self-reliance.[115] The Western world, through its intelligence agencies, had arrived upon the conclusion that the Soviet Union was heading to a severe economic, social and political crisis. The failure in controlling the Chernobyl nuclear power plant accident fallouts badly exposed the inherent weaknesses on the USSR's domestic front. It was time for Mikhail Gorbachev to move to the centre stage of Soviet politics. President Gorbachev unleashed policies of 'Glasnost' and 'Perestroika' that brought an end to the new cold war with the collapse of the Soviet Union in 1991 and the beginning of a new world order, in the words of President Bush (Sr.).

It was imperative for India to take note of the changing world order and take appropriate measures so as to ensure that it was not caught unprepared under the changed circumstances. Thus, Indira Gandhi's visit to the USA marked the beginning of a new chapter in Indo-US relations; her visit also generated a better climate of goodwill for India in the USA. The most vexing problem of resumption of fuel supply for the Tarapur Atomic Power Station (TAPS) was settled. Any improvement in Indo-US relations was bound to get affected by the issue of supply of sophisticated military equipment to Pakistan.

INDO-US NUCLEAR COOPERATION
(THE COLD WAR PERIOD)

Indo-US relations, throughout the period of the Cold War, had been a casualty of India's and the USA's divergent perceptions about the nuclear issue. India's nuclear policy was formulated to meet the fundamental problems facing the country after independence. India's first PM Jawaharlal Nehru[116] foresaw the utility of the energy in augmenting power generation and its possible use in agriculture, industry and medicine. Since India's independence, its nuclear policy has been: first, to abjure from making nuclear weapons; second, to develop

---

[115] Dixit, *Across Borders*, 151.

[116] Nehru, *Speeches* (September 1946–May 1949), 24–25.

and use nuclear energy for peaceful purposes; third, to work for and support nuclear disarmament and nuclear arms control measures; and fourth, not to accept the discriminatory international inspection and safeguards in respect of national nuclear facilities.[117]

The first occasion causing an eruption of differences on the nuclear issue between India and the USA was the creation of the International Atomic Energy Agency (IAEA) on 23 October 1956, and the issues of safeguards and control and India's and the USA's divergent stands on the NPT constantly served as irritants between the two nations.

India reacted strongly to the 'Atoms for Peace' proposal of President Dwight Eisenhower, which it saw as an attempt at using the safeguards of the IAEA to maintain and prolong the predominant position of countries already advanced in nuclear science and technology. India and the USA differed on many crucial issues while negotiating the scope and powers to be given to the IAEA. The differences were so predominant that India had emerged as a leading critic, on behalf of newly independent countries, of the US-led IAEA safeguards system at the international level.

India and the USA adopted conflicting positions on the nuclear non-proliferation issue that was several decades old, dating back to 1968, when the NPT treaty was finalized. The US administration wanted India to be a signatory to the NPT, which India did not accede to. The matter became much worse when India carried out a peaceful nuclear explosion (PNE) in 1974. The USA considered India's nuclear explosion as a challenge to the nuclear non-proliferation regime built around the NPT. India condemned the series of actions taken by the US government as discriminatory and as an effort to slow the progress of the country.

Differences over the nuclear issue greatly complicated the overall course of the Indo-US relationship since the late 1960s. During the 1970s, this issue became much more complicated, as well as vexing. The two countries came to a sort of clash on the USA's reluctance to supply fuel to India for TAPS. It was a reflection of their ideological

---

[117] Kaushik, 'India's Nuclear Policy', 23–24.

stands on the NPT 1968 taken at the global level.[118] India had not been a signatory of the NTP, stating it to be discriminatory. The differences over the NPT placed India and the USA poles apart, as India emphasized the need for achieving the goals of time-bound disarmament, the CTBT, a complete freeze on the proliferation of nuclear weapons and the means of delivery and a substantial reduction in the existing stocks.

India favoured an early solution to the problem of non-dissemination of nuclear weapons, because it felt that if a large number of countries were allowed to emerge as nuclear powers, it would contribute to an increase in instability and insecurity. It wanted the non-nuclear states to refrain from manufacturing nuclear weapons.[119] India consistently maintained that the continuous production of nuclear weapons by the nuclear powers would always remain a source of temptation for others to start an independent nuclear weapons programme of their own. India's nuclear policy was not to make nuclear weapons; it was to develop and use nuclear energy for peaceful purposes only. India worked for and supported nuclear disarmament and nuclear arms control measures. It continued to refuse signing the NPT. It felt that the treaty only allowed the existing nuclear powers to pile up their stock of nuclear warheads, neither moving towards disarmament nor removing the threat of nuclear attack on non-nuclear states. Thus, India was against any kind of proliferation, be it 'horizontal' or 'vertical'.

In October 1972, Indira Gandhi gave the green signal to the chairman of the Atomic Energy Commission (AEC) and the director of the Bhabha Atomic Research Centre (BARC) that they could go ahead with their PNE project.[120] The nuclear test carried out by India on 18 May 1974 at Pokhran[121] brought significant strains in Indo-US relations.

---

[118] Goheen, 'Indo-US Relations', 3–4.

[119] Chopra, *India's Policy on Disarmament*, 153–155.

[120] Subrahmanyam, 'Nuclear Policy Perspective', 45.

[121] The peaceful nuclear explosion (PNE) gave India a deterrent capability in Asia. By not going in for a nuclear weapons programme, India legitimized this nuclear capability and retained the diplomatic advantage of a non-nuclear power. Paranjpe, *U.S. Non-Proliferation Policy in Action*, 28.

The relations got complicated because of the reluctance of the USA to supply fuel for TAPS[122] until it received satisfactory assurances regarding nuclear safeguards and the handling of spent fuel from the plant. During the initial agreement with the USA in 1963 for the construction of two light-water reactors (LWR) in Tarapur, India had succeeded in preserving the safeguards-free status of the LWRs in Tarapur.

The issue of disposition of spent fuel became contentious after the PNE, because India's emphatic and repeated assertions that its detonation of a nuclear device was 'peaceful'[123] and that it had no intention of producing bombs or using nuclear energy for any other purpose did not succeed in allaying the fears of nuclear proliferation. India's nuclear test led the USA to realize that peaceful nuclear technology had brought India closer to nuclear weapons technology. By this time, India had emerged as a leading critic, on behalf of newly independent countries, of the US-led IAEA safeguards system. The USA insisted to link up the issue of full scope safeguards, as a precondition for the continued supply of fuel for TAPS, the safeguard issue throughout remained the main source of dispute.

This issue became even more complicated after the US Congress passed the Nuclear Non-Proliferation Act (NNPA) of 1978. The NNPA made the supply of nuclear fuel to any non-nuclear country conditional to its acceptance of IEAE safeguards.[124] The Carter administration, with the objective of limiting nuclear arms, pressurized non-nuclear states to adhere to the NPT. The US Congress pressed even harder, calling for a cut in economic aid to countries not accepting international safeguards against the spread of nuclear weapons, including intrusive inspection.[125]

President Carter's visit to India in January 1978 seemed to mark a new beginning in Indo-US relations, as minor irritants and suspicions that had marred them in the past were sought to be removed.

[122] Clausen, 'Non-proliferation Illusions', 744–5.

[123] Bose, 'Nuclear Proliferation', 34.

[124] Noorani, 'Indo-US Nuclear Relations', 399–416.

[125] Brands, India and the United States, 162.

There was a new rapport and understanding between the leaders of the two nations.[126] PM Morarji Desai visited the USA in June 1978 and made highly successful appearances before the Senate and House Committees dealing with foreign affairs. It was seen that the PM Desai government's initiative to normalize relations with the USA was to correct its policy of non-alignment, which had tilted to the Soviet Union's side after the 1971 Indo-Soviet Treaty.

Notwithstanding strong opposition within the country, the Carter administration authorized the sale of 38 tons of nuclear fuel to India for its Tarapur reactor in September 1980.[127] President Carter, wishing to maintain the favourable momentum in the Indo-US relations and believing that the Desai Government was negotiating in good faith on the matter, set aside the Nuclear Regulatory Commission opposition to the sale of nuclear fuel and authorized the sale as a once-only exception.[128] However, very soon, serious differences with the USA emerged over the decision of the Carter administration to offer arms worth $400 million to Pakistan.

It is important to note that during this period, the USA was much harsher on Pakistan for the first time, invoking the Symington–Glenn Amendment[129] for achieving its nuclear non-proliferation objectives, than on India, even after the adoption of the NNPA in 1978. This step of the US administration was directly related to the insecurity in South and West Asia caused by the turmoil in Iran and Afghanistan in 1979 and the need for the USA to promote peace and stability in the region. It would have been prejudicial to the US non-proliferation objectives had the USA wished to do so.

The Indian nuclear test of 1974 and the apparent determination of the Government of India to minimize the impact of IAEA safeguards

[126] Vajpayee, 'India's Foreign Policy Today', 5.

[127] Bose, 'Indo-US Security Relations', 108–109.

[128] Brands, *India and the United States*, 162.

[129] The Symington–Glenn Amendment required that the USA cut off economic assistance to any country that did not accept internationally approved safeguards for its nuclear facilities or which embarked on a programme that seemed to be designed to develop nuclear weapons capabilities.

and keep them distant from India's own nuclear plants provoked Pakistan during the 1970s and 1980s to continue with a clandestine nuclear programme with the concept of the 'Islamic Bomb'. Unlike India's policy of remaining independent, Pakistan was using both open and secret methods to acquire fissile materials, facilities and nuclear devices. Speaking about India's nuclear policy in the Lok Sabha, Indira Gandhi[130] informed the house on 24 February 1983 that 'the policy of Government of India was to utilise atomic energy for peaceful purposes and continued to be the same'.

Pakistan, apprehensive of India's nuclear programme, signed an agreement with France, under which the latter agreed to build a larger nuclear processing plant at Chashma. This led to President Carter to invoke the Symington–Glenn Amendment (The International Security Assistance Act of 1961), which stopped the flow of military and economic aid to Pakistan, but it was resumed a year later when France decided to cancel the reprocessing project.[131]

The Symington–Glenn Amendment (section 670) dealt with nuclear reprocessing transfers and was to be used for providing military assistance or granting military education. Further, no military credits were to be made or guarantees given to countries that delivered nuclear reprocessing materials to any other country or those who were not nuclear weapons states, as defined by the NPT,[132] but this was not applicable to Pakistan.

However, under a law adopted in 1985, also famously known as the Pressler Amendment, the US aid and assistance programme could continue each year only if the president gave Congress a formal assurance that Pakistan did not possess nuclear weapons. Five years later, the Bush administration expressed its inability to provide such a certification, stopping the economic aid to Pakistan, and this step was interpreted in India as official confirmation by the USA that Pakistan had nuclear bombs.[133] Such discriminatory US policies were sufficient

[130] *Lok Sabha Debates*, Session 11 (February 24, 1983), c. 56.

[131] Fisher, *Towards 1995*, 5.

[132] Pande, *Pakistan's Nuclear Policy*, 54.

[133] Ibid.

to mar the USA's relations with India, which were also antagonistic to US non-proliferation policies.

Over the years, the USA pursued its nuclear non-proliferation goals more vigorously at the global and regional levels. It halted the spread of nuclear weapons and completely dedicated itself to prevent the horizontal proliferation of nuclear weapons among non-nuclear states.[134] Despite serious differences with India over the nuclear issue, the deadlock over non-supply of fuel for Tarapur was settled during PM Indira Gandhi's visit to the USA in 1982 when President Reagan agreed to France's resumption of fuel supply to India on the USA's request.

On the whole, therefore, conflicts on the nuclear issue between the USA and India during the 1980s included their disagreement vis-à-vis the limit for disarmament, ban on nuclear weapons tests and moratorium on underground tests, prohibition of the use of nuclear weapons, reduction in and elimination of nuclear weapons and their delivery vehicles and the problem of controls and verifications. Besides these, there were other divergences in relation to the NPT, turning of South Asia into a Nuclear-Weapons-Free Zone (NWFZ), the USA's and India's interpretations of the 1963 agreement and nuclear deterrence. Chapters 3 and 4 analyse the paradigm shift in US nuclear policy towards India after the culmination of the historical 'Indo-US Civil Nuclear Cooperation Deal 2005' and 'Indo-US Civil Nuclear Cooperation Agreement 2008'.

INDO-US RELATIONS: THE INDIAN OCEAN REGION

India and the USA have many common interests in the Indian Ocean region, including those of preventing conflict and promoting economic development, social cohesion, political stability, freedom of navigation and supporting democratic regimes, human rights and human betterment. However, from a geographical perspective, India and the USA have had divergences of interest in the Indian Ocean during the period under study.

---

[134] U.S. Department of State, *Security and Arms Control*, 58–59.

Issues such as the US naval build-up, continuing US military presence in the Indian Ocean, the development of Diego Garcia as a substantial naval base and the declaration of the Indian Ocean as a zone of peace have acted as irritants in Indo-US relations.[135] Despite the Indian Ocean being declared as a zone of peace by the UN General Assembly in December 1971, it could not become a zone of peace due to the indifferent attitudes of the major powers to the proposal, the Cold War between the superpowers and their rivalry for strategic gain in the Indian Ocean.[136]

India and other littoral states repeatedly opposed the naval presence of the superpowers in the Indian Ocean region, which had the potential of exacerbating tensions, both regionally and globally. India, with the support of the non-aligned nations, was in the favour of the UN resolution to declare Indian Ocean as a zone of peace. India made formal protests to the USA and the UK expressing its concern and anxiety about the development over the Diego Garcia base, where the naval military presence of the superpowers had increased significantly.

Since the mid-1970s, the Soviet Union maintained a permanent squadron of 17–22 vessels in the Indian Ocean. US naval activity in the Indian Ocean also increased substantially between 1979 and 1980 in response to the Iranian Revolution and the Soviet Union invasion of Afghanistan. The US naval presence comprised two carrier task forces constituting some 30 combat and support vessels as part of the expansion of facilities in Diego Garcia. It resulted in increased superpower rivalry in the Indian Ocean, which ran counter to India's foreign policy interest in two important respects: first, the shadow effect of extra-regional naval power undercut Indian politico-military primacy on the sub-continent; and second, such deployment, for India, accelerated the transformation of South Asia into a possible arena of Cold War confrontation.[137] Immediately

---

[135] Palmer, *The United States and India*, 193.

[136] Mohite, *Indo-US Relations*, 102.

[137] Litwak, 'The Soviet Union in India's Security Perspectives', 127.

after becoming PM for the second time in 1980, Indira Gandhi, on the US expansion of the naval base at Diego Garcia, said, 'it was an attempt to create a nuclear base in the Indian Ocean. However, the USA went ahead with the development plan of the Diego Garcia base'.[138]

On the one hand, the Soviet Union's naval presence in the Indian Ocean was varyingly attributed to a number of factors: first, the desire to develop a defensive capability to counteract possible US intercontinental ballistic missile (ICBM) deployments in the Indian Ocean; second, the growing economic and strategic importance of the Indian Ocean as a commercial waterway; and third, the political utility and prestige derived by the Soviet Union via the projection of its naval forces.[139] On the other hand, the US foreign policy was, by and large, determined by its oil interests in the Middle East. Its geopolitical interests in the Indian Ocean had assumed great significance, and the US military build-up in the Indian Ocean increased the security threat to India.

India, as a major littoral state, was concerned about the superpower rivalry in the Indian Ocean in the 1980s. It could hardly remain immune to the effects of the massive military build-up, especially by the USA, which had established the US Central Command (CENTCOM) in 1983, with jurisdiction over the territories of a large number of littoral states.[140] India's experiences with the USA in the Indian Ocean Region region are to be held responsible for the historic turnaround in Indo-US strategic cooperation in the region under the new, US-led formulation of the 'Indo-Pacific' policy in the 21st century. The US-led defence and strategic cooperation in the newly defined 'Indo-Pacific' region is responsible for providing a bulwark to Indo-US defence and strategic cooperation at the end of the second decade of the 21st century. These aspects of their bilateral relations are discussed in Chapter 7.

---

[138] Bhattacharya, 'Indian Ocean', 933.

[139] George, *Security in Southern-Asia 2*, 127.

[140] Singh, 'Can the US and India be Real Friends?' 1023.

CONCLUSION

As analysed in the preceding sections, for almost four decades (1947–1984), Indo-US relations experienced several ups and downs. In the post-Second World War era, the basic objectives of the US foreign policy were to contain communism and Soviet Union expansionism. India followed a positive and dynamic policy of non-alignment. It did not align with either power bloc and firmly followed the policy of non-alignment, thus avoiding getting enmeshed in the Cold War politics of military alliances. However, the three consecutive wars in 1962, 1965 and 1971 placed India in direct confrontation with the USA because of their divergent views on the outcomes of the Cold War goals and objectives. The Kashmir issue also remained a major source of conflict in Indo-US relations because of controversies around Kashmir's merger with independent India and attempts of Pakistan to wean it away from India on the grounds that Kashmir had a majority Muslim population, by virtue of which it should be part of Pakistan. The new dynamics of Kashmir, that is, the era of Pakistan-supported proxy war, separatists' movement and nuclearization of Kashmir, is discussed in subsequent chapters.

The discussions in this chapter highlighted the involvement of the two superpowers, the USA and the USSR, in the region. They exposed the limitations of India in dealing with them, even as Pakistan was ready to ally with both the superpowers and China, thus complicating things for India. India was made to fight three successive wars with neighbours—in 1962, 1965 and 1971—within a short period of just 10 years, which badly affected its development. The USA–Pakistan military alliance and the subsequent military aid by the USA to Pakistan remained the single most important complicating factor in Indo-US relations throughout the period of the Cold War. The nuclear factor assumed critical significance in the 1970s and 1980s. Indo-US relations remained strained throughout but did not ever break. The two countries have always maintained a minimal level of relations at all times, despite major differences and divergences of interests.

To deal with the circumstances thrown up after the beginning of the new cold war towards the end of the 1980s, the renewed ties between Pakistan and the USA and the threat to India's national security, India embarked on building a strong defence force and steadily increased the pace of military modernization. India avoided becoming overly dependent on the Soviet Union for its military supplies and technologies and made military hardware purchases from the UK, France and Sweden. It sought improvement in its relations with the USA, which was necessary to gain recognition of its primacy in the region by both the superpowers. In pursuit of these objectives, Indira Gandhi met President Reagan in Cancun in 1981 and made an official visit to the USA in 1982, which successfully resolved the important issue of the Tarapur nuclear fuel. It also marked the beginning of a new phase of relationship between India and the USA. The process finally kicked off during PM Rajiv Gandhi's tenure, and the momentum is still being continued under PM Narendra Modi's administration. The next chapter captures the nature of and causes that led to the transition of Indo-US politico-strategic relations to the 21st century, which turned them into 'natural allies'. The Indo-US defence and strategic cooperation under the US-led 'Indo-Pacific' policy is historical, and the factors that led to this stage are analysed in the chapters to follow.

Politico-Security Dynamics

1985, A New Beginning

The invasion of Afghanistan by the erstwhile Soviet Union and the commencement of a new Cold War following the end of the Cold War and emergence of a new world order had brought unparalleled changes in international relations, which necessitated rethinking and restructuring the relationship between India and the USA. This chapter primarily deals with the Indo-US relations in the context of politico-security dynamics and changes in the South Asian region in the 1980s and the 1990s. It presents analyses of the divergent approaches of the two countries on the Kashmir issue in the post-Cold War period. The impacts of USA–Pakistan relations and USA–Soviet rapprochement on Indo-US relations are discussed.

As stated in the preceding chapter, PM Indira Gandhi was keen on establishing a sound working relationship with the USA, as there were many fundamental interests of India whose fulfilment depended on a positive equation with the USA. J. N. Dixit,[1] an Indian diplomat, believed that the presence of Soviet forces at the Pakistan–Afghanistan border was not good for India's security and larger interests. Sustaining an equation with the USA was important for reducing India's over-dependence on the Soviet Union for defence supplies. India was also conscious that defence technology available in the USA and the West would contribute more to India's technological capacities, not only for the defence sector but also for other sectors of India's economy. India was keen to improve its relations with the USA while being a Soviet friend, as the USA was also a friend of China. The Cold War started getting diluted from the mid-1980s onwards, because of President

---

[1] Dixit, *Across Borders*, 151.

Gorbachev's policies announced during his Vladivostok speech. Growing USA–Soviet rapprochement also required adjustment by India and other developing countries.

INDO-US RELATIONS: THE 1980s (TOWARDS THE END OF THE COLD WAR PERIOD)

Gorbachev's policies of glasnost and perestroika were increasing pressure on Soviet forces to withdraw from Afghanistan. Such a withdrawal would increase the US and Pakistani influence and options for the USA and Pakistan in the Gulf and the West Asian region. A thaw in Sino-Soviet relations would also result in a change in China's approach towards India and other neighbours. Apart from Pakistan acquiring nuclear weapons capability, India's other neighbours such as Nepal, Bangladesh and Sri Lanka, were also forging political and defence relationships with the USA, China and Israel, which could change the military balance in South Asia. Thus, India needed to readjust its relations with both the superpowers, the USA and the Soviet Union. PM Rajiv Gandhi prioritized technological and resources inputs for modernizing the Indian economy and sustaining India's defence capabilities to meet possible security challenges emanating from transitions and new alliances in the international strategic environment.

The diplomat Dixit considered that Rajiv Gandhi was not tied to the ideological, political or socialist orientations of Indira Gandhi, Jawaharlal Nehru and others. Nor was he excessively subject to the influence of events and memories of the 1950s, 1960s and 1970s, which carried a strong anti-USA strain. He was inclined towards acquiring the most effective state-of-the-art technology and adopting the latest management methods for India's development and modernization.[2] PM Rajiv Gandhi, being a pilot himself, understood the importance of science and technology for a developing country like India. He had the enormous task to ensure that India grew by leaps and bounds in the area of science and technology and did not enter into the 21st century as a laggard nation. He was very clear about seeking

[2] Ibid., 172.

cooperation with Western nations, including the USA. However, the international relations theory suggested the 'quid pro quo' maxim in countries relationships. As Cold War conditions were fast approaching their end, the USA was also keen to work together with India by shedding its past burdens.

Indo-US relations were bound to witness a more congenial atmosphere as PM Rajiv Gandhi moved further to remove a number of economic controls and allowed greater scope to the private sector. India's desire for a better relationship with the USA was enthusiastically reciprocated by the Reagan administration.[3] The Indian leadership under Rajiv Gandhi understood the importance of blending security policies with the economic needs of India through adopting policies of neoliberalism. US President Ronald Reagan himself turned out to be one of the protagonists of policies of neoliberalism in the late 1980s. A blend of security, economic, scientific and technological concerns on the part of India and the USA was sufficient for providing a common ground for the convergence of interests of the two nations. This resulted in a multifaceted relationship between the two countries, involving security, economic, scientific, technological and defence cooperation.

The Signing of the 1985 MOU: Beginning of a New Era

PM Rajiv Gandhi's historic visit to the USA during 11–15 June 1985 was in many ways a 'landmark' in Indo-US political–strategic relations. The signing and finalization of the MOU between the two countries was to become the basis for the export of the USA's advanced 'dual' technology to India, and it was to open new avenues for Indo-US cooperation.[4] As mentioned earlier, there is always a 'quid pro quo' phenomenon in international relations. It was going to be true in the case of Indo-US relations too.

The Reagan administration developed more sophistication in its behaviour towards India; there was a higher inclination on its part to

[3] Dutt, *India's Foreign Policy*, 124. Also see Jain, 'Indo-US Relations', 126–128.

[4] Government of India, Ministry of External Affairs, *Annual Report 1985–86*, 32.

understand the limits of the Indo-Soviet relationship. There was clear evidence of India being given greater prominence in US foreign policy considerations. Immediately after the 1984 crisis, the US administration acknowledged the immense value of Indian unity and stability. Statements made by US officials to the Congress and other forums explicitly stated, 'we support India's unity, territorial integrity, and non-alignment and recognise its pivotal role and its responsibilities for regional peace and stability'.[5] Another US official, Robert Peck, also emphasized the US policy towards South Asia to be that of 'seeking a relationship of trust and friendship with all nations in the region and supporting efforts of the states in the region to achieve greater regional co-operation and have no intention of upsetting the military balance among the states of the region'.[6] It appeared from the statements of various US officials that there would be a change in US policies towards the South Asian region, including towards India. There was an effort on the part of the USA to de-emphasize global security considerations in its relations with India, which was in part a result of its recognition of India as a major regional power and a potential global power.

The changes in US perceptions were evident what the former US Under Secretary of Defense policy, Fred Ikle, had stated way back in 1980 that India could be a power that contributes to the world stability as the USA will see it and want to shape it in 1995 and the year 2025 and a power with which they could work together.[7] Richard Armistice, at a briefing in advance of Secretary Weinberger's visit to India in 1986, reiterated the same sentiment: 'We recognize India as a regional power and becoming a World Power'.[8]

It was in recognition of this future potential of India that the US National Security Council (NSC) had issued National Security Decision

---

[5] Armacost, 'South-Asia and US Foreign Policy', cited in Mansingh, 'New Directions in Indo-US Relations', 189.

[6] Robert Peck, Deputy Assistant Secretary, Bureau of Near Eastern and South-Asian Affairs Department of State, Before the Sub-Committee on Asian and Pacific Affairs, US House of Representatives, 20 February 1985, cited in Mansingh, 'New Directions in Indo-US Relations', 189.

[7] *The Washington Post*, 4 May 1985.

[8] *International Herald Tribune* (Bangkok), 14 October 1985.

Directive (NSDD) 147 on 11 October 1984, which underlined to all concerned agencies the importance of building a better relationship with India, particularly by accommodating its request for sophisticated technology, subject to export controls.[9] NSDD 147 could be attributed to the beginning of the institutionalization of new emerging partnerships between India and the USA towards the end of the Cold War period, and finally, the two nations crossed their thresholds and have become 'natural allies' in 2020. After beginning efforts to strengthen their relations in 1984, the two countries took another 35 years to attain the goal of 'natural allies.' One had started witnessing a clear departure from the earlier USA-led Cold War policies. There was a greater realization on the part of US officials[10] about India's growing military potential and that India, on the way to becoming a world power, was a country alongside which the USA could work.

A view was emerging on both sides that India–Soviet Union ties did not preclude a constructive relationship of India with the West, because many Indian needs were better met through Western (US) sources. Despite deeper Soviet connections in the economic, political and military areas, India was expected to keep in mind the interests of Western nations, led by the USA, to retain its fullest possible access to them.

Thus, US policy in the region was directed at improving the USA's non-strategic ties with India in the framework of regional balance and maintaining its strategic ties with Pakistan in the context of its larger military objectives. Despite India's bold move in 1985 and the Reagan administration's reciprocal support, the USA agreed to a second $4.02 billion aid package to Pakistan[11] consisting of $2.28 billion in economic aid and $1.74 billion in military sales credit at highly reduced rates and covering 6 years (1987–1993). There was no change in

[9] Mukherjee, 'US Weaponry for India', 601 and Subramaniam, 'Indo-US Security Relations During the Decade 1979–89', 166.

[10] Ikle, 'Under Secretary of Defence for Policy'. See India as an Emerging World Power 'Appeared' in a State Department Background Paper on Indo-US Relations, cited in *the Times of India*, 16 July 1987.

[11] Jain, 'Indo-US Relations', 130.

the USA's pursuance of the 'zero-sum' game policy in South Asia till the end of the Cold War. India appeared to have accepted the USA's special relationship with Pakistan and tried to develop its own level of relations with the USA without emphasizing much on US relations with Pakistan. However, 35 years down the line, the USA, in the 21st century, officially pronounces that it does not pursue the 'zero-sum' game policy in South Asia. It favours independent relationships with India and Pakistan.

US Military Hardware to Pakistan Ran Contrary to Closer Indo-US Cooperation

The reasons for the USA going ahead with a second military aid to Pakistan clearly indicated that 'the complexes and suspicions harboured by the USA about India's links with the Soviet Union and the dynamics of India's own relations with Pakistan remained an influential factor in Washington's attitude towards India'.[12] The developments in West Asia, the Gulf and Afghanistan only increased Pakistan's importance in the strategic perception of the USA. Arms and economic aid to Pakistan bore testimony to such developments.[13] The ongoing Iran–Iraq war in the 1980s had been exerting its own set of pressures on US security policymakers. Undoubtedly, the extensive military assistance given to Pakistan by the USA with the prime objective of pushing the Soviet Union out of Afghanistan ran contrary to Washington's stated willingness to have a closer relationship with India. There were other hurdles too. For instance, India's somewhat ambivalent stand on the Afghanistan crisis, its support for the Sandinista government in Nicaragua and its good relations with the pro-Vietnamese Heng Samrin government in Cambodia generated antagonism in the US Congress and the US establishment towards India. As a result, the US Congress progressively reduced direct developmental assistance between 1985 and 1988. All such issues acted as pins and pricks and never allowed the normalization of Indo-US relations.

[12] Dixit, *Across Borders*, 173.

[13] Government of India, *Annual Report 1982–1983*, 1–2.

India still needed to overcome Washington's prejudicial assessment that India remained a Soviet ally and an aspirant for regional hegemony in South Asia. Pakistan's increasing nuclear weapons capabilities evoked a matching Indian response, which only heightened the differences of opinion between India and the USA on the nuclear non-proliferation and disarmament issues.[14] It was only after the end of the Cold War and the collapse of the USSR in 1991 that one could see a drastic change in US policies towards India. The new world order was unipolar, as the USA was not faced with any challenger, from any corner of the world, to its dominance at the global level. Even China was badly preoccupied with its domestic affairs that had emerged in the aftermath of the Tiananmen Square episode in 1989. It was the dawn of a new world order after the collapse of the USSR, which was supposed to have provided new opportunities for building a stronger Indo-US politico-strategic partnership.

Taking into account the role of the Pakistani factor, the basic problem of Indo-US relations had been the conflicting and divergent security interests of the two states emerging from the Western neighbour of India. The continuance of US arms transfers to Pakistan had become a matter of embarrassment for the Government of India (GOI), inside and outside the Parliament, which struggled to justify its relations with the USA and defend its efforts for an improvement in their bilateral relations.

For India, the continued supply of sophisticated arms by the USA to Pakistan adversely affected Indo-US relations, inspired an arms race in the subcontinent and jeopardized the normalization of relations between Pakistan and India. India further maintained that it would 'introduce a new level of weapons sophistication in the region which would affect the existing balance'[15] not only between India and Pakistan but also in the entire South Asian region.[16] India's Defence Minister R. Venkataraman stated categorically that 'the supply of military hardware on a massive scale by the US was in excess of Pakistan's

---

[14] Dixit, *Across Borders*, 175.

[15] *Lok Sabha Debates*, Session 14, cc. 207–208.

[16] Government of India, *Annual Report 1983–1984*, 1.

legitimate defense requirement'.[17] Further, State Minister of External Affairs A. Rahim, in a statement in March 1984 in the Lok Sabha, confirmed that the USA had committed to a 5-year security assistance programme to Pakistan under the US International Military Education and Training (IMET) program.[18]

India maintained that the induction of external military influence in and around South Asia was deleterious to the peace, stability and development of the countries of this region.[19] Minister of External Affairs P. V. Narasimha Rao stated:

> according to US Report Pakistani Government had promised to allow US Planes to use Pakistani Airfields in the event of certain contingencies in the Persian Gulf. In return, Pakistan was to benefit from the ongoing security assistance program with the US joint intelligence sharing and the training of its military personnel.[20]

The US action of setting up its military bases not only in Pakistan but also in Bangladesh and Sri Lanka posed grave threats for Indian security.

The 6-year US economic and military aid package worth $3.2 billion consisted of two parts: (a) sale to Pakistan of 40 F-16 aircraft and other military equipment, including tanks, missiles, howitzers, helicopters and armoured personnel carriers; and (b) economic aid through fiscal year 1987. Most of the military aid went into the financing of arms sales. During the late 1980s, India continuously raised its concerns on all possible platforms. Minister of External Affairs P. V. Narasimha Rao stated:

> We don't want strategic consensus being built; we don't want this consensus to be built in this area; we want the countries of the region to live peace fully in good neighbourly relations. Government of India is pursuing the policy of peace, at the same time following the policy of preparedness.[21]

---

[17] *Lok Sabha Debates*, Session 14, cc. 375–76.

[18] Ibid., cc. 207–208.

[19] Ibid.

[20] Ibid., cc. 374–75.

[21] Ibid., cc. 419–22.

Thus, India's policy remained one of building a strategically secure, politically stable and friendly and advantageously shared neighbourhood.[22] India remained concerned about Pakistan's growing capability and maintained that most of the weapons acquired by Pakistan from the USA, including naval vessels, Harpoon missiles and Vulcan and Phalanx guns, were meant less for landlocked Afghanistan and more to be used against India for causing a disparity of forces in the Indian subcontinent.[23] Thus, the US stakes in Pakistan continued to be high in the late 1980s.

There was a strong feeling in India that the US strategy to involve Pakistan as a military–political bridgehead was also directed at increasing pressure on India. India, because of its independent foreign policy and aspirations for a regional role, was seen as an obstacle to accomplishing US strategic, political and military aims in South Asia. It has been seen in the past that whenever Pakistan received open US military help, it emboldened the country to pursue misadventurism in the Indian state of Jammu and Kashmir. There are several writings that point to Pakistan's misadventurism in the Indian state of Jammu and Kashmir. A new era of Pakistan-led proxy war (incursions by mujahedeen inside Jammu and Kashmir) was about to begin in the state of Jammu and Kashmir. A book written by former Jammu and Kashmir Governor Jagmohan, *My Frozen Turbulence in Jammu and Kashmir*, provides a better understanding about the role of non-state actors in aggravating the security scenario in Jammu and Kashmir and causing India–Pakistan relations to deteriorate further.

There was a rise in India's feeling that the arms supplied by the USA to Pakistan were being used against India rather than against the Soviet Union or Afghanistan.[24] It was contended that the Reagan administration supplied weapons to the Zia regime without applying any strict test of 'offensive' versus 'defensive' weapons or ascertaining whether these were to be used for combatting the Russians or the Indians.[25]

---

[22] Muni, 'India and Its Neighbours', 189.

[23] Kathpalia, *National Security Perspectives*, 28–29.

[24] Pasricha, 'Military Balance Between India and Pakistan', 137.

[25] Cohen, 'US-Pakistan Security Relations', 25.

India's ambassador to the USA, K. R. Narayanan, conveyed to Sharon Butler when he stated 'that supply of arms to Pakistan was injurious due to four reasons: first, it makes Indo-Pakistani relations more difficult; second, it would come in the way of Indo-US relations; third, India feels that it also affected internal development in Pakistan; fourth, it introduces a cold-war element into the region.[26] He further explained to the US administration that 'the sale of arms would have multifarious consequences. Even if the US cannot see today, it is something which will have incremental effect in all these areas [four reasons] over the future'.[27] Undoubtedly, the words of K. R. Narayanan were proved right 20 years later, on 9 September 2001, when the World Trade Center in New York got completely destroyed by the al-Qaeda and US forces were compelled to attack Afghanistan on 5 October 2001. The USA-led war against Afghanistan exposed Pakistan's dual role to US policymakers, who accused Pakistan several times of aiding such terrorist organizations against US interests in the region. US forces are present in Afghanistan even in 2020, because a deal concluded by the USA with Afghan Taliban leaders has run into trouble. One of the important areas of the Indo-US strategic partnership in 2020 is cooperation on GWOT.

There was no big change in US policy, as the Pentagon officials seemed to believe that the USA–Pakistan military tie-up would force India into a tight corner and that India would be left with no option but to seek a military understanding with the USA. The irony of the situation was that India was constrained to spend an additional ₹7,000–8,000 crores a year on defence,[28] simply because of the environment around its borders, particularly the threat emanating from Pakistan and the activities of the superpowers in the Indian Ocean. Notwithstanding India's moves for seeking an improvement in Indo-US relations, particularly Rajiv Gandhi's visit to the USA, the Reagan administration offered a second aid package to Pakistan worth $4.02 billion[29] during 1987–1993.

---

[26] *The Telegraph*, 21 February 1984.

[27] Ibid.

[28] *Lok Sabha Debates*, Session 2, cc. 296–297.

[29] Jain, 'Indo-US Relations'.

The signing of the Indo-US MOU in 1985 did not stop the 6-year assistance programme for Pakistan, despite its involvement in the making of nuclear weapons. Moreover, the US administration gave a 30-month waiver to Pakistan from the application of its non-proliferation legislation, notwithstanding the fact that Pakistan was, without doubt, engaged in a vigorous, clandestine, weapon-oriented nuclear programme. An official report of the GOI[30] stated clearly that the USA's non-proliferation concerns had made it yield to the need for ensuring Pakistan's continuance as its strategic ally. The important element in such aid and assistance was that the USA tried to delink its military aid to Pakistan from the Soviet presence in Afghanistan and merited it on its own grounds. Pakistan had become a strategic ally, with its armed forces being viewed as part of the US CENTCOM based in Miami. US officials went to the extent of describing India's objections to arming Pakistan as an irritant and as an undue interference in the conduct of US foreign policy.[31]

Much to India's discomfort, Pakistan made it clear that its nuclear capability was a reality, only a few turns of the screw away, and that the decision to go nuclear awaited a political decision.[32] It was clear that US pursuance of its military objectives continued to fuel the arms race between India and Pakistan. The USA's massive supply of military aid enabled Pakistan to narrow the gap in its military strength vis-à-vis India's from 1:5 in 1971 to 1:3 in 1988.

DIVERGENCES ON INDIA'S INTERNAL SECURITY ISSUES

Apart from the US arms transfers to Pakistan, the activities of extremist leaders in the USA and their support for the Khalistan movement in India had emerged as a contentious issue in Indo-US relations. Such extremist elements disturbed the official Indian Independence Day celebrations in the USA in August 1984 and hurled abuses at the

---

[30] Government of India, *Annual Report 1987–1988*, 2.

[31] Armacost, 'South-Asia and the US', 75–79.

[32] *The Times of India* (Bombay), 10 February 1984.

Indian team during the Los Angeles Olympic games.[33] US authorities failed to deter them from doing so. India's concerns could be observed from Indira Gandhi's interview given to *The Sunday Times* (London) published in *The Indian Express* (New Delhi), dated 11 June 1984, in which she said, 'Forces of destabilization and possibly a foreign hand was at work in Punjab. There is some method in the whole thing. It has just not been a series of isolated events'.[34]

The issue had become shriller in India as Indian Members of Parliament (MPs) unequivocally condemned the interference in the country's internal affairs by the US Congress's Human Rights Caucus, which had held a briefing in the US Congress annexes on the human rights issue in Punjab, as it provided a platform to spread anti-India feelings with the vociferous participation of extremist Khalistan leaders like Ganga Singh Dhillon and Jagjit Singh Chauhan.[35] In India, this issue was highly debated, as political leaders were of view that US agencies were by and large responsible for the grim deterioration of the situation in Punjab.[36] Minister of State for External Affairs Khursheed Alam Khan agreed that in certain countries like the UK, Canada and the USA, overindulgence was being shown to Sikh terrorists.[37] Indian MPs took seriously the views expressed by Ms Kirckpatrick, the USA's ambassador in the UN, who had stated, 'There is a noticeable growth of separatist movements to the extent, there is a real possibility of the balkanization of India, which would destroy its influence in the Third World and else-where'.[38] India's demand that the Sikh leaders involved in the bombing of Air India's Kanishka aircraft and operating from the USA, UK and Canada be handed over to it for trial also was not heeded on the grounds of non-existence of an extradition treaty with India. India considered such activities as interference in the internal affairs of a sovereign country. The attempt to distort the picture with

[33] Government of India, *Annual Report 1984–1985*, 84.

[34] *The Indian Express*, 11 June 1984.

[35] *Lok Sabha Debates*, Session 2, cc. 343–346.

[36] Ibid.

[37] Ibid., c. 396.

[38] Ibid., cc. 346–347.

a view to achieve certain geostrategic and political objectives was also unacceptable to India.

The issue of training being given to Sikh separatists and that of a full-fledged hearing by the US Congress on the human rights issue in Punjab were enough to create diplomatic and political embarrassment for India just prior to the visit to the USA by PM Rajiv Gandhi during 11–16 June 1985.[39] India's categorical rebuttal to the USA was made known by the Minister of State for External Affairs Khursheed Alam Khan, who stated, 'Terrorism is a hydra-headed monster which is apparently brutal, barbaric and cruel. We do not agree with a view of the US Administration that these schools are for training mercenaries and they conform to the laws of country'.[40]

All such issues were of deep concern to India, which was conveyed to the US administration by Rajiv Gandhi during his visit to the USA. After such talks, India was assured of the US government's cooperation with India in curbing the international dimension of terrorist violence against India. The discussions reflected the reservations that the Indian government and citizens had on the issue of any support, direct or indirect, being provided to terrorist organizations working against the interests of India. It is pertinent to mention here that India and the USA rarely shared a common platform on the issues of terrorism in Punjab and Kashmir during the 1980s and 1990s, respectively. Both the issues remained bones of contention between the two countries for a fairly long period of time. It was only after the al-Qaeda attack on the World Trade Center in New York on 11 September 2001 that prospects of sharing common views on the issue of terrorism grew between India and the USA.

CONVERGENCES ON EXTERNAL SECURITY ISSUES AFTER THE 1985 MOU

Notwithstanding several irritants in Indo-US relations, India continued its efforts for maintaining a sustained dialogue with the USA for the enhancement of their relations in the fields of commerce, scientific

[39] Ibid., cc. 390–346.
[40] Ibid., c. 354 and c. 356.

cooperation and transfer of technology. The new procedures under the MOU signed in 1985 had enabled the clearance of transfer of several computer systems to India. The MOU had prepared grounds for defence cooperation becoming a reality in Indo-US relations from the mid-1980s onwards.

In line with the emerging contours of the strategic cooperation, the Indian Naval Frigate INS Godavari, for the first time ever, participated in the Centenary Celebrations of the Statue of Liberty in June–July 1986.[41] There was a greater realization in the USA about the Indian capability to project its power beyond its shores, largely because of India's naval expansion and the Indian Air Force (IAF) modernization under PM Rajiv Gandhi.[42] Another US official pronouncement stated that the USA intended the 'natural weight' of India to assert itself,[43] and it was in recognition of this that the USA approved India's role in Sri Lanka's devastating ethnic conflict during the mid-1980s. Once again, India's power projection beyond its shores was seen when the Indian Navy conducted a successful commando operation on the high seas and rescued Maldivian hostages who had been seized by fleeing mercenaries.[44] Prospects of a substantial jump in strategic cooperation between India and the USA were going to become a reality in the late 1980s and mid-1990s.

A new thinking had started emerging in the USA that it was trying to avoid making a choice between India and Pakistan by dealing with Pakistan in the contexts of the Persian Gulf, Afghanistan and the Islamic World and dealing with India in the contexts of South Asia, non-alignment and the Third World. Any such change reciprocated with actions on the ground needed appreciation. This new approach was more visible in the post-Cold War period. Such trends of improvement in Indo-US bilateral relations were cumulative results of the visits of Indira Gandhi to the USA and return visits of Secretary Schultz and Vice President Bush to India. Undoubtedly, Rajiv Gandhi's visit to the USA added a new dynamic to Indo-US relations.

[41] Government of India, *Annual Report 1986–1987*, 41–42.

[42] Subramaniam, 'Indo-US Security Relations During the Decade 1979–89', 165.

[43] Mansingh, 'New Directions in Indo-US Relations', 189.

[44] Government of India, *Annual Report 1988–1989*, 2.

India, conscious and aware of its natural status and role in the South Asian region, had been resisting US moves, during the Cold War period, of propping up Pakistan as a counterweight to India. India had always emphasized that its neighbours recognized this natural fact; it saw the South Asian region as its sphere of influence and viewed any external interventions as a challenge to its regional role and status and a threat to regional security.[45] The Indian leadership had always favoured the line of thinking that India had larger stakes in South Asia and that all South Asian countries needed to maintain restraint insofar as their engagements with major powers were concerned. The 'Indira Gandhi' doctrine and 'Rajiv Gandhi' doctrine favoured the recognition of India's primacy in South Asia. Indo-US relations in the late 1980s and early 1990s demanded more accommodation in India's and the USA's policies towards each other. It is analysed in subsequent sections that the USA was getting ready to acknowledge India's natural power status in the region. With more steps taken by the USA in this direction, prospects of enhanced strategic cooperation were going to become a reality.

Post the 1985 MOU, a clear change in the US policy towards India started emerging in their bilateral dealings. The USA wanted India to play an effective role in the South Asian region. A US expert foresaw that, in the long term, the Indo-US relationship was likely to grow in intensity and that the Reagan administration and the Pentagon were to forge closer ties with India in the military sphere, apparently on the assumption that India would become a major military power.[46] The analyst was also considered that the regional level of the USA–India relationship overshadowed bilateral matters as a determinant of the relationship. India is primarily a regional power, and the US response to the Tamil insurgency in Sri Lanka was a model of deference to Indian primacy.[47] The USA appreciated the way India had approached the problem, at least since it had stopped fuelling the insurgency in Sri Lanka. The US press was perhaps more supportive of the Indian role

---

[45] Mohite, *Indo-US Relations: Issue in Conflict and Cooperation*, 25.

[46] Thornton, 'US Role in South-Asia', 159.

[47] Thornton, 'US Role in South-Asia', 163. For the evolution of this approach, see Mansingh, 'New Directions in Indo-US Relations'.

than the Indian press, and the public opinion too was sympathetic to India's actions and problems.

The USA supported Indian actions in Sri Lanka and in the Maldives, thus giving limited support to India's own perception of its position and status in the region. During his second visit to the USA in October 1987, Rajiv Gandhi acknowledged the US support to the Indo-Sri Lankan Accord at the White House.[48] President Ronald Reagan praised the statesmanship shown by Rajiv Gandhi and the Sri Lankan President J. R. Jayawardene in signing the agreement to end the ethnic conflict in Sri Lanka.[49] PM Rajiv Gandhi's Sri Lankan policy evoked fulsome acclaim from wide sections of the US public, including endorsement by President Reagan.[50] All such gestures at the highest levels between India and the USA were going to help the two nations build a new era of Indo-US strategic cooperation in the post-Cold War period. Reagan also expressed his 'appreciation' for the prompt action taken by India in Maldives in thwarting the attempted coup against the Maldivian government.[51]

It is argued that both India and the USA tried to minimize the damage done to their relations during the Afghanistan crisis because of the USA–Pakistan nexus. Reagan's approach was that the USA should make efforts to reduce the Soviet influence on India and have a greater appreciation for India becoming a large military power. All these steps yielded bigger results in times to come. On the economic front, the USA's need for new markets, India's opening of its private sector to global market forces and, most importantly, the growth of India's military establishment added to US interests. The US policy towards India clearly indicated that the USA was ready to allow India to play its natural role of a dominant country in the South Asian region. It was also reflected in the convergence of interests on important political and strategic matters. India too had been seeking a similar kind of

---

[48] Government of India, Ministry of External Affairs, *Foreign Affairs Record* xxxiii, no. 10 (21 October 1987).

[49] *The Hindu*, 21 October 1987.

[50] *Deccan Herald*, 10 November 1987.

[51] *The Times of India*, 6 November 1988.

recognition from the USA, that it be considered a power in the region, with no external power's interference in subcontinental affairs.

PAKISTAN'S PROXY WAR AS AN IRRITANT

By the early 1990s, the internal strife in India had taken a very serious turn because of Pakistan's continuous abetment of insurgency in Kashmir and Punjab. The issue of Pakistan's proxy war also raised serious tensions on the Indo-Pak border. *India Today,*[52] a reputed national magazine, in its cover story described the situation as very explosive, needing just one spark to explode, in the early months of 1990. The Indo-Pak crisis on the border began as the temperature was raised with a provocative statement, made during the second week of February 1990, by Pakistan's PM Benazir Bhutto, who declared open support for the people of Kashmir and 'unleashing a thousand years war with India for the liberation of Kashmir'.[53] As the situation worsened on the Indo-Pak border, the scope for US interference allegedly increased. The more the USA interfered, the more the Kashmir issue would get internationalized. Under the Shimla Agreement, the Kashmir issue had been declared a bilateral matter between India and Pakistan, but in the early 1990s, Pakistan restarted a vigorous campaign against India for the internationalization of the Kashmir issue. Any precipitation of crisis on the India–Pakistan border created conditions for US intervention in the region's politics, which always posed threats to the improvement in Indo-US bilateral relations. During this period, India's defence strategists were of the view that while a conventional war was unlikely, Pakistan's covert involvement in stoking the flames in Jammu and Kashmir was certain to escalate the issue.

The cover story in *India Today* carried viewpoints of several veterans who considered that India was going to see a low-level confrontation in Kashmir that could escalate. The real issue of concern for India was Pakistan's development of nuclear weapons clandestinely.[54]

[52] Gupta, 'India-Pakistan', 28 February 1990.

[53] Ibid.

[54] Ibid., 22–23.

The precipitation of the Indo-Pak crisis in early 1990 led to the publication of a provocative article in 1993 by Seymour Hersh[55] stating that Pakistan 'openly deployed its main armoured tanks units along the Indian border and, in secret, placed its nuclear-weapons on alert'. As a result, 'the Bush Administration got convinced that the world was on the edge of a nuclear exchange between Pakistan and India'. Hersh, in his story, quoted Richard J. Kerr, a CIA official, as saying in 1990, 'It was the most dangerous nuclear situation and frightening than the Cuban Missile Crisis of 1962'. Another US official, Robert M. Gates, said that he was convinced that if a war started, it would be nuclear.[56]

Hersh's story was later rejected by many top military officials in India, but subsequently, the nuclearization of Kashmir got internationalized. Concerns about escalating tensions between India and Pakistan were also raised inside the Indian Parliament, and the Minister of External Affairs I. K. Gujral assured the members:

> Government was fully alive and alert to the threat posed by Pakistan. Reacting about the Prime Minister Benazir Bhutto's threat that she would carry out a 1000-year war for Kashmir, Gujral replied that they will not be able to take Kashmir from India by war or subversion in thousand years, or in a million years.[57]

Events in the subcontinent in early 1990 had become very dangerous. Internationalization of the Kashmir issue and nuclearization of Kashmir had become a reality with Pakistani PM Benazir Bhutto going to Pakistan-occupied Kashmir (PoK), making a $5 million pledge and warning of waging a 1,000-year war to free the Muslim state. To this, Indian PM V. P. Singh hit back by telling his own countrymen to prepare psychologically for war. The nuclearization[58] aspect was also evident from the reports of the CIA and National Security Agency, and it was feared that nuclear bombs would be used during the crisis. The number of debates inside the Lok Sabha proved the gravity of the

---

[55] Hersh, 'On the Nuclear Edge'.

[56] Ibid., 56–57.

[57] *Lok Sabha Debates*, c. 590.

[58] Burrows and Windrem, *Critical Mass*, 81–83.

situation on the Indo-Pak border.[59] Even GOI assured the MPs that it was keeping a close watch on all developments having a bearing on India's national security and was taking appropriate measures to ensure full defence preparedness.[60]

It is pertinent to mention here that during the debate, Indian MPs wanted GOI to appeal to the US administration that the latter use its leverage to tell the Pakistan government to stop the infiltration and bring the proxy war to an end.[61] Considering the gravity of the situation, the USA asked India and Pakistan to enter into a constructive dialogue for solving the Kashmir problem in an open manner. As part of such an initiative, several US State Department officials, such as Robert Gates, John Kelly and Richard Hass, visited India and exchanged views on the Indo-Pak situation. US Congressman Stephen Solarz revisited India for the same purpose, and Senator Allan Cranston was another important visitor who came to discuss the Indo-Pak situation.[62] All these visits pointed out that both India and Pakistan had been accepting the US role in diffusing the crisis indirectly, even as they asserted that no third-party mediation was acceptable on the issue of Kashmir. In the years to come, the US role on the Kashmir issue would become all-important.

Hersh quoted Oakley, who accompanied Robert Gates during his visit to the subcontinent, as saying that 'the essential goal of the meeting was to get the message'—that Pakistan could not win a war with India—to President Khan. Oakley also recalled to Hersh that Gates had warned Khan that if war broke out, 'Don't expect any help from US'.[63] These visits reflected a greater understanding on the part of the USA of India's problems, which had been aggravated because of Pakistan's role. An important shift in the US approach towards South Asia could be seen when Robert Gates said that the USA would remain neutral if Pakistan started a war with India. He also reportedly told the

[59] Lok Sabha Debates, c. 483.

[60] Ibid., c. 537.

[61] Ibid., cc. 550–555.

[62] Government of India, Ministry of External Affairs, Annual Report 1990–1991, 48.

[63] Quoted in Hersh, 'On the Nuclear Edge', 65.

Pakistani leaders that aid and spare parts would not be forthcoming for the US-supplied weapons if a war was started with India.[64]

According to Hersh, India allowed the American attaché to visit its borders and report back that the Indian units, including its vaunted strike corps, were in the process of closing down their exercises. This information was passed to the leadership in Pakistan, and over the next few days, both armies moved their troops away from the borders and the foreign ministries of both countries opened discussions on CBMs. By the end of June, the crisis was over.[65] It is important to mention here that the history of Indo-Pak relations has been such that US involvement in them never reduced. The US role was all-important, even during the Kargil crisis between Indian and Pakistan in 1999.

Many scholars in South Asia and in the West rejected the theory of the imminence of a nuclear war in the region. Even in India, officials, experts and leaders negated this theory.[66] The speculations made by Hersh had a clear message for India that any tensions on the border might involve an exchange of nuclear warheads and that the Kashmir issue was moving to the centre stage of international relations; henceforth, the Kashmir issue stood intertwined with the threat of a nuclear war breaking out between the two hostile neighbours India and Pakistan. Agreeing partially with Hersh's story, Devin T. Hagerty maintained that a fourth Indo-Pak war was indeed a possibility; however, Hersh had misinterpreted the nuclear dimension.[67] Some scholars were of view that 'the USA overestimated the risk of a nuclear war in 1990, and they strongly disagreed that the consequences of an outbreak of a nuclear conflict between India and Pakistan would have been greater than the Cuban crisis, which could have destroyed all mankind and not just millions of innocent civilians in densely populated region of South Asia'.[68] Even Hersh's story was raised inside

[64] *The Times of India* (New Delhi), 4 May 1990.

[65] Hersh, 'On the Nuclear Edge', 68.

[66] Burrows and Windrem, *Critical Mass*, 85.

[67] Hagerty, 'Nuclear Deterrence in South-Asia', 79–114.

[68] Bajpai et al., *Brasstacks and Beyond*, 85.

the Indian Parliament, and MPs demanded that GOI needed to think about its nuclear policy and straighten it out.[69]

The Indo-Pak border crisis' diffusion in the month of June 1990 did help in setting the future course of Indo-US relations in the 1990s. Two important takeaways were: Pakistan was told in clear terms that it could not expect of any US help during the war with India and scope for the US playing a role of mediator between India and Pakistan, henceforth. It must be pointed out that US intervention in India–Pakistan affairs since then has become a routine feature. The Kargil crisis would not have ended soon without the USA's help to India and snub to Pakistan.

The way the US officials, the CIA and other intelligence agencies exaggerated the Indo-Pak border crisis in 1990 in the region, it can be inferred that by presenting a distorted picture before the world, they hoped to put pressure on the Indian and Pakistani governments to make them sign the NPT. On the whole, the most important outcome of the 1990 border crisis was that it brought the Kashmir problem to the centre stage of international relations and linked it with the threat of nuclear war. The US administration since then started linking the problem of Kashmir with nuclear proliferation as well as with the issue of human rights violation in Kashmir by Indian forces. The nuclearization aspect of Kashmir is discussed in a later section of this chapter.

END OF THE COLD WAR: A NEW BEGINNING

The signing of the Intermediate-Range Nuclear Forces (INF) Treaty between the USA and USSR in 1988 resulted in enhancing the climate of mutual trust between the two. It had a favourable impact on regional conflicts in West Asia and Southeast Asia. The crisis in Namibia, Palestine, Iran and Iraq, and Afghanistan and Cambodia—all were brought somewhat closer to a solution. The general climate of 'détente' affected the Sino-Soviet, Sino-Indian and Indo-Pak relations. Added to these, the signing of the Geneva Accord on Afghanistan

---

[69] *Lok Sabha Debates*, cc. 346–353.

was very important.[70] The most important implication of the steady improvements in USA–USSR relations was that it lessened the strategic significance of the 'USSR–USA–China' triangle as compared to that in the 1970s.

An Indian government report acknowledged the transformations at the world level because of the bold initiatives of President Mikhail Gorbachev, who initiated a new thinking in Soviet foreign policy that resulted in the end of the Cold War and beginning of a new world order.[71] For India, Gorbachev's foreign policy initiatives had important lessons that henceforth, the Soviet Union would not be getting dragged to the Indian side in any of its military or political disputes with Pakistan and China.[72] This declaration was very important in correcting the course of future Indo-US relations and creating complementarities between India and the USA.

The end of the Cold War and the collapse of the Soviet Union in December 1991 left India with the daunting task of coping with a transformed world order, which had become more complex because of the domestic difficulties on the economic, political and social fronts. The crises had compounded, as India was facing major challenges because of the insurgency in Punjab and Kashmir that considerably deteriorated the security of the country.[73] Hence, it was time for India to mend its relations with only remaining superpower, the USA. It was fully aware of the emergence of a unipolar world after the collapse of the former USSR.

Describing the situation arising because of the changes witnessed due to the end of the Cold War and its implications for the region, a noted South Asian expert stated that 'South-Asia, has been undergoing a number of changes in terms of national dynamics, bilateral relationships and regional concerns, all making for a multilayered set

[70] Government of India, Ministry of External Affairs, *Annual Report 1988–1989*, iii; and Kumar, 'India and the World', 11.

[71] Government of India, *Annual Report 1988–1989*, iii.

[72] Muni, 'India and the Post-Cold War World', 866.

[73] Mohan, 'India's Relations with the Great Powers', 78.

of challenges and opportunities for the region'.[74] All such developments were expected to impinge on Indo-US relations in the post-Cold War period.

The post-Cold War period threw up new challenges and fresh opportunities for India's foreign policy and diplomacy. The collapse of the USSR and dissolution of the Warsaw Pact increased the importance of the Asia-Pacific region in place of the Euro-Atlantic region. Pakistan was no longer the strategic frontline state deciding US perceptions of India and South Asia.[75] The loss of the frontline status of Pakistan in the post-Cold War period was going to be a positive indicator for the strengthening of the Indo-US strategic cooperation in the years to come, and it would help US policymakers de-hyphenate the USA's bilateral relations with India and Pakistan. The USA was also expected to stop pursuing the 'zero sum' game policy in South Asia.

It was expected that the post-Cold War period would free Indo-US relations of past burdens and help the consolidation of the strategic cooperation of India and the USA. An Indian diplomat strongly felt that a real possibility for a mutually beneficial Indo-US security cooperation relationship existed despite differences over the nuclear issue.[76] The later decades witnessed a very important understanding being arrived at between India and the USA. In 2020, both the countries have been dealing with each other as 'Natural Allies'. The use of terminology 'Indo-US strategic partnerships' in the Indo-Pacific region has been historical. Both countries are fully geared up to meet any eventuality from any corner of the world, in general, and from China, in particular. The importance of the China factor in the consolidation of Indo-US defence and strategic partnerships in the 21st century is analysed in Chapters 6 and 7.

Describing the fallout of the end of the Cold War and US policy in South Asia, an Indian expert was sceptical about the improvement of relations between India and the USA. He considered that the superpower

---

[74] Jetly, 'South Asia in Post-Cold-War Period', 190–192.

[75] Rasgotra, 'India's Foreign Policy', cited in Jetly, 'South Asia in Post-Cold-War Period', 29.

[76] Ibid.

détente remained generally confined to European issues, on the one hand, and strategic nuclear weapons, on the other hand. Issues of regional conflicts in the Third World remained on the agenda of the USA, which sought linkages between the regional issues and strategic arms limitations, but the outcome of superpower agreements on the regional issues had not gone far enough to get them resolved on a permanent basis.[77] The expert added that the effective US presence in Asia did not decline after the end of the Cold War. There were important indications by which one could conclude that US military presence was going to remain in Asia, especially in South Asia.[78] The events of 9/11 proved that US forces remained present in Afghanistan since 2001. US forces even occupied Iraq after the invasion in 1991, and again in 2003.

Similar apprehensions were cast by others too. As the editor of *Foreign Policy* mentioned,

> On the horizon perhaps there are other states that may some day pose new challenges to American power or pride. Perhaps states like India will develop regional aspirations and capabilities that bring them into conflict with an America still trying to maintain a global reach.[79]

The editor was emphatic in stating that there was very little likelihood of any significant decline in the USA's strategic stakes in South Asia and the adjoining regions.

A. P. Rana was of the view that 'the United States may eventually need to depend on regional stabiliser, through a policy of delegated peace (the "pax delegata") to tackle its worldwide stability problematic.' He added,

> US can count on regional stabilizers to undertake this for her. India may constitute such a stabilizer for the United States in South-Asia and was optimist about a congruence that would have made partnership between India and the United States a natural consequence of shared national interests.[80]

[77] Muni, 'Global Developments', 3–4.

[78] Ibid., 4–5.

[79] Maynes, 'America Without the Cold-War', 3–25, cited in Muni, 'Global Developments', 6–7.

[80] Rana, 'Indo-US Relations', cited in Jetly, *India's Foreign Policy*, 258.

He affirmed that India, in the 1990s, had evolved a greater realism and a conscious strategy of re-engaging the great powers of the international system, based on mutual benefit rather than ideological notions of the past.[81]

With the end of the Cold War, New Delhi recognized that the USA was the sole superpower in the international system. India paid particular attention to building a new relationship with Washington. It needed an intensification of cooperation with all the great powers, without being tied down to the rigours of a strategic alliance with any one or a group of them. For India, the pursuit of an independent foreign policy that would maximize its freedom of manoeuvre in all directions was the foremost consideration while developing its relations with any of the powers, including the USA.[82]

Throughout the 1990s, redefining the relationship with the USA emerged as one of the principal objectives of Indian policy. Raja Mohan considered that the USA could have promoted several Indian interests, including trade and economic development, technology transfers, national security and India's relations with its neighbours, despite the fact that 'Indian expectations from the United States in the 1990s oscillated wildly from optimistic forecasts of a strategic partnership to pessimistic fears about the American determination to prevent India from acquiring its rightful place in the world order'.[83]

Except a few years after the end of the Cold War, US policy reversed in the aftermath of the Iraq–Kuwait war in early 1991, which raised the prospect of renewed US arms sales to Islamic countries that joined the USA-led allied coalition. This coalition included Pakistan and one of its strongest Arab supporters, Saudi Arabia.[84] It was clear that global conflict issues continued to have a bearing on the military balance in the subcontinent, which in turn had a bearing on the outcome of any future Indo-Pak relations, particularly in relation to the core issue of conflict, the Kashmir issue.

[81] Ibid., 259.

[82] Mohan, 'India's Relations with the Great Powers', 87.

[83] Ibid.

[84] Thomas, 'Reflections on the Kashmir Problem', 27.

US officials were upbeat about an upward swing in Indo-US relations. The USA no longer viewed the South Asian region as a subset of its relations with the USA, USSR or China but rather saw it as a key political and economic entity in itself. The USA was to do everything to resist making its relations with India and Pakistan an 'either/or' zero-sum proposition, and US interests in the region would be direct and not derivative of USA–USSR relations.[85] Thus, during the 1990s, for the first time, there was an opportunity that while the USA's interest in South Asia would be close, and perhaps because of that, its relations with India might be good as well.

As for India, Richard Hass stated, 'we begin with the recognition of its position in the region'. Its 'substantial capabilities' should serve not only 'our bilateral interests but also of all those of all the countries of the people and countries of the South-Asia'. Hass foresaw 'a more developed set of consultations with India on matters of regional and indeed security consultations that are commensurate with India's growing role, and that in my opinion are long overdue'.[86]

Despite strong indications of transformations in Indo-US relations, in the mid-1990s, India, during President Clinton's tenure, had begun coming under tremendous pressure to adhere to the NPT, despite the fact that China was a nuclear power with IRBM and ICBM capabilities. Further, Pakistan had nuclear weapons capability, and it frequently threatened waging a nuclear war against India. Additionally, even after the collapse of the USSR, Central Asian republics continued to have tactical nuclear weapons on their soil.[87] Thus, the changes in the US administration's policy towards India that indicated a significant improvement in Indo-US relations in future were perhaps short-lived, and with the arrival of President Bill Clinton in office, the warming up of the relations eventually slowed down because of direct Indo-US confrontation over issues such as the NPT, nuclear proliferation concerns and the Kashmir issue, which are discussed in the next section.

---

[85] Speech of US Assistant Secretary Richard Hass made in 1990, cited in Dixit, 'India Pakistan and the Great Powers', 36–37.

[86] Chopra, *The Crisis of Foreign Policy*, 113.

[87] Dixit, 'India's Security Concerns and Their Impact', 150–151.

INTERNATIONALIZATION AND NUCLEARIZATION OF KASHMIR ISSUE AND THE USA'S ROLE

As pointed out in Chapter 1, the US position on Kashmir had been largely determined by its Cold War strategy. The main concern of the USA in the 1950s had been the containment of communism, and Kashmir had got involved in US Cold War policies because of Pakistan's strategic location in Western and Eastern Asia in the event of a war with the erstwhile Soviet Union and China.[88] Pakistan had also received huge economic and military aids, which had improved its military capability and intensified Indo-Pak tensions.[89] It had been raising the Kashmir issue at every conceivable global forum and, at the same time, maintaining the international focus on Kashmir by ensuring that militant strife and murderous mayhem were kept alive in the Kashmir valley.[90] Pakistan also continued with its hostile, anti-India propaganda, misrepresenting the situation in Jammu and Kashmir, and sought to spread distorted and exaggerated accounts of alleged atrocities by Indian security forces.

The increasingly visible shift in the US position on Indo-Pak issues in favour of India was indeed the positive aspect of Indo-US relations during the period under survey. The shift was particularly notable with the USA urging Pakistan not to encourage the Punjab and Kashmir secessionists and to seek instead a political and negotiated solution to the Kashmir dispute on the basis of the 1972 Shimla Agreement.[91] When Indian Ambassador to the USA Abid Hussain presented his credentials to President Bush, the latter reiterated the US support for using the Shimla Agreement as a framework for resolution of the dispute.[92] The USA asked India and Pakistan to initiate a constructive dialogue to solve the Kashmir problem in an open manner. It, however, had no intention of being the mediator

---

[88] Bindra, *Indo-Pakistan Relations*, 32–33.

[89] Singh, *India and Pakistan*, 3–8.

[90] Government of India, Ministry of Defence, *Annual Report 1989–1990*, 2.

[91] Muni, 'India and the Post-Cold War World', 866.

[92] *The Hindustan Times*, 27 September 1990.

between the two countries.[93] Most significant was the USA's blunt warning that if Pakistan started a war with India, the USA would remain neutral. US official Robert Gates told Pakistan leaders that aid and spare parts would not be forthcoming for US-supplied weapons if a war was started.[94]

Senator Daniel Moynihan warned Pakistan that it would be a dreadful mistake to start a war over Kashmir with India. He predicted that after a possible initial success by Pakistan, the Indian forces would eventually defeat it. There would be a rebellion in Baluchistan and total chaos in Pakistan. No help would come from anywhere. Even China might not help, as it would not like to risk its improving relations with the Soviet Union.[95] The change in the US stand over the issue of Kashmir and its communication to Pakistan thus in strong words also sent a signal to non-state actors indulging in acts of terrorism who had been operating far away from Indian territory. It also led to a greater understanding between India and the USA on the need to adopt measures against international terrorism.

India wanted the US administration to put pressure on Pakistan for not indulging and providing assistance to terrorist organizations active in India. India made continuous efforts in trying to get the USA to declare Pakistan a 'terrorist state', which later became a cause of disagreement between USA and Pakistan. Some US Congressmen were, however, of the view that the US administration should stop all kinds of economic aid to India, as there were a lot of violations of human rights taking place in various areas, such as Kashmir, Punjab and Northeast India.

As the situation between India and Pakistan worsened and the two were unable to break the deadlock on the issues of Kashmir and Punjab, the Bush administration urged Pakistan to settle the Kashmir issue on the basis of the Shimla Agreement and desist from morally and materially egging on secessionists in Punjab and Kashmir.[96]

---

[93] Ibid.

[94] *The Times of India*, 4 May 1990 and Hersh, 'On the Nuclear Edge', 65.

[95] *The Times of India*, 20 May 1990.

[96] Muni, 'India and the Post-Cold War World', 866.

It was the first time after the end of the Cold War that the USA made its stand explicit, that the Indo-Pak dispute over the issue of Kashmir ought to be settled in a bilateral manner within the framework of Shimla Agreement[97] of 1972. The most important aspect of such a US pronouncement was that the USA thought it fit not to emphasize the UN resolution on the Kashmir issue. It was again important because such a step by the USA also made other countries like Britain, Germany, Japan and China adopt a similar stand on the Kashmir issue.

Although the USA was still keen on retaining its cooperative relationship with Pakistan, New Delhi was greatly encouraged by the US stand[98] since the early 1990s that the Kashmir problem needed to be resolved bilaterally between India and Pakistan within the framework of the Shimla Agreement.[99]

It has been India's constant effort to muster enough support at the international forum, as well as the support of all friendly countries, to accept Kashmir as an integral part of the country and condemn Pakistan's undertaking of a proxy war in Kashmir by providing 'non-state actors' moral and material support. It was in this context that the US administration's pronouncement on Kashmir and declaration of Pakistan as a terrorist state helped India in overcoming its inhibition in mending its relations with the USA. However, with the change in its political leadership, the USA reverted to its old policy on Kashmir in terms of emphasizing the UN resolution for the settlement of the Kashmir dispute. For the Clinton administration, the issue of human rights had a lot of importance from the US foreign policy point of view. As militancy continued in Kashmir, the USA went ahead with condemning Indian violations of human rights in Kashmir and other places. This started the era of US official pronouncements that worked in the direction of lowering the level of relations that had been attained between India and the USA after the signing of the MOU in 1985.

---

[97] For details of Shimla Agreement, see Bindra, *Indo-Pakistan Relations*, 259–261.

[98] Gopalan, 'Indo-US Relations', 373.

[99] For details, see Shimla Agreement in Singh, *India and Pakistan*.

Reflecting on the general US thinking, a US expert on South Asia held the decline of political institutions in India, the erosion of Kashmir's special status enshrined in Article 370 of the Indian Constitution,[100] the electoral frauds and abuses by a number of national governments and the emergence of a new generation of leaders in Kashmir as the important factors responsible for the origins and evolution of the insurgency there.[101]

As the separatist movement in Kashmir raged on through the 1990s, much of India's energy was devoted to preventing the 'internationalization' of the Kashmir problem. For India, the priority was to cope with the situation in Kashmir, but the diplomatic activism of the Clinton administration on this issue, the determined bid by Pakistan to get the UN and the USA involved in an early resolution of the conflict and the pressure from international human rights groups queered the pitch for India.[102] By late 1991, the militancy situation in Punjab had been brought under control, but there was no respite in the situation in Kashmir. A totally new dimension of Pakistan providing open support to terrorist organizations like Hizbul Mujahedeen and Lashkar-e-Taiba (LeT) was unfolding in Kashmir. Once again, chances of the USA slipping back to its past policies of extracting more Indian concessions on the NPT and the proposed CTBT by siding with Pakistan on the Kashmir issue had risen very high. In a candid manner, one could say that the Kashmir issue was brought to the centre stage of global agendas without caring much for its long-term impact on Indo-US relations.

Under the Clinton administration, there was a growing international perception that Kashmir was a major international flashpoint, and the sense that the Indo-Pak tensions could drift into a conventional war that could escalate to the nuclear level gave a new salience to the Kashmir question in the eyes of the West.[103] The linkage that was established between Kashmir and the nuclear questions resulted in increased pressures from the USA and the West on India's nuclear

[100] Ganguly, *The Origins of War in South-Asia*, 107.

[101] Ganguly, 'Avoiding War in Kashmir', 67–73.

[102] Mohan, 'India's Relations with the Great Powers', 80.

[103] Ibid.

and missile programmes. C. Raja Mohan[104] opined that US pressures were centred on proposals to cap the nuclear programme of India and prevent the deployment of its short-range missile Prithvi and the further testing and development of its medium-range missile Agni. A variety of negotiating forums—multilateral, regional and bilateral—were promoted by the USA and the West to persuade India to freeze, if not roll back, its nuclear and missile capability. This aspect of the nuclear proliferation question is analysed in greater detail in Chapter 3. India also had started experiencing greater difficulties with the US administration on the issue of human rights, which had gained salience in the USA's relations with South Asian nations, especially since the seemingly worldwide trend towards 'self-determination' had also reached the region. An US expert[105] viewed it, 'situations in Punjab and Kashmir were as the worst cases, where Indian Federal Government Forces were charged with brutality as the worst cases'. Another US analyst declared that 'in India, democracy is so marred by political violence, human rights abuses, corruption and group conflict that Freedom House has downgraded its rating to "partially" free'.[106] All such writings went against India, and the Clinton administration had taken a tough stand on issues of human rights violations across the world. As a result, India also came under US pressure.

India maintained on its part that the USA was using human rights abuse as an effective arm-twisting strategy to browbeat India. GOI Annual Report (1992–93) underlined the fact that 'Human Rights has become a priority issue for both the US Administration and Congress. Pakistan supported Kashmiri groups and proponents have joined hands and have employed professional lobbyists to intensify their propaganda campaign against India in the US'. As a result of this lobbying and one-sided reports by international human rights organizations, some US Congressmen were influenced to introduce anti-India bills related to human rights. Attempts were also made to cut the major developmental aid to India over alleged human rights

[104] Ibid, 81.

[105] Thornton, 'The United States and Asia', 116–117.

[106] Diamond, 'Promoting Democracy', 26–27.

violations in Punjab and Jammu and Kashmir, though eventually no bill or amendment that specifically targeted India was passed.[107]

The US State Secretary Warren Christopher made the US stand clear in Washington on 1 February 1994, where he stated, 'they help shape our decisions on our assistance program, trade, and foreign policies itself. Most important, we use them, as well weave human rights and democracy more tightly into the activities of all our missions abroad'.[108] President Clinton, while underlining human rights as fundamental to US foreign policy in his speech to the 48th UN General Assembly, equated Kashmir with Angola and the Caucasus, as a place where 'bloody ethnic, religious and civil wars rage',[109] which raised a huge controversy back in India.

The internationalization of the Kashmir issue and nuclearization of Kashmir led to the creation of a recurring rift in Indo-US relations in the mid-1990s. India made its position clear that it would not brook any outside influence from any quarter over Kashmir and would only discuss the Kashmir issue bilaterally with Pakistan within the framework of the Shimla Agreement. Despite overwhelming evidence of Pakistan's continuing support to terrorism in India, the US government announced in July 1993 'that listing of Pakistan as a state sponsoring terrorism was not warranted'.[110]

On the whole, India's bilateral ties with the USA got vitiated over the issues of alleged human rights violations by Indian security forces in Kashmir and Punjab and the anti-India propaganda and lobbying by 'Khalistan' and pro-Pakistan Kashmiri groups. President Clinton's letter of 27 December 1993 to the anti-Indian Kashmir American Council and to Congressman Gary Condit on the Punjab issue was seen as being highly objectionable in India.

---

[107] Government of India, Ministry of External Affairs, *Annual Report 1992–1993*, 77–78.

[108] Christopher, 'America's Commitment to Human Rights', 53.

[109] Singh, 'An Irritant', *The Hindustan Times*. And also see, Alam, Clinton's India Policy, 17.

[110] Government of India, Ministry of External Affairs, *Annual Report 1993–1994*, 71.

GOI was quick to reiterate that India's commitment to human rights and democracy was axiomatic to India's existence, and no external prescriptions were acceptable in this regard. It also conveyed that such official pronouncements by the US government, including at the highest level, could not but have a negative impact on Indo-US bilateral relations.[111]

A clear shift in US policy became more evident when Deputy Secretary in the US State Department John Mallot visited New Delhi and said, 'the Kashmir problem could no longer be left to be resolved bilaterally by India and Pakistan and insisted that there is a third party, the People of Kashmir'.[112] He asserted that the 'whole of Kashmir on both the sides of the Line of Control (LOC), was disputed territory'.[113] Such pronouncements of US officials on Kashmir were sufficient for marring Indo-US relations.

The Clinton administration's aim was clearly to force India to give in by consent or under UN pressure. This was made more explicit by Robin Raphel's statement, 'that in the last twenty years the Shimla Agreement has not been used in any way, really to deal with the Kashmir question, and as such new ways have to be found'.[114] She too repeated that the people of Jammu and Kashmir had the right to self-determination and that a new, genuine leadership in Kashmir was emerging. She added that 'any solution that is going to stick and going to be meaningful must take into account what the Kashmir people want for their political future'.[115]

It could be argued that the actions of the US administration were mostly directed at embarrassing India through international propaganda, by agencies such as Amnesty International and Asia Watch, on the question of alleged human rights violations. The human rights issue also provided the US administration ample leverage to get India to go along with the US proposal of extending the NPT indefinitely and to pressurize India to sign it.

---

[111] Ibid.

[112] Rasgotra, 'America Needles in Kashmir Again'.

[113] Dua, 'Kashmir'.

[114] Dua, 'Kashmir', 118; also see, Malviya, 'An American Approach to India's Kashmir'.

[115] Dua, 'Kashmir', 118.

The US pronouncements on the issues of human rights in Kashmir only encouraged sub-national forces that proclaimed the right to nationhood based on religion or ethnicity. The US administration did not label Pakistan as a 'terrorist state'. It soft-pedalled on various reports by the US governmental and other agencies on human rights violations in the Sindh and Karachi provinces of Pakistan. H. N. Singhal writes that India's diplomacy, however, achieved a major success: 'India was able to mobilize the world opinion in its favour forcing Pakistan to withdraw its pernicious resolution from the United Nations Human Rights Commission at Geneva in April 1994'.[116] Henceforth, the US stand on Pakistan-sponsored terrorism always would remain on the agenda of Indo-US diplomatic engagements. However, post 9/11, the USA emerged as the biggest crusader against GWOT.

It was alleged that the USA considered informing the World Bank, and Asian Development Bank continue to defer new credits to India, the International Monetary Fund placing tough new conditionally on new accommodation for India in 1994–95 and the international investment and trade with India be slowed down.[117] All such allegations and counter allegations were enough to derail the normalization of Indo-US relations that had begun in the post-1985-MOU period.

It is mentioned here that under US pressure, India set up the National Human Rights Commission (NHRC) in September 1993, which was to examine the statutes having a direct bearing on human rights and to recommend changes in them wherever necessary.[118] India was careful about relations with the USA in the light of the latter's policy of globalization and liberalization. The USA had become the largest trading partner of and investor in India, and hence India accommodated the USA's concern on the issue of human rights. India did not have many options, as it was a unipolar world.

[116] Shingal, 'Kashmir'.

[117] Majumdar, 'The Vexed Issue of Human Rights'. And also see, Kumar, 'The Human Rights Issue in Pakistan's Kashmir-Strategy', 840–845. The USA has domestic laws of US Special 301 and Super 301 legislations of taking punitive measures over trade issues. It was a sort of diplomatic move.

[118] Majumdar, 'The Vexed Issue of Human Rights', 840–845.

India, however, remained firm on the Kashmir issue, despite all the pressures. Reiterating India's stand on Kashmir, PM P. V. Narasimha Rao, in his address to the nation on 15 August 1994 from the ramparts of the Red Fort, declared, 'with you, without you, in spite of you, Kashmir is an integral part of India and this will not change'.[119] PM Rao, during his US visit in May 1994, re-emphasized India's stand on the human rights issue in Kashmir inside the US Congress and said:

> India is trying its best to improve the situation in Kashmir, unaware of the local conditions the forces sometimes resort to some strict measures achieve quick results and during the course of duty certain violations do take place but authorities have not hesitated in taking action against such personnel.[120]

On balance, Indo-US relations in the years immediately after the end of the Cold War remained stable, notwithstanding the USA taking a rather harsh stance on the human rights violations in Kashmir and the resolution of the Kashmir problem in light of its own linkages with Pakistan and its overall agenda for South Asia.

THE 1991 GULF CRISIS: A MISSED OPPORTUNITY

The Gulf War in 1991 posed severe challenges before regional, as well as global, players. India sought a non-military solution to the Gulf crisis. The matter was discussed during two Non-Aligned Movement (NAM) meetings convened in Belgrade and India in September 1990 and January 1991, respectively, on India's initiative. India, as a UNSC member, in January 1991 adhered to all the 12 mandatory UNSC resolutions on the sanctions against Iraq and took effective steps to implement them.[121] The Indian external affairs minister met Secretary of State James Baker in Washington and apprised him of the human aspect of the Gulf crisis. The US expressed sympathy and understanding in assessing the impact of the Gulf crisis on the Indian economy.[122]

---

[119] Jagmohan, 'Kashmir'.

[120] United States Information Service (USIS), *Backgrounder*.

[121] Government of India, *Annual Report 1990–1991*, i.

[122] Ibid., 49.

In light of NSDD 147, and in an attempt to transcend irritants in their relations and evolve a framework for a cooperative relationship encompassing various fields, including defence cooperation, GOI took a strategic decision when it entered into a limited cooperation with the USA in ending the Gulf war by allowing the refuelling of US Air Force fighter aircraft in Bombay. P. M. Kamath[123] writes that despite irritants in their relations, the two countries had made a substantial improvement towards military cooperation, and the decision to allow refuelling of US jets in India had to be weighed accordingly. It was also remarkable that the Pentagon then regarded India as a friendly country that would have permitted overflight rights to the USA not only for transport aircraft but also for fighter aircraft. The USA entering into a limited defence cooperation with India reflected a change in the US approach towards India. It is to be noted here that the limited defence cooperation that had started between India and the USA took almost another 30 years to stabilize, with the Logistics Exchange Memorandum of Agreement (LEMOA) and Communications Interoperability and Security Memorandum of Agreement (CISMOA) being signed on 30 August 2016 by the two countries and operationalized on 8 September 2018. These agreements were similar to the security arrangements that existed among North Atlantic Treaty Organization (NATO) members, but India and Pakistan both enjoy such arrangements with the USA outside NATO. Details on this are provided in Chapter 7.

However, whether India, which was a leader of the NAM group of nations, would accept defence cooperation with the USA or not was still not very clear. The beginning of this cooperation, made through India allowing the refuelling of US fighter planes, was of a limited nature; because of a huge political outcry in India, PM Chandra Shekhar's government was forced to terminate the refuelling facilities granted to US Air Force jets. However, the US administration understood the political compulsions of India and sought a settlement of differences without acrimony. The then Foreign Secretary of India Muchkund Dubey,[124] in an interview to the author, said that this

---

[123] Kamath, 'The End of the Cold War', 62–63.

[124] Author's interview with Professor Muchkund Dubey on 15 April 1997.

decision of allowing US aircraft to refuel in India had nothing to do with any security cooperation between the two countries and that it was done purely on humanitarian grounds.

As a close neighbour, India had an abiding international role in the Gulf region and any future regional security arrangements that were sought to be put into operation should have been based upon the initiative of the regional countries themselves, worked out under the overall aegis of the United Nations, guaranteed by the United Nations Security Council and United Nations Peace Keeping Forces and underpinned by disarmament measures that were global in character.[125] In the light of the emerging world order in 1991, a GOI report highlighted new orientations in India's foreign policy initiatives. India established full diplomatic ties with Israel, which was a positive factor in the enhancement of Indo-US relations. The GOI report added:

> India's foreign policy focused on three important objectives: maintaining the territorial integrity of India ensuing her geo-political security by creating a durable environment of peace and stability in the region and to build a framework for the economic well being of the people by encouraging a healthy external environment.[126]

Sino-Soviet rapprochement also had important implications for Indo-US relations in the post-Cold War period. Such developments reduced the USA's strategic ties with China and Pakistan against the Soviet Union. It also provided an opportunity for both India and the USA to look into their bilateral relations on a realistic basis and not through the Cold War prism. Since the new Russian government had established good working relations with both China and the USA, it provided India the chance to move ahead and seek a better relationship with the USA as well as with China, without the fear of potentially damaging consequences for its relationship with the erstwhile Soviet Union.

India continued to work towards restructuring its foreign relations with different countries of the world, which was reflected in the

---

[125] Government of India, Ministry of Defence, *Annual Report 1990–1991*, 1.

[126] Government of India, Ministry of External Affairs, *Annual Report 1991–1992*, ii.

1992–1993 annual report of the Ministry of External Affairs, GOI.[127] It continued to forge closer economic and scientific cooperation with the USA without surrendering its independence in political and strategic initiatives on global issues. However, disappointments manifested over trade relations, economic assistance and technology transfer cases, which had appeared to be the strongest pillars on which Indo-US political–strategic relations depended.

Having gained economic primacy with its acquisition of territories in the Pacific, the USA was now as much an Asian power as it was a Western power. Its security and commercial interests were focused sharply on the Asia-Pacific region. Because of the inevitable commercial rivalry and political–strategic interaction among the world's four leading countries, China, Japan, Russia and the USA, this region remained the centre of the world's attention for much of the beginning of the 21st century. India, being an important part of Asia, needed to strengthen its economic, political and security links with its neighbouring Association of Southeast Asian Nations (ASEAN) countries. Member countries of ASEAN sit astride the eastern part of the Indian Ocean and so are vital to India's future security.

As discussed earlier, India and the USA continued to have differences over important political and security matters, like the continuing US arms aid and assistance to Pakistan, which continued to impinge on their relationship. The issue of Kashmir, upon which the US policy had changed considerably over a period of time, raised a lot of heat between them, bringing India and the USA to a virtual conflict. Both countries were busy trying to cope with the harsh realities of the new world order. The flexible approach of the USA towards the Kashmir issue and its linking of the same with the nuclear non-proliferation and human rights issues made things very difficult for India.

THE KARGIL CRISIS AND THE US ROLE

The 1990s were not very conducive for Indo-US relations. There were some positive outcomes on the economic front, but eliminating negative outcomes on security matters such as the Kashmir and nuclear

---

[127] Government of India, Ministry of External Affairs, *Annual Report 1992–1993*, 4.

issues was very difficult. The deterioration of the security scenario led to the conduct of nuclear explosions by India and Pakistan in May 1998 and the beginning of the Kargil war in 1999, which did not augur well for Indo-US relations.

Despite setbacks from the USA on the Kashmir and nuclear issues, the US diplomacy during the Kargil conflict was appreciated by the Indian government, as it had yielded positive results. As a result of it, Pakistan was forced to withdraw its forces from the LOC and Kargil mountains, which led to the declaration of ceasefire in the Kargil sector. The US pressure on Pakistan forced the latter to change its hard-line position towards India, and it agreed to carry forward its relations in the aftermath of the failure of the Lahore and Agra summit processes. All these developments in the South Asian region had important bearings for the Indo-US strategic relations. India showed a lot of restraint by taking a conscious decision to not cross the LOC, which could have resulted in full-fledged war between India and Pakistan. There was greater realization on the part of the Indian military and Indian public of the neutral role played by the USA during the entire crisis, which led to a change in the long-held negative perceptions about the USA. It also enabled India and the USA to overcome their differences that had come out into the open in the aftermath of the conduct of a nuclear explosion by India in May 1998. It can be said that the relations between the world's two largest democracies began to improve during and after the Kargil crisis in August–September 1999.

During the 1990s, the USA continued to press New Delhi and Islamabad to resolve bilateral differences, especially over Kashmir, and enter into a dialogue. At the same time, the USA did not acknowledge forcefully enough the fact that Pakistan had blatantly been sheltering, training and arming Kashmiri militants and even foreign nationals to carry out subversive and violent activities in Kashmir. The outcomes of such meetings definitely helped India in stopping the internationalization of the Kashmir issue. The linkage between the Kashmir issue and the nuclear issue was slowly getting evaporated. Once again, the USA began acknowledging the Kashmir issue as a bilateral issue between India and Pakistan. The USA also had started paying attention to the problems of terrorism in India more seriously, and after a gap of several years, it formed a joint task force to counter terrorism.

Allegations are still being made that the US government has developed friendly ties with Pakistan. In India, a large section of the elite still thinks that it needs to strengthen its security, either with the USA or without it. A secure national environment is possible only if India pays sufficient attention towards political, economic, technical, social, cultural and national progress. A sustained economic growth of 7–8 per cent, with a special focus on manufacturing and agricultural productivity, accompanied by reduced regional and social inequalities, is critical to India's national security. It must narrow down its gap in all respects vis-à-vis China.

President Bush (Jr.) accelerated and intensified the process of USA–India rapprochement. After the 9/11 attacks in the USA, he lifted the Glenn sanctions imposed after the 1998 tests and welcomed PM Vajpayee to the Oval Office. During the same period, US relations with Pakistan substantially improved because of the Musharraf government's role in the war against the Taliban and Osama Bin Laden. The USA–Pakistan relations continue to grow stronger despite recent revelations about Pakistan's assistance to North Korea and Saudi Arabia in their nuclear weapons programmes.

Six meetings of the Joint Working Group on Counter terrorism have been held so far, with the latest being held in New Delhi on 31 August 2004. These have proved fairly useful. Apart from ongoing cooperation in the area of anti-terrorism training, agencies from both India and the USA have been engaged in intelligence sharing. Both sides have also initiated cooperation in the area of cyberterrorism. The first plenary meeting of the India–USA Cyber Security Forum[128] was held in Washington on 9–10 November 2004 to identify areas for collaboration in the combat against cybercrime, cyber security research and development, information assurance and defence cooperation, standards and software assurance and cyber incident management

---

[128] Embassy of India, Press Release, 29 April 2002; also see Embassy of India, Press Release, 22 January 2002.

and response.[129] During the conference, the USA and India reaffirmed their commitment to cooperation on cybersecurity by establishing five joint working groups and identifying action plans for each. Future efforts will include workshops in New Delhi and Washington and scientific exchanges. Representatives of private industries that took part in the meeting similarly identified areas in which to strengthen cooperation.[130]

Indo-US relations have significantly transformed in the past few years. India is now seen as a world power with which the USA has common strategic interests. It is a key partner in the USA's efforts to stabilize the Asia-Pacific region; ensure free access to oil reserves in the Indian Ocean region; maintain freedom of sea lanes, particularly in the Indian Ocean region; and combat the spreading menace of terrorism. The recent cooperation between the two countries, especially between the two navies, in the wake of a tsunami disaster in Sri Lanka, Maldives, Indonesia and Thailand has added a new dimension to Indo-US bilateral and multilateral cooperation.

The two countries have agreed recently to have an enhanced strategic, energy and economic dialogue, in addition to building up the Next Steps in Strategic Partnership (NSSP), underway since January 2004.[131] The USA announced in March 2005 that it would respond positively to India's request for information from US companies willing to sell their next generation of multi-role combat aircraft to India and would be ready to discuss even more fundamental issues of the defence transformation with India, including transformative systems in areas such as command and control, early warning and missile defence.[132] The energy dialogue would include cooperation in civil, nuclear and nuclear safety issues. There has been an agreement to establish a working group on trade. The economic dialogue is to be

---

[129] United States Information Service (USIS), 'The Fact Sheet'.

[130] United States Information Service (USIS), 'The Fact Sheet' and Embassy of India, Press Release, 10 November 2004.

[131] USA and India to Expand Cooperation in Energy, Space and Trade, Statement by President, *Washington File*, 12 January 2004.

[132] *The Hindu*, 24 March 2005.

revitalized with discussions on energy, trade, commerce, environment and finance. The relationship between India and the USA consolidated further with meetings between President Bush and PM Manmohan Singh during the latter's visit in July 2005 to the USA and President Bush's return visit to India in March 2006.[133]

During their first meeting in New York on 21 September 2004, on the sidelines of the UN General Assembly session, PM Dr Manmohan Singh and President Bush noted with satisfaction that Indo-US bilateral relations had never been as close as they were then, and they set the direction for further development of the India–USA strategic partnership. The two leaders welcomed the implementation of Phase 1 of the NSSP, which led to the removal of the Indian Space Research Organisation (ISRO) headquarters from the US Commerce Department's Entity List, marking the beginning of a new era of cooperation and trust. Expanded defence cooperation was perceived as an integral aspect of the expanding ties. They also agreed that policies encouraging greater integration of the two economies and with the global economy would offer opportunities to expand and strengthen cooperation on international economic issues, including the World Trade Organization's (WTO's) Doha Development Agenda, and on bilateral efforts such as the USA–India Economic Dialogue and the High Technology Cooperation Group.[134]

The pace of bilateral interactions between the two countries has been extensive. Prime Minister Manmohan Singh met President Bush in New York on September 21, 2004 on the sidelines of the UN General Assembly session. Other important bilateral meetings/ visits included former PM and Home Minister L. K. Advani's visit to Washington in June 2003, External Affairs Minister Natwar Singh's visit to Washington in June 2003 and April 2005, former External Affairs Minister Yashwant Sinha's visits to Washington in June 2003 and January 2004, former Commerce Minister Arun Jaitley's visit to Washington in June 2003, Foreign Secretary Shyam Saran's visit to

[133] Mulford, 'From a Strategic to a Comprehensive Relationship'.

[134] *The Hindu*, 22 September 2004, also see *Backgrounder,* 22 September 2004.

Washington in September 2004 and November 2004, former Chief of Army Staff General N. C. Vij's visit to the USA in March 2004 and Chief of Naval Staff Admiral Arun Prakash's 19–28 March 2005 visit.[135]

From the USA's side, Secretary of State Condoleezza Rice visited Delhi on 15–16 March 2005; Secretary of Defence Donald Rumsfeld visited Delhi on 8–9 December 2004; Deputy Secretary of State Richard Armitage came to India in March 2003, July 2003 and July 2004; Chairman of the Joint Chiefs of Staff General Richard Myers in July 2003; and Chief of Army Staff General Eric Sinseki in February 2003.[136] At present, all such visits and the holding of periodic military exercises and training programmes between the armed forces of India and the USA stand institutionalized. Different aspects of nuclear and defence cooperation are analysed in later chapters.

Since 2005, India and the USA spent around one decade thrashing out the nitty-gritty of the nuclear agreement of 2008. The finalization of the nuclear deal in 2005 and the nuclear agreement of 2008 were jointly responsible for the restoration of mutual trust and willingness to work together on a long-term basis on the part of the two countries. The result is that the USA, in 2020, is the largest trading partner of India, and the annual bilateral trade is worth around $145 billion. It has the prospect of reaching up to $500 billion in the next few years, which would be very significant. The world witnessed the comfort level that the leaders of the two countries enjoyed with each other when PM Narendra Modi addressed the Indian diaspora in Houston, USA, in October 2019 and President Trump received a warm welcome at Ahmedabad when he visited India in February 2020.

Visits of high officials from defense, state and commerce departments, besides visits of all US Presidents to India since 2000 including the recent visit of President Donald Trump had become the hallmarks of 21st century Indo-American bilateral relations. Finally, India has

[135] *US Embassy Handout.*

[136] Ibid.

appeared on the radar of US foreign relations at all levels: global, multilateral, regional and bilateral. It is no ordinary achievement for two nations who have had a long history—almost five decades—of differences. The first two decades of the 21st century have witnessed a historic transformation in their multifaceted relationship.

India has gained a lot in all important sectors of its development. The way Indo-US relations have grown stronger at the end of the second decade of the 21st century, India's importance has been well recognized all over the world and at all international forums. In the last two decades, the Kashmir issue has seen emergence of a new level of cooperation between India and the USA. All such changes have led to the institutionalization of the Indo-US politico-strategic partnership that has moved beyond the stage of being transactional and hence is very significant. It has resulted in establishing a stronger strategic relationship between India and the USA independent of Pakistan. The process of de-hyphenation is complete. The process was expedited when al-Qaeda chief Osama Bin Laden was killed on 2 May 2011 in Pakistan by US marines. The exposure of the involvement of Pakistan with terrorist organizations like al-Qaeda, LeT, JeM and others definitely played an important role in the consolidation of the ongoing strategic partnership between India and the USA. The exposure of Pakistan as a state supporting non-state actors has enabled India to emerge on the global stage for fighting the menace of global terrorism. It has infused a lot of energy in India's diplomacy at the global level. India, with the help of the USA and Western nations, has succeeded in exerting pressure on the Pakistan government to end its support to non-state actors in Jammu and Kashmir. The policies of the Manmohan Singh government of not holding any official dialogue with Pakistan, maintaining international pressure on Pakistan and making no compromises on the issue of Pakistan supporting the ongoing terrorism in India's Jammu and Kashmir have been continuing under the Modi administration since 2014. It is important to note that it is after several years of understanding that today India and the USA are on the same page on almost all global, regional and bilateral issues. There was a perceptible change in the US approach towards India after the culmination of the Indo-US nuclear deal in 2005 and the signing of the Indo-US nuclear agreement in 2008. At the end of the second decade of the 21st century, the Indo-US relationship has entered a golden era since its beginning in 1947. The historic trans-formations in the aftermath of the Indo-US nuclear deal in 2005 and the Indo-US nuclear agreement in 2008, leading to the unfolding of a higher level of strategic partnership, in general, and under President Obama, President Trump and PM Narendra Modi, in particular, are discussed in the chapters to follow.

Nuclear Cooperation

Past and Present

This chapter seeks to make an evaluation of the factors guiding India's nuclear policy since the resumption of diplomatic ties between India and the USA. It analyses India's response to the US-led global, regional and international regime's pressures on India's stand on the NPT and the CTBT and its overall nuclear programme in the 1980s and 1990s. It analyses the role of external powers in assisting Pakistan in acquiring nuclear weapons capability and thereby indulging in cases of nuclear proliferation. It also highlights various disarmament proposals made by India for making the region safe. Finally, factors leading to the finalization of the historical Indo-US civil nuclear cooperation deal of 2005 and the diplomatic and theoretical framework aspects of the nuclear deal and its transition into the Indo-US Civil Nuclear Cooperation Agreement of 2008, reflecting a complete reversal in the US global nuclear non-proliferation goals towards India in the 21st century, are analysed. The delay in the operationalization of the historic Indo-US civil nuclear cooperation agreement of 2008 over India's nuclear liability bill, and its implications for India's energy security, are analysed comprehensively in Chapter 4 on 'energy cooperation'.

INTRODUCTION

Keeping in view the changed external security environment in South Asia in the post-Cold War period, it had become imperative for a country like India, a non-nuclear country, to take appropriate measures for safeguarding its security. Despite the fact that by the late 1980s India had developed considerable expertise in nuclear and missile technologies, it ensured that this did not lead to proliferation. India's nuclear programme often came under US pressure, as the USA had been trying to clamp down conditions and restrictions on India in the name of preventing the spread of 'dual-use' nuclear technology that violated the NPT. India had been against any control of access to dual-use technologies by the US-led ad hoc international regimes known for dictating terms and restricting India's access to high technology. During the period 1984–2005, India's nuclear policy by and large remained in direct conflict with the US nuclear policy. Their divergence on the nuclear issue continued to be an important irritant in overall Indo-US relations.

The developments in Afghanistan at the end of 1979 and the outbreak of armed conflict between Iran and Iraq in September 1980 had greatly aggravated the situation. The presence of the USA's and USSR's navies in the Indian Ocean and the Gulf region had always had ramifications for security and stability in the region. India, in previous decades, had been a protagonist for converting the Indian Ocean into a zone of peace.[1] The presence of extra-regional powers in the Indian Ocean region had always remained a matter of concern for India. China's defence modernization programme had aggravated security implications for the country. China's involvement with Pakistan's nuclear programme was equally a serious issue for India. In the post-Cold War period, Sino-Russian rapprochement, China's rise as a global power and its seeking of a greater balance in its relations with the USA were responsible for impinging on India's security environment. The quest of Pakistan to acquire greater military capabilities with the USA's and China's help, besides moving close to acquiring nuclear weapons, was good enough for India's security planners to prepare India to meet all challenges to its security from different corners.[2]

Despite India's continued efforts to improve relations with the USA during Rajiv Gandhi's tenure from 1984 to 1989, issues such as Indo-US divergence on the NPT, Pakistan's nuclearization and the proposal for declaring South Asia as an NWFZ continued to act as serious irritants in Indo-US relations. However, throughout the 1980s and 1990s, India did not relent on its position on the nuclear issue and

[1] Government of India, Ministry of Defence, *Annual Report 1981–1982*, 1.
[2] Ibid., 2.

opposed any US attempt to contain its nuclear programme by asserting itself despite several pressures. The divergence of interests on the nuclear issue often forced India and the USA to take different stands at global and regional forums. The reasons behind their divergence on the nuclear issue were India's decision to keep its nuclear option open versus the US nuclear non-proliferation agenda and their differences on the NPT and CTBT. The USA wanted a regional solution to the global problem, whereas India sought a solution to this regional problem at the global level, which included even China.

Despite serious differences over the nuclear issue throughout the 1980s and 1990s, there was a perceptible change in Indo-US nuclear cooperation in the 21st century. In order to strengthen its strategic partnership with India under the NSSP in 2004, the USA finalized the Nuclear Civil Cooperation Deal with India in 2004. The deal was converted into the Indo-US Civil Nuclear Cooperation Agreement in 2008. The nuclear agreement with the USA was a historic achievement for Indian diplomacy, and it was supposed to have ramifications for the entire South Asian region, including China. The agreement led to the opening of nuclear commerce and trade between India and the rest of the world. The developments were so enormous that after the agreement, India got entry into the IAEA, Missiles Technology Control Regime (MTCR) and Nuclear Suppliers Group (NSG), those very international nuclear regimes that it used to accuse for obstructing its nuclear programme through several decades in the past. Post the nuclear agreement of 2008, India finalized similar nuclear agreements with several countries of the world. The historic transitions in Indo-US nuclear cooperation are analysed in subsequent sections.

INDO-US NUCLEAR COOPERATION: REGIONAL FACTORS (1980s–1990s)

PM Indira Gandhi's visit to the USA in 1982 had successfully resolved the important issue of the TAPS nuclear fuel supply. France had agreed to supply fuel with USA's consent. Indira Gandhi,[3] laying emphasis

---

[3] Lok Sabha Debates, Session 11, c. 56.

on India's nuclear policy inside the Parliament, stated that the policy of GOI was to utilize atomic energy for peaceful purposes and that it would continue to be the same. PM Rajiv Gandhi also emphasized the policy of use of nuclear power for peaceful purposes, as laid down by his predecessors. Addressing a press conference in Geneva, Rajiv Gandhi made a categorical statement on the nuclear issue in relation to Pakistan:

> We are worried that the United States which can do more in stopping Pakistan from developing nuclear weapon is not doing so. The Americans know about the program and we still feel that the United States can do more to put pressure on Pakistan to stop this program.[4]

The Pakistan factor was going to emerge as a constant irritant in any future Indo-US nuclear cooperation. Since the enforcement of the NPT in 1970, India's stand on it had always been guided by global considerations and not by any bilateral or regional considerations. India remained completely committed to nuclear non-proliferation, but it was not willing to be party to any discriminatory arrangement regarding non-proliferation as enshrined in the NPT. India was, however, willing to work bilaterally and multilaterally to achieve the objective of global and complete disarmament, particularly nuclear disarmament, within a definite time framework and on a non-discriminatory basis. India's nuclear policy issue was definitely shaped by its effort to attain a great-power status, apart from its security considerations. As a potential great power, India followed an independent policy in terms of its own national interests, and it refused to succumb to any kind of pressure from nuclear powers. It is important to mention that since decades of 1980s–1990s, India has been compelled to consider the China and Pakistan factors into its overall nuclear policy.

The Pakistan Factor

The 1980s and 1990s witnessed Pakistan's pursuit of nuclear weapons with the help of external powers and its implications for India's security, which always acted as a source of conflict between India and the

---

[4] Gandhi, *Selected Speeches and Writings*, 459.

USA. Pakistan's clandestine quest for attaining nuclear capability in the 1980s in full knowledge of the US administration while also being aided and assisted by China in terms of design and know-how was a matter of serious concern for India. The vitiated nuclear environment, which was directly linked to India's security scenario, was sufficient for raising the pitch of the nuclear debate in India over the two decades. As discussed in Chapter 2, after the Soviet intervention in Afghanistan, the US nuclear non-proliferation policy was relegated to the background. For instance, Senators Glenn and Percy, ardent advocates of aid cut earlier, opined that in view of the Soviet action in Afghanistan, Washington should make an exemption to its nuclear policy and accept Pakistani assurance on its nuclear plans.[5] A leading US expert stated that the crux of US-Pak nuclear cooperation was the furtherance of the US policy to contain Soviet influence. Pakistan cherished its relationship with the USA as a means to acquire the equipment to deter Indian aggression, but India's intransigence on bilateral disputes and overwhelming nuclear superiority forced Pakistani leaders to seek nuclear weapons in order to stay in the game.[6]

India, under PM Rajiv Gandhi (1984–1989), was not willing to sign the NPT with Pakistan, because it thought that it would not be effective enough in stopping Pakistan from developing nuclear weapons.[7] On the other hand, Pakistan continued its clandestine nuclear programme. By 1984, it had made considerable progress in the enrichment field. Pakistan announced the commissioning of its uranium enrichment facility at Kahuta Plant in 1984[8] and succeeded in producing enriched uranium. On 13 March 1985, the Reagan administration agreed to supply Pakistan with sophisticated air-to-air missiles to bolster its defence against Soviet and Afghanistan incursions.[9] Meanwhile, the US pressure on Rajiv Gandhi's government to sign the NPT became more discernible.

[5] Pande, 'US Non-Proliferation Policy Failures', 749.

[6] Kemp, 'Powder Keg', cited in Cohen, *Nuclear Proliferation in South Asia*, 346.

[7] Gandhi, *Selected Speeches and Writings*, 461.

[8] Ali, 'A Framework for Nuclear Agreement and Verification', cited in Cohen, *Nuclear Proliferation in South Asia*, 266. Also see Pande, 'US Non-Proliferation Policy Failures', 751.

[9] *Financial Times* (Bombay), 14 March 1985.

The USA had a feeling that Rajiv Gandhi, on account of the deep internal problems in Punjab and Kashmir, would be more amenable to pressure regarding the NPT than the strong-willed Indira Gandhi.[10] This had been the set practice of the USA—seeking concessions from India on issues when the latter was faced with domestic problems.

While Pakistan continued its clandestine weapons-oriented nuclear programme, it continued to prod India, on many occasions, to sign the NPT, or go for a South Asian NWFZ in order to keep the region free from nuclear weapons. India always resisted US bilateral moves asking India to take the initiative to halt the nuclear race with Pakistan.[11] It appealed to the USA to put pressure on Pakistan so that the latter did not acquire nuclear weapons capability. India persisted that it was committed to peace, and 'if Pakistan can also be similarly committed and the US could assist in the process, there was no need for a regional agreement'.[12] This practice of equating India with Pakistan would become the set practice of the USA for several decades to come. It was only after 2005 that there was an important shift in US policy, after the signing of the Indo-US nuclear deal in 2005 and the Indo-US nuclear agreement in 2008.

The China Factor

The revelation of the China–Pakistan nuclear collaboration had been a very serious issue for India's security planners since the mid-1980s. Undoubtedly, the fallout of this nexus had to be factored in India's nuclear policy since the 1980s. P. V. Narsimha Rao drew attention towards the testimony of Howard Schaffer before the US Senate in 1983 confirming that there was a nuclear relationship between China and Pakistan. In early March 1984, Paul Leventhal also testified that China had transferred sensitive nuclear weapons design information to Pakistan.[13] The minister assured, 'Government is vigilant in the matter,

---

Indian Scientists are keeping abreast of all aspects of R&D connected with modern and relevant technologies'.[14] The China factor continued to remain important for Indian policymakers after the debacle of the 1962 war with China and the latter becoming a nuclear power in 1964.

China's help to Pakistan in the nuclear energy sector was a very big issue for the Indian political class. The Indian political class, till date, has not been able to move forward from the 1962 war, and it continues to see China as an adversary because of its annexation of a large chunk of Indian territory in the state of Jammu and Kashmir, which is known as the Aksai Chin area. The concerns of the Indian leadership are not baseless, as India has been engaged in a warlike situation with China in the Ladakh area, close to the LAC—in China's occupied Aksai Chin area—since March 2020.

India has been wary of China's design for it—to cultivate Pakistan in such a manner that it acts as a balancer to India. China does seek the creation of a multipolar world at the global level, whereas it strongly favours a unipolar Asia to be dominated by itself. Despite past differences, towards the end of the Cold War period in the late 1980s, India had been working for the normalization of its ties with China. Since India's 1993 agreement with China for maintaining peace and tranquillity on the borders, their bilateral relations had been witnessing a gradual improvement and summit-level meetings between them had become a regular feature. However, no doubt, China continued to cause major uncertainties in India's future strategic scenario.

India continued to maintain a close watch on China's military modernization programme, as well as its military relations with Pakistan. It needed to remain vigilant with regard to China's missile and nuclear technology transfers, which would have vitiated the regional security scenario.[15] China's assistance to Pakistan's missile programme and its probable cooperation with Pakistani nuclear activities had been proved by many American experts.[16] CIA Director James Woolsey

[14] Ibid., c. 398.

[15] Government of India, Ministry of Defence, *Annual Report 1991–92*, 4–5.

[16] Spector, *Nuclear Proliferation Today*, 319, and also see *Nucleonics Week*, 15 August 1991, 14–16.

stated, 'Beijing has consistently regarded a nuclear armed Pakistan as a crucial regional ally and as a vital counterweight to India's growing military capabilities', and he added that prior to signing the NPT in 1992, China probably provided some nuclear weapons-related assistance to Islamabad, which included nuclear technology.[17] Although in August 1991, the USA had applied sanctions on both China and Pakistan because of the transfer of M-11 missile-related technology from China to Pakistan,[18] India could not afford to drop its guard and had to remain prepared to face any eventuality.

It is important to mention here that the USA in the 1980s had not been very forthright in using its influence in dealing with the nuclear collaboration between China and Pakistan, which had increased India's apprehension as far its security was concerned. Chinese assistance to Pakistan in the area of unconventional weapons and their delivery system have shaped its nuclear policy. Such assistance to Pakistan affected India's security directly and was therefore a matter that engaged the attention of all sections of the Indian public. It is an open truth that the China factor has found a lot of prominence among Indian security planners, who openly attributed India's May 1998 nuclear explosion to emerging Chinese threats to India's security. With the passage of time, the maturing of Pakistan's nuclear programme and the relaxation of tensions between the erstwhile USSR and China altered the nuclear weapon environment for India in the post-Cold War period.

GOI was dismayed over the statement of a former PM of Pakistan that the country possessed an atomic bomb, and this was the first ever explicit statement by a Pakistani leader.[19] The most unfortunate thing was that the USA never paid attention to India's apprehensions about Pakistan becoming a nuclear state. In the backdrop of the US–Iraq war in 1991 and the USA's efforts of positioning itself at the global level in the post-Cold War period, one needed to analyse

[17] Jammes, *Director of CIA's Testimony.*

[18] *The Statesman*, 5.

[19] *Lok Sabha Debates*, Session 13, cc. 385–386.

Indo-US approaches to the nuclear question. On the whole, it was the USA's reluctance to take into account these developments and address India's complaint of nuclearization of the region, as well as its inability/unwillingness to stop countries such as China and Pakistan from acting against the interests of India, which had compounded the problems for both India and the USA. There was a complete failure by the USA to initiate any kind of domestic legislative action against erring countries, whereas under President Clinton, it continued putting pressure on India to adhere to the NPT and forego its nuclear option in the mid-1990s.

NUCLEAR COOPERATION: GLOBAL FACTORS

Divergent Stand on Nuclear Disarmament Issues

Indo-US nuclear cooperation had been a casualty of the two countries' antagonistic stands on nuclear issues at the global level. The USA always tied the attainment of global goals with bilateral and regional issues. Issues like complete nuclear disarmament and achievement of nuclear non-proliferation goals on a global basis were very significant for the shaping of Indo-US bilateral nuclear cooperation or confrontation throughout the period of study. The GOI report of 1984–1985 reflected deep concerns over the escalating arms race, the rise in international tensions and the absence of willingness for constructive dialogue among the major nuclear weapon powers, which had increased the risk of outbreak of a nuclear war.[20]

India's commitment to global nuclear disarmament has remained firm over the years. Disarmament and promotion of world peace were the basic objectives of India's foreign policy. India, from time to time, conveyed its stand on disarmament at the global level. During the UN General Assembly (UNGA) Special Session on Disarmament (SSOD) II in 1982, PM Indira Gandhi proposed a programme of action for cutting down on existing nuclear stockpiles, demanding a freeze on nuclear weapons, a ban on further production of nuclear weapons,

[20] Government of India, *Annual Report 1984–85*, iii.

a cut in the production of fissionable material and suspension of all nuclear weapons tests.[21]

India's commitment to disarmament measures was also reflected in another peace initiative by PM Indira Gandhi along with the heads of five governments—Argentina, Greece, Mexico, Sweden and Tanzania—launched on 22 May 1984, which called upon nuclear states to halt the testing, production and deployment of nuclear weapons and their delivery systems, to be followed by a programme of arms reduction, leading to general and complete disarmament. It also insisted on measures to strengthen the UN system and to ensure the urgently needed transfer of substantial resources from the arms race to social and economic development.[22] The peace initiative led by the six nations continued. Reviewing India's efforts for disarmament in January 1985, again, the group of six nations called for an immediate halt to nuclear testing preparatory to the CTBT. The leaders quoted Gorbachev's famous phrase: 'a nuclear war cannot be won and must never be fought'.[23] It could be argued that though India's nuclear policy in the 1980s and 1990s was directly related to its security environment, India also had been a staunch champion of disarmament at the world level. India believed that given the political will, a nuclear-weapon-free world was possible. It was of the view that one of the first steps towards elimination of nuclear weapons from the world would be to delegitimize nuclear weapons.

Carrying forward the legacy of his predecessor, PM Rajiv Gandhi, in his address to the 40th Anniversary Commemorative Session of the UN in New York, stressed, 'the need to cure the world of the insanity of the nuclear militarism and let man's creative genius be enlisted on behalf of enrichment and not destruction'.[24] His meetings with the US and Soviet leaders provided an occasion to re-emphasize the importance India attached to disarmament, both as a long-standing objective of

[21] Rao, 'Address at the SSOD-II of United Nations General Assembly', 12–13.

[22] Kashyap, National Policy Studies, 304.

[23] Government of India, Ministry of External Affairs, Foreign Affairs Record, 239.

[24] Government of India, Annual Report 1985–86, iii.

its foreign policy and as one of the main aims of the NAM.[25] India's commitment towards the goals of complete disarmament continued in the years to come.

India continued its efforts in working for global disarmament; Rajiv Gandhi, on 22 May 1987 in New Delhi, in a 'New Appeal for Nuclear Disarmament', emphasized and urged the USA and the Soviet Union to conduct their current negotiations with a view to bringing them to a successful conclusion.[26] The Six-Nation Five-Continent Peace Initiative warmly welcomed the global elimination of all land-based, intermediate nuclear missiles, and the six nations' joint statement added that 'this is a historic first step in the direction of our common goal, namely total disarmament'.[27] These proposals always got marred because of serious differences between the USA and the USSR till the end of the Cold War in 1991.

Rajiv Gandhi, in his second visit to the USA on 20 October 1987, stressed, 'my country has a consistently recognised that a secure world order cannot be built on nuclear weapons. Our actions have spoken louder than any words in expressing our commitment. We do not want nuclear weapons in our neighbourhood'.[28] Despite India's constant efforts for global disarmament, it did not succeed much in persuading the nuclear powers to abandon their nuclear weapons in the larger interest of the world and humankind. The policies of nuclear powers, particularly the USA's policy, continued to be guided by their global and regional interests. The USA remained more concerned about regional proliferation than about global disarmament. Hence, India and the USA held divergent viewpoints on the nuclear issue at the global, regional and bilateral levels.

Meanwhile, Rajiv Gandhi's efforts led India in bringing an 'Action Plan for Nuclear Disarmament' during the UNSSOD-III on 08 June 1988 where he directed the attention of the world towards the development of

---

[25] Ibid.

[26] Government of India, Ministry of External Affairs, *Foreign Affairs Record*, 152–153.

[27] Ibid., 311.

[28] Ibid., 340.

'third generation nuclear weapons' and reminded the world body about submission of an Action Plan which emphasised: binding commitment by all nations to eliminate nuclear weapons by the year 2010; all nuclear weapons states to participate in the process of nuclear disarmament; all other countries also to be part of the process; all nations must achieve tangible progress at each stage towards the common goal; changes were required in doctrines, policies and institutions to sustain a world free of nuclear weapons; finally, to establish a Comprehensive Global Security System under the aegis of the United Nations.[29]

Emphasizing the relevance of the Action Plan presented by PM Rajiv Gandhi in June 1988, PM P. V. Narasimha Rao once again reminded world leaders about the ideas put forward in it at the UNSC in 1992. All these measures consistently showed India's commitment to global efforts for achieving total disarmament goals. However, at the same time, it always asserted its sovereign right to take care of its security by all means, which included through nuclear means also. Till date in 2020, the goals of total nuclear disarmament remain unfulfilled. Both India and Pakistan have become open nuclear powers since May 1998. Still, the USA lacked trust in India and continued to pose obstacles in India's nuclear programme because of a divergent stand on the nuclear issue with the country.

Divergent Stand on Nuclear Proliferation Issues and Nuclearization of South Asia

India's main contention was that in any debate on the nuclear issue in the South Asian region, it was the India–Pakistan equation that became important, whereas India's immediate concern was China, which was also a nuclear weapon power. India also opposed the US practice of equating India and Pakistan at par as far as the two countries' nuclear policies were concerned. It had also been opposing US pressures to sign the NPT. The USA had also been maintaining silence over roping China into any kind of regional disarmament arrangements.

In the coming years, India was to witness extra US pressure to sign the pending NPT. The Minister of State for External Affairs, on 16 March 1992, assured the members on India's stand on the NPT—that India had consistently taken a principled stand to the effect that while the NPT was discriminatory, what was needed was total and complete nuclear disarmament.[30] The 5-Power Conference (US, Russia, China, India and Pakistan) proposal put forward by the USA for discussing security issues, including nuclear non-proliferation in South Asia, was not acceptable to India, as it was not a solution for a global problem. India, time and again, resisted US moves to seek a regional solution to a global problem. India's stand was that without involving China in any kind of discussions on the nuclear non-proliferation issue in the South Asian context, there could not be any exercise in finding a solution to it. India's rejection of this proposal was because it felt that Pakistan's proposal had a different political purpose, that is, to clearly publicize the 'unfair treatment' it was receiving at the hands of USA.[31] Citing the potential threat from China's nuclear weapons, India had in the past opposed the establishment of a Southeast Asian Nuclear-Weapon-Free Zone unless China was included in that arrangement, a condition China was certain to reject.[32] All such pressures on India showed the USA's keenness to apply different tactics at different levels for making India and Pakistan sign the pending NPT in the 1990s. It was evident that there were no major changes in India's nuclear policy during late 1980s and mid-1990s. However, things changed after the Bush administration decided to invoke the Pressler Amendment against Pakistan in 1991. It established the fact that Pakistan's nuclear programme was not a peaceful one. It was against this background that the Bush government decided not to certify the annual aid and assistance programme meant for Pakistan before the US Congress.

NPT Review and Extension Conference, 1995: Divergent Views with the USA

Another issue that had cropped up amidst the existing Indo-US nuclear cooperation complexities was the outcome of NPT Review and Extension Conference in 1995. The NPT was due for renewal in

---

[30] Government of India, Ministry of External Affairs, *Foreign Affairs Record* 38, 140–142.

[31] Mahapatra, 'US Policy Towards Nuclear Issues in South Asia', 526–527.

[32] *Carnegie Endowment for International Peace Report*, 70.

1995, and the preparatory work for this had commenced in 1993. India was of view that the occasion should be utilized to review the contents of the NPT for making it non-discriminatory and universally applicable.[33] Divergence of approaches with respect to achieving non-proliferation goals persisted. While the USA sought a universal and indefinite extension of the NPT, India's long-standing position was that the treaty was discriminatory in character and the issue of non-proliferation could only be addressed through measures that were comprehensive, universal, non-discriminatory and verifiable.[34] As there was no scope for change in India's stand on the NPT, it was going to act as a bone of contention between India and the USA, as was the issue of CTBT too in the mid-1990s.

An important development during the mid-1990s was the exposure of China's assistance to Pakistan in the development of the latter's missiles programmes, particularly Hatf I and Hatf II, in reply to India's Integrated Guided Missile Development Programme (IGDMP) that neutralized US nuclear proliferation efforts in the region. The GOI report of 1995–1996 confirmed this nexus[35] and stated that China had continued with an extensive defence collaboration with Pakistan. China was already associated with Pakistan's nuclear programme. The acquisition of sophisticated weapons systems by Pakistan, including missiles, as well as uranium enrichment equipment, from China had a direct bearing on India's overall security environment.

During President Bush's (Sr.) administration, India and the USA had moved towards a cooperative relationship in the economic and military hardware spheres. However, soon after President Clinton's arrival, according to Raj Chengappa[36], India was confronted with one of the most determined initiatives by the USA to pressurize India and Pakistan to foreclose their nuclear option. The US pressure on India continued according to the US policy on non-proliferation during the 1990s, which had assumed greater importance and was high on the

[33] Government of India, *Annual Report 1992–93*, 10.

[34] Government of India, *Annual Report 1993–94*, 70.

[35] Government of India, *Annual Report 1995–96*, 4.

[36] Chengappa, 'Nuclear Dilemma', 42.

agenda of the US foreign policy. It sought to cap, roll back and eventually eliminate the nuclear capabilities of India and Pakistan.[37] The US policy could also be attributed to the ongoing arms race between India and Pakistan. James Woolsey stated, 'the arms race between India and Pakistan poses perhaps the most probable prospect for future use of weapons of mass destruction, including nuclear weapons. A nuclear exchange in the subcontinent would be devastating. Millions of innocent civilians in this densely populated region would be vulnerable'.[38] The USA was pushing for a system that would cap existing nuclear assets at the current level, freeze the production of fissile materials and then roll back on existing fissile and weapons production facilities.[39] There was no respite for India, as the pressure to sign the NPT came from even friendly countries like Russia,[40] which 'called on India and Pakistan to join in the negotiations on NPT and become original signatories to the treaty'.

Over a period of time, US interests in 'strengthening nuclear non-proliferation' and the various regimes aiming to prevent nuclear proliferation became increasingly coercive and had a direct bearing on threshold countries like India, which, during the course of an impending NPT review conference, were under tremendous pressure to surrender their nuclear option.[41] Till the end of the NPT Review and Extension Conference in 1995, differences over nuclear issues persisted between India and the USA, but they also continued their efforts to resolve their differences. Many rounds of negotiations and talks were held between the officials of both countries to resolve the deadlock over the vexed issue of nuclear non-proliferation.

On the eve of PM Narasimha Rao's visit to the USA in June 1994, an Indian newspaper broke the news of secret talks being held between India and the USA in London, which was sufficient for putting domestic pressure on the Indian government not to bow under any other

[37] Ibid.

[38] Senate Governmental Affairs Committee, 'To Examine Nuclear'.

[39] Nair, 'The Nuclear Policy'.

[40] Singh, 'The Moscow Message'.

[41] Singh, 'US Nuclear Non-Proliferation Policy', 533.

power's pressure, in general, and that from the USA, in particular. According to newspaper reports, a grave suspicion had arisen in the country that India was going to diverge from its well-established and well-accepted policies on the NPT. It reflected the mood of the country on the vexed issue of India's stand on the NPT. Members of the lower house of Parliament wanted to know from GOI why such meetings between India and the USA were taking place in a third country.[42] They wanted to know India's stand on the NPT and changes to be incorporated in the government's policy. However, GOI clarified its stand on the controversy in the Rajya Sabha on 29 April 1994 and assured the MPs that there had been no shift in its policy.[43] Thus, it was clear that India was not going to bow under any kind of bilateral or international pressure. India always was in favour of disarmament, but reports of any kind of pressure or discrimination were sufficient for the Indian people to put pressure on the government not to succumb to any kind of external pressure. It was evident that the nuclear issue, which had become an important issue between India and the USA, had linkages with domestic politics too.

PM P. V. Narasimha Rao, during his visit to the USA in May 1994, was able to stand firm on India's position on the nuclear proliferation issue. It was President Clinton who accepted that differences persisted between them. However, there was no major outcome of this visit except for either leader putting forth his views on difficult issues. There were no indications that the USA would relent on the issue of nuclear proliferation. A US assistant secretary for state emphasized on 4 February 1994 that 'our approach to the knotty problem of non-proliferation in South Asia will continue to combine firm application of our global policy and US law, as with the ISRO-Glavkosmos and M-11 sanctions, with a search for effective ways to move ahead'.[44] The USA was very clear about not making any compromises with its set goals of tightening nuclear proliferation loopholes. It had become easy for

---

[42] *Lok Sabha Debates*, Session 9, cc. 417–419.

[43] *Rajya Sabha Debates*, cc. 300–302.

[44] Text of Raphel's prepared statement, as submitted to the panel hearing, on 4 February 1994, of the Senate Foreign Relations Sub-Committee on Near Eastern and South-Asian Affairs, p. 4.

the USA to influence even India's space and missiles cooperation with friendly countries like Russia by forcing the latter to scrap their past contracts with India. It was not a very easy task for Indian officials to resist the US onslaught during the mid-1990s.

US efforts to ramp up pressure on India continued when Raphel told the Senate Committee on Foreign Relations (SFRC) on Near East and South Asia (NESA) that South Asia was the one area of the world where regional conflict had the potential to escalate to a nuclear exchange with devastating consequences for the region and beyond.[45] It was evident from US actions and the statements of its officials that the USA was still soft towards Pakistan and was ignoring India's advice that Pakistan was responsible for the situation in Kashmir. India also felt that Pakistan's efforts to become a nuclear power with China's assistance did not deter the US administration from going ahead with providing arms aid under the Brown Amendment.

India continued to defend its right to differ with the USA on the question of the NPT. It believed the treaty should emphasize the need for tangible progress towards disarmament, a comprehensive test ban, a complete freeze on the proliferation of nuclear weapons and the means of delivery and a substantial reduction in the existing stocks.[46] It wanted the non-nuclear powers themselves to refrain from manufacturing nuclear weapons.[47] There was not much of a change in India's stand on the issue of the NPT, as it knew that any compromises on the NPT would force it to make bigger compromises on the issues of the proposed CTBT and Fissile Material Cut-off Treaty (FMCT) in discussions inside the UNGA.

India insisted that any obligation placed on it was 'discriminatory', and the country expressed its strong preference for universally applicable regimes. On the other hand, Pakistan expressed its willingness to sign the NPT on the condition that India agreed to do so simultaneously.[48] India's stand was that despite having developed considerable expertise

[45] Raphel, 'United States Policy Toward South-Asia', 248.

[46] Vinod, 'Idealism and Self Interest in Conflict', 222–23.

[47] Chopra, *India's Policy on Disarmament*, 153.

[48] Bose, 'The United States and South Asia', 1604.

in nuclear, space and missile technologies, none of its actions had led to proliferation. At the same time, India was against any ad hoc regimes or cartels that tried to restrict access to high technology, and it was India's opinion that it would only lead to the formation of technological colonialism. Regimes like MTCR and NSG were arbitrary, unequal and patently discriminatory.[49] India's opposition to the role of technology denial regimes is analysed in Chapter 7.

India had always been of the view that the NPT had failed to achieve its objective, as evident from the fact that nuclear weapons had proliferated in geometric proportions. New generations of nuclear weapons had been invented and deployed, and nuclear countries had achieved greater sophistication in destructive power. However, India was left behind during the 1995 NPT Review and Extension Conference, as it was not party to the ongoing deliberations wherein the US administration left no stone unturned to make all the member countries agree to the proposal of indefinite extension of the NPT by linking it with their bilateral foreign relations. By resorting to threats of stopping aid and assistance programmes and various other measures, the USA managed to get the treaty extended for an indefinite period in May 1995.

For India, this development was a far-reaching event with serious implications for the prospects of a nuclear-free world. India regretted that there was no move towards global de-nuclearization. In effect, this unconditional and indefinite extension of the NPT had legitimized major weapons of mass destruction and allowed a few countries to have complete monopoly over them.[50] Differences persisted between India and the USA over the issue of nuclear non-proliferation throughout the period of study. C. Raja Mohan[51] considered that if India and the USA shed their rigid approaches and looked at nuclear weapons as part of the larger balance of the power system in the world, they might be in a better position to find cooperative solutions to their nuclear dilemma. With the indefinite extension of the NPT in 1995,

[49] Sibal, 'India', 9–11.

[50] Government of India, Annual Report 1995–96, 2.

[51] Mohan, 'Non-Proliferation', 14.

a new debate started in India regarding the USA's determination to get the CTBT adopted by the members of the UN.

Mohan added[52] that in the absence of any prospects for alliances that could secure India's interests, either one with the USA or a revival of the partnership with Russia, or an alliance of India, China, Russia and Iran, self-reliance and expansion of India's own national capabilities remained the sole option for India. His conviction was that the basic case for India's overt acquisition of nuclear weapons rested not only on immediate security threats from either Pakistan or China but also on the structural aspects of the current international system.

It is necessary to mention here that India's determination and consistent stand on the NPT and nuclear proliferation issues throughout the 1990s compelled the USA, after a gap of almost 10 years, to conclude the historic Indo-US Civil Nuclear Cooperation Agreement in 2008. Thereby, the USA was made to accept India's claim to entry to international nuclear regimes like the IAEA, MTCR and others without being party to the NPT, and it allowed the resumption of India's nuclear commerce with member countries. The nuclear deal of 2005 was later converted into the Indo-US Nuclear Agreement of 2008, and since then, Indo-US relations have been growing stronger, reaching the peak in 2020, and India and the USA have not looked backwards. These details are analysed in Chapter 4, which covers the developments between India and the USA in the post-nuclear agreement period.

Divergent Approaches on the CTBT, 1993

As discussed earlier, India always supported achieving the goals of complete nuclear disarmament in a time-bound manner. Till the NPT extension in 1995, India had been an enthusiastic supporter of both NPT and CTBT. It had co-sponsored a resolution with the USA in the UNGA in 1994 calling for a global ban on the production of weapon-grade fissile material. India was also one of the original proponents of the CTBT way back in the 1950s. Once again in the mid-1990s,

[52] Ibid.

GOI was of view that India's accession to the proposed CTBT must be linked to a schedule for universal and complete disarmament. It was this decision of India that brought it into a direct conflict with the USA in the mid-1990s, as the latter was keener on getting the treaty finalized before the beginning of the second term of President Clinton in 1996. The Clinton administration devoted much of its energy to ensure that the final draft of the treaty was adopted without any dissension or abstention in the Conference on Disarmament, which was authorized by the UNGA to conclude the final draft of the treaty.

The CTBT[53] is a comprehensive treaty that prohibits countries from carrying out any kind of nuclear tests—above ground, underground, under sea or even in space. India was one of the countries, along with the USA, to put forward this resolution inside the UNGA in 1993. It was to come into force in 1996, but because of provisions related to its entry into force (EIF) clause, it is yet to come into force. Its non-ratification by the US Senate itself has been a very important reason for the CTBT not coming into force. It consists of a preamble, 17 articles, two annexures and a protocol for the signatory countries. Though India supported this resolution initially, it later boycotted it and did not sign the CTBT.

In the aftermath of the NPT Review and Extension Conference in 1995, India's position on the issues of NPT and CTBT reflected a substantive change; earlier, its policies had been guided by goals of disarmament, total elimination of nuclear weapons, etc., whereas the mid-1990s onwards, they were openly linked with the question of the country's security. Since 1995, the issue of security had assumed tremendous importance for policymakers, and India's stand on the CTBT was a result of this new policy vision. When the CTBT was being finalized at the UN level, India witnessed intense debates over the issue of closing India's nuclear option after it had carried out a nuclear explosion. It is noteworthy to mention that no major power's pressure ever worked in making India change its stand on the nuclear option.

---

[53] Available at https://www.armscontrol.org/factsheets/test-ban-treaty-at-a-glance, accessed 25 September 2020.

It was also certain that no government in India would ever compromise on its nuclear policy. Chances were remote that the fear of US economic sanctions and India's isolation at the global forum would deter India from keeping its nuclear option open. It was amply clear that India's decision to keep its option open was not because of any single reason but rather the culmination of many factors, such as security, prestige and power, and its emergence as a major power. It was because of all these factors that the 1990s saw an intense reconsideration of the role of nuclear weapons in India's strong security policy.

INDO-US CONFRONTATION OVER INDIA'S MAY 1998 NUCLEAR EXPLOSION

It was against the backdrop of mounting US and international pressure on India to be part of the NPT and CTBT that India, under PM Atal Bihari Vajpayee, took the historic decision to explode five nuclear devices at Pokhran on 11 and 13 May 1998[54] after its first PNE in 1974 and to weaponize the nuclear option in the name of 'national security' and the danger from China and Pakistan. Soon after the conduct of the nuclear explosions, the then PM Vajpayee declared, 'India is now a nuclear weapon state, the tests have given India Shakti, they have given strength, they have given India self-confidence'.[55] However, several USA- and UN-led sanctions were imposed against more than 500 companies, which led to India's declaration of self-imposed moratorium on the conduct of fresh nuclear tests in future.

Pakistan also followed India and conducted six nuclear explosions, despite international efforts to dissuade it. The tests created a global storm of criticism and represented a serious setback in Indo-US relations. Following the tests, the US administration imposed full restrictions on non-humanitarian aid to both India and Pakistan. The UNSC also passed Resolution 1172 (June 1998), which condemned the two countries' nuclear tests and called upon India and Pakistan to immediately stop further nuclear tests and sign and ratify the NPT and

---

[54] *The Times of India* (New Delhi), 12 May 1998.
[55] Ram, 'What Wrong this Man Do?'

the CTBT.[56] It had become clear that Indo-US relations were going to be the biggest causality in the post-May 1998 nuclear explosion period. It would not be wrong to say that nuclear controversies continued to haunt Indo-US strategic cooperation throughout President Clinton's 8-year (1993–2000) tenure.

The Clinton administration set five key 'benchmarks' for India and Pakistan in the aftermath of their nuclear tests in May 1998.[57] These were:

1. Signing and ratifying the CTBT; 2) halting all further production of fissile material and participating in Fissile Material Cut-off Treaty negotiations; 3) limiting development and deployment of WMD delivery vehicles; 4) implementing strict export controls on sensitive WMD materials and technologies; and 5) establishing bilateral dialogue between India and Pakistan to resolve their mutual differences.

The post-May 1998 nuclear explosion period could be summed up as one witnessing the weakest Indo-US relations so far. All sorts of cooperation between companies of the two countries came to a complete standstill. The normalization of the relationship that had started during the 1980s, strengthening especially after Rajiv Gandhi's visit to the USA in May 1995, evaporated completely. Most of the Indian defence, missile and space projects started suffering, as many of these projects had been under different stages of completion with the USA's cooperation. In August 1999, the Vajpayee government released a draft nuclear doctrine that specified India's commitment to maintaining a 'minimum credible deterrent' (MCD) based upon a triad of delivery systems. India also pledged that it would not be the first country to use nuclear weapons in a conflict and that it would adhere to the 'no first use' (NFU) policy. In January 2003, India also announced the creation of the Nuclear Command Authority, and it vowed to consolidate its nuclear deterrence.

India conducted a series of missile tests after the nuclear test and made its intention very clear that it was not going to succumb to any

---

[56] Kronstadt, 'India–U.S. Relations', 1–16.

[57] Ibid.

kind of US or other international pressure. It made it clear to the USA that it would not make any compromise on building a minimum nuclear deterrence. The uncertainty in their bilateral relationship continued until 2002. For India, it had become imperative to break its isolation at the international level after the May 1998 by entering into negotiations with the USA and to convince the Clinton Administration under which circumstance India was forced to go for nuclearization.

Singh–Talbott Talks, 'Indo-US Strategic Dialogue' and President Clinton's Visit to India

In order to end the stalemate in Indo-US relations that had emerged after the nuclear explosions in May 1998, a very important beginning in this direction was made when a behind-the-scenes dialogue between US Deputy Secretary of State Strobe Talbott and then Indian External Affairs Minister Jaswant Singh started, which ended in 2002. After more than 14 rounds of talks, a sort of understanding was reached that the USA would accept the new reality and India would also take into account the USA's nuclear proliferation concerns. The US stand on India regarding signing the CTBT was eased when the US Senate failed to ratify the CTBT and jeopardized the very possibility of it ever coming into force. As a result of this ongoing dialogue between the two countries, the USA was also able to play a crucial role in defusing the crisis between India and Pakistan in the Kargil sector in the summer of 1999. The US role during the Kargil crisis is discussed in Chapter 2.

The Talbott–Singh dialogue[58] laid the ground for President Clinton's visit to India in March 2000, which reflected an important indication of a likely turnaround in Indo-US strategic relations. The importance of the visit could be gauged from the fact that a US president was visiting India after a gap of 20 years; the last visit had been in 1979. It must be inferred that because of the weaker-than-normal relationship between India and the USA over the 1980s and 1990s, no US president had ever thought of visiting India. President Clinton's visit led to the

---

[58] For details, see Talbott, *Engaging India*.

release of an important 'Vision Document' laying the future roadmap for Indo-US relations. It did not help in easing or lifting the sanctions on India by the US administration. However, Indo-US relations started normalizing after Clinton's visit. It did help to end the stalemate after several years. The two countries had the opportunity to commit to each other for strengthening Indo-US strategic cooperation as visualized in Vision Document 2000 and the MOU of 1985.

An important transformation in Indo-US relations was witnessed when Indian PM Vajpayee made a return visit to the USA in October 2000 and declared that India and the USA were 'Natural Allies'. Two summit-level meetings in 2000 tried to get their strategic cooperation process back on track. The USA also realized that India's emergence as a rising world power and its development into a mature market economy were significant to the South Asian region and the world. As the largest country in South Asia, India had a vital role to play in helping secure a stable, peaceful and prosperous Asia.

It was President George W. Bush (Jr.) who was the Republican president of the USA in 2001 when the 9/11 attack led by al-Qaeda happened, which led to the beginning of a new era as the USA launched the GWOT. In the aftermath of the 9/11 attack, Indo-US relations started improving. The US Congress, through a series of legislative measures, lifted restrictions against Indian public sector undertakings (PSUs), and finally, the Bush administration waived all the remaining sanctions on 28 September 2001.[59] It was an indication of the strengthening of Indo-US strategic relations that India gave its assurance to President Bush's announcement of missile defence proposals and conveyed that they were 'significant and far-reaching'. In 2001 itself, Deputy Secretary of State Richard Armitage visited India to talk about the missile defence system. India's National Security Advisor Brijesh Mishra also visited Washington, and a number of other high-level visits took place that helped both countries to improve their relations significantly, especially on the contentious issues of nuclear proliferation and the CTBT.

---

[59] Kronstadt, 'India-U.S. Relations'. Also see, *Washington File, Fact Sheet: Sanctions on India and Pakistan*, dated 28 September 2001, CRS 8–15.

A new era of Indo-US defence and strategic cooperation began in 2002 when the two countries were engaged in an unprecedented joint military cooperation. The USA agreed to supply 12 AN-TPQ-37 Firefinder counterbattery radars to the Indian army. Important beginnings were also made in the direction of civilian nuclear technology cooperation. The US Nuclear Regulatory Commission (NRC) Chairman Richard Meserve[60] visited India in 2003 to discuss civil nuclear cooperation between the two countries. It resulted in the revival of the 'India-US Defence Policy Group', which had been moribund since India's 1998 nuclear tests. There was a resumption of and increase in high-level visits of military and political leaders to each other's country.

BEGINNING OF A NEW ERA IN INDO-US NUCLEAR COOPERATION

Summit-level Meetings Leading to the NSSP and Indo-US Nuclear Deal 2005

It was during PM Vajpayee's visit to the USA in September 2004 that he and President Bush announced the 'NSSP'. As part of it, progress was to be made in three very crucial areas: easing of export restrictions on India on dual-use technology goods, increase in civilian nuclear and civilian space cooperation and missile defence, which was added to the list later on.[61] In January 2004, President Bush issued a statement indicating that the USA–India 'strategic partnership' included expanding cooperation in the above-mentioned three areas, as well as expanding dialogue on missile defence. US Under Secretary of Commerce for Industry and Security Ken Juster called this agreement a 'major milestone in the US-India relationship'.[62]

As part of the ongoing cooperation under the NSSP, India signed with the USA a landmark strategic civil nuclear cooperation agreement

---

[60] *The Times of India*, 27 February 2003.

[61] Kumar and Singh, 'Dynamics of Indo-US Nuclear Deal and Its Strategic Implications', 43–70.

[62] Ibid.

having far-reaching consequences for India's nuclear programme faced with stagnation and uncertainties about fuel, during PM Manmohan Singh's summit meeting with President George W. Bush on 18 July 2005. The Indo-US nuclear deal of 18 July 2005 emphasized US cooperation in the field of civilian nuclear power under the condition that it would persuade its Congress to make amendments in its NNPA 1978 and other laws, and that it would also persuade NSG members to facilitate a waiver for India on a reciprocal basis.[63]

In a way, the nuclear deal legitimized India as a responsible state with advanced nuclear technology. It was also a recognition of India's status as a de facto nuclear state by the USA without being a signatory to the NPT. The deal was important for another reason, as the USA was ready to reconcile with India's position on nuclear issues and also ready to cooperate with India on civil nuclear energy issues. The origin of the deal could be seen in the NSSP signed in 2004. The agreement[64] stated that the USA would work to achieve full civil nuclear energy cooperation with India. It would help India in goals of promoting nuclear power and achieving energy security. It expressed the USA's commitment to get conflicting US laws amended by the Congress and also to get laws of various international regimes like the IAEA, NSG and others made compatible with the nuclear deal, so as to enable full civil nuclear energy cooperation and trade with India. The USA was also to seek concessions with friendly countries for considering India's participation in the ITER (International Thermonuclear Experimental Reactor). Then onwards, India and the USA were going to experience a paradigm shift in their bilateral nuclear and strategic cooperation.

According to the nuclear deal signed on 18 July 2005, India was also bound to reciprocally assume 'the same responsibilities and practices and acquire the same benefits and advantages as other leading countries with advanced nuclear technology, such as the United States'. Under these obligations, India accepted the separation plan of its civil and military nuclear installations as per the IAEA norms.[65]

---

[63] *The Hindu*, 19 July 2005.

[64] Kumar and Singh, 'Dynamics of Indo-US Nuclear Deal and Its Strategic Implications'.

[65] Ibid.

The announcements made by PM Manmohan Singh and President Bush on 18 July 2005 were to write a new history of Indo-US nuclear cooperation and, in turn, strategic cooperation. A new beginning was made between India and the USA 2005 onwards, thereby paving a new milestone for the strengthening of the Indo-US strategic partnership and realizing the goals of them being 'Natural Allies'. Both countries needed to cover an extra mile in order to implement the provisions of the Indo-US nuclear deal in letter and spirit. Things were not going to be easy for either the USA or India to convince its people about the rationale behind the major departure from their past policies. Both countries were expected to satisfy their citizens that the deal was the need of the hour and that it would not be against the national interest of either country. People in both countries had high expectations from their respective governments. The media was also expected to exert an enormous amount of pressure on their decision-makers. This turnaround was going to raise the eyebrows of many detractors of the USA and India both. It was the first case of the divided world. There were supporters and a good number of opponents of this new arrangement between India and the USA that was going to be operationalized. The next section helps us in understanding the transition of the nuclear deal of 2005 into the Indo-US Civil Nuclear Cooperation Agreement 2008, also called the '123 Nuclear Agreement' between India and the USA.

Transition from the Indo-US Civil Nuclear Cooperation Deal 2005 to the Indo-US Civil Nuclear Cooperation Agreement 2008 (123 Nuclear Agreement)

The July 2005 nuclear deal announcement led to ferocious debates taking place in both India and the USA. There were serious doubts on the part of experts and policymakers in both countries, who started sharing concerns about the deal since the day it was announced. The Bush administration was keen to ensure that all hurdles in the US Congress were overcome by persuading key US congressmen about the deal's political, strategic and economic virtues. However, congressmen saw the deal as a challenge to the US policy of nuclear non-proliferation. Others opposed the deal saying that the USA did not get anything in return from India for putting a curb on its nuclear assets. To Stephen Cohen,[66] the USA should have bargained for placing certain limits on India's nuclear programme. US scholars like Chris Smith, George Perkovich and others opposed any nuclear cooperation with India on the ground that it would defeat the NPT objectives. They were of the view that the deal with India had weakened the international nuclear non-proliferation regime, as it was awarding India non-adherence to the NPT, CTBT and other nuclear regimes. Many were worried that making an exception for India would crack open the international non-proliferation regime, the rules and norms that until then had kept the world secured from widespread proliferation.

Cohen added[67] that similar doubts were shared by some conservatives in the USA, who defied their own president and dismissed the argument that India might be a natural strategic ally or a reliable partner in containing China (one of the implicit strategic underpinnings of the agreement, at least as seen by US officials). Apprehensions about support from Indian officials were also cast by protagonists of the deal. A few also saw it as a betrayal of an old US ally, Pakistan.

However, there was a group of US businesses that favoured the agreement, as it was seen as promoting a more favourable atmosphere for US investment in India. Thus, officials of the US companies did show their interest in becoming suppliers of technologies that were essential for giving a boost to India's civilian nuclear programme. Meanwhile, for India, the views of the strategic community were positive, as it felt that if the deal went through and if strategic military cooperation between the two states increased, then the prospects for major military sales to India would become a reality. Similar sentiments were expressed by business delegates who accompanied President Bush during his visit to India in March 2006. It is important to note that this deal brought an enormous transformation in the overall Indo-US strategic cooperation, which enabled both countries to finalize defence deals worth more than $18 billion between 2008 and 2020.

---

[66] Cohen, 'Deal Gone too Far'.

[67] Ibid.

Back in India, the nuclear deal received widespread support from the United Progressive Alliance (UPA) coalition government led by PM Manmohan Singh. However, the deal was vehemently opposed by the principal opposition party, the Bharatiya Janata Party (BJP), and other smaller groups. Inside India, even the scientific community stood divided on the issue of the nuclear deal. Anil Kakodar, the topmost official of Atomic Energy Commission (AEC), also approached the media opposing the negative impact it was to have on India's nuclear programme because of the separation of civilian and military nuclear installations. A number of other former scientists who had worked with BARC or other government agencies in India started putting a lot of pressure on the government to renegotiate the deal, concerned about serious implications for India's nuclear programme.[68]

As discussed earlier, many US legislators and supporters of non-proliferation, in the past, had always tried to undercut, weaken and terminate India's military nuclear programme. Despite all the sanctions and various types of proliferation and technology denial regimes, Indian scientists succeeded in producing a nuclear weapon. A good number of scientists had been fearful of US intrusions into the country's nuclear programme. The strategic and scientific community insisted that 'technology transfer' should be the touchstone of US-Indian relations, as US records in the past had not been very good—this is analysed in detail in subsequent sections. On most occasions, denial of technology always dominated the negotiations between Indian and US officials. The role of international technology regimes in the denial of high-end technologies to India is discussed in Chapter 7.

Some experts were also of the view that the Indo-US nuclear deal would raise the financial and political costs of the Indian nuclear weapons programme, though it did not impose a legal bar on the production of fissile material or the testing of nuclear explosive devices by India.[69] Many were not convinced by the deal offered by the USA to India and cited examples of Iraq and Iran—though both were the USA's friends, the USA did not hesitate in taking revenge on them

[68] *Frontline,* 'Cover Story'.

[69] Vardarajan, 'The Nuclear Deal and "Minimum Deterrence"'.

when conflicts of interest with them arose. There was no guarantee for India too. It is noteworthy to mention here that thousands of pages were published by different media organizations debating the pros and cons of the Indo-US nuclear deal of 2005. Over several decades prior, rarely any such issue had consumed so much space in newspapers and magazines in India as the debates regarding the Indo-US nuclear deal did in the 21st century.

In the words of Cohen, a group in the USA believed that strategic autonomy would give India even greater leverage over the USA than it had ever had and, even more importantly, would have forced Pakistan to bend and required China to deal with India as a strategic equal.[70] Much controversy was generated in India over the alleged US pressure on Iran and a host of other issues. There seemed to be a major departure from the long-practised policy of the Clinton administration of putting enough pressure on India to 'cap, roll back, and *eliminate*' the Indian nuclear programme in the mid-1990s. The second Bush administration, in the aftermath of the 9/11 incident, seemed to have accepted a modest and stable Indian nuclear force and that it would not mind seeing India acquire a major force that would in some way balance out China's nuclear arsenal. The USA under President Bush actually wanted to see a strong and vibrant India playing a role in the global balance of influence. It could be seen that while India remained under tremendous US pressure during the Clinton administration (1993–2000) to sign the NPT and CTBT, all pressures on its nuclear programme were eased when Clinton's successor President Bush assumed office in the USA (2001–2008).

Slowly, the euphoria over the nuclear deal started evaporating, and misunderstandings over the issue of separation of civilian nuclear reactors from the military ones and the acceptance of full safeguards by India under the IAEA cropped up. The statements of Indian and US officials indicated that these issues were thorny and needed a lot of understanding. Both the governments had to tell their country-men that the nuclear deal was in the interest of both countries. For India, meeting future energy requirements, ending the USA-imposed

[70] Cohen, 'Deal Gone Too Far'.

nuclear sanctions and seeking US cooperation in this crucial area were a must. For the USA, achieving certain foreign policy goals, as well as encouraging India to rely more upon clean energy and adhere to non-proliferation regimes, was very crucial. The issue of a separation plan hinged on whether India would complete its separation plan before the US president readied congressmen for getting other necessary legislative changes made to enable the deal getting converted into a full-fledged nuclear agreement. Doubts were also raised over whether US cooperation would ever get extended to the military sphere.

Robert G. Joseph testified that the Bush administration expected that the 'separation of civil and military leaf infrastructure must be conducted in a credible and transparent manner, and be defensible from a non-proliferation point of view'. He added, 'we indicated at the recent G-8 and NSG meetings that we do not view a voluntary offer arrangement as defensible from a proliferation standpoint or consistent with the Joint Statement'. That India was to maintain its nuclear-testing moratorium was mentioned as one of the conditions for full civil nuclear cooperation.[71] Difficulties still persisted over the interpretation of the provisions of the deal, and several rounds of dis-cussions were held for months between the officials of both countries. India and the USA being the two largest democracies of the world, it was quite natural that the deal having the potential of ending India's nuclear apartheid was going to generate much heated debates in both countries for several months to come. It was for this reason that the nuclear deal of 2005 took another 3 years to be converted into the nuclear agreement in 2008.

On either side, there were hawks and peaceniks. It was not easy for the officials to get the deal converted into a full-fledged agreement. Several legislative and administrative steps needed to be taken by both countries before the deal could be converted into an agreement. This suggested that the deal, before finally getting converted into an agreement, had to pass through several tests in both the countries. It exerted an enormous amount of pressure on all those who were part of the decision-making process. They were expected to remove all

---

[71] For details, see *Factsheet*.

hurdles so that a decision could be implemented to the satisfaction of both parties.

Some nuclear critiques like Robert Joseph even suggested renegotiation of the entire deal while responding to demands made in the hearings that India should accept moratorium on production of fissile material, ratify CTBT and sign NPT as a non-nuclear weapon state.[72] The Indo-US nuclear deal of 2005 demanded that India place all its nuclear installations under the supervision of the IAEA by accepting IAEA safeguards and formalizing an India-Specific Safeguards Agreement with IAEA. There were problems at this stage also. For the IAEA, India in 2005 was still a non-nuclear state. Its 35-member Board of Governors, of which India had been a member ever since the establishment of the agency, had to be persuaded to recognize India as 'a responsible state with advanced nuclear technology'.[73]

Indian negotiators were expected to overcome another obstacle before their case for membership of the NSG could be approved. The 45 members of the NSG, having the role of regulating nuclear trade among the members and with other countries that were signatories to the NPT, were also expected to make a similar decision as the IAEA. While Britain, France and Russia were ready to support India's membership, China's objection raised doubts about the NSG's willingness to adjust to the new framework for nuclear energy cooperation with India.[74] Till date, India has not been able to become a member of the NSG because of China's ambivalent stand on India's membership, as China supports the idea of Pakistan also being given NSG membership.

An Indian expert stated that Indian purchase of natural uranium from abroad was to be under IAEA safeguards. Zuberi quoted PM Manmohan Singh's joint statement speech in Washington on 29 July 2005 and said, 'The only commitment that we have taken additionally is "It will be an autonomous Indian decision as to what is 'civilian' and what is 'military'". Our strategic policies and assets will remain outside

---

[72] Ibid.

[73] Mohan, 'N-Deal'.

[74] C.R.S. Report, 'US Nuclear Cooperation with India: Issues for Congress'.

the scope of our discussions with any external interlocutors.'[75] The controversy over the separation of civilian and military nuclear reactors was not going to settle down very soon. PM Singh assured the country that the government would not allow any fissile material shortages or any other material limitations on India's strategic programmes in order to meet current or future requirements. In light of India's three-stage nuclear programme, the deal would need sequential implementation in an integrated manner. No conditions were acceptable to India.[76] The slugfest over the interpretation of the deal's contents continued in both countries at the legislature level. PM Singh's statement made amply clear that India would not accept any condition whereby its strategic autonomy was likely to come under pressure. The nuclear issue has been a very emotional issue in India for several decades. The USA was solely blamed for obstructing the growth of the Indian nuclear sector in the aftermath of the 1974 PNE and May 1998 nuclear tests and the sanctions imposed thereafter against more than 500 Indian companies.

As discussed, it became explicit that on all possible occasions, Indo-US nuclear cooperation would be guided more by politico-strategic factors and less by any other factor. US administrations had always pursued such policies whereby it would become difficult for the Indian government to achieve self-reliance in crucial sectors like defence and the nuclear field. Promising to offer substantial coopera-tion initially and then dragging its feet in due course of time had, more often than not, been true on the part of the US administration. Apprehensions were also cast in India regarding the import of foreign reactors, which would involve a long-term process of tenders, licens-ing hurdles and construction delays. It would make India dependent on foreign supplies of enriched fuel. The developments regarding the operationalization of Indo-US Civil Nuclear Agreement 2008 and its implications for India's energy security policy are analysed in the next chapter.

The nuclear deal of 2005 was to be converted into a nuclear agree-ment after all necessary legislative and administrative steps were

---

[75] Zuberi, 'The Nuclear Deal: India Can't be Coerced'.

[76] Ibid. *The Hindu* (New Delhi), 9 July 2006.

completed by both India and the USA. The issue, to a very large extent, was settled after the decision of GOI was announced just a few days before the arrival of US President Bush in India in March 2006. GOI declared that only 14 out of the total 22 reactors were civilian nuclear installations, which showed amply that all concerns expressed by the strategic and scientific community in India were taken care of, decisions had accordingly been made and India's stand was made clear to the US administration.[77] During Bush's visit, a joint statement was issued, and the US president expressed the firm commitment of his administration to the implementation of the Indo-US nuclear deal shortly after the passing of the necessary legislation by the US Congress. He also expressed satisfaction over the necessary steps taken by GOI for fulfilling its obligations, as required under the deal of July 2005 for ensuring its smooth sailing through both houses of the US Congress.

The delay in the process of getting the deal passed as a legislation and the attempts by US congressmen to introduce amendments and a number of conditionalities to the original bill generated a lot of hue and cry in the country. Even the Indian government became serious and expressed concerns about the proposed amendments, equating them to 'change of the goalposts' just before the match. PM Manmohan Singh tried to address the misgivings of the scientific community by assuring that India would walk away from a 'deal' that did not conform to the July 2005 framework and/or was deemed to be not in accordance with the national interests.[78] He assured the members of both the houses on 17 August 2006 that in no manner 'India is going to accept any fresh conditionalities and change in the provisions of the July 18, 2005 and March 02, 2006 joint statements'. He categorically assured that India would not settle for anything less than the resumption of 'full civil nuclear energy cooperation'.[79] As discussed earlier, one could understand the reasons that were responsible for the 3-year-delay in the nuclear deal of 2005 finally getting subsumed under the 123 Nuclear Agreement of 2008.

[77] *Frontline*, 'Cover Story'.

[78] *The Hindu*, 13 August 2006.

[79] *The Hindu*, 20 August 2006.

Just before the US Congress elections in November 2006, the bill for the implementation of the nuclear deal was passed by both the houses. However, it appeared difficult that the Republican Party of President Bush suffered loss of majority in both the House of US Congress raising fresh doubts that whether the Bush Administration be able to get the Bill passed jointly by the US Congress during the Lame Duck Session often called immediately after the elections for completing the necessary formalities of newly chosen Congressmen or not.

Finally, on 9 December 2006, the Joint Conference of the United States Senate and House of Representatives passed the much-debated H.R. 5682—the Henry J. Hyde United States-India Peaceful Atomic Energy Cooperation Act of 2006. The act permitted the resumption of US nuclear trade with India after 32 years, which had ended in 1974 over the latter's nuclear test. The deal now had to be supported by the 45 members of the NSG, which needed to change its guidelines and grant a waiver to countries for resuming nuclear cooperation with India. Once it was done, India and the USA were also expected to finalize the bilateral '123 Agreement' for making the deal operational.[80] India also managed to sign an India-Specific Safeguards Agreement with the IAEA. This was how the deal became a full-fledged agreement in 2008. The author has analysed the Indian government's response to the pending issues and the role of the then main opposition party, the BJP, in 2006 in Chapter 4.

CONCLUSION

On the whole, the chapter concludes that the changes during the mid-1980s reflected the US desire to accommodate India's interests in emerging as a global power. Because of the change in the USA's policies towards India, it started giving importance to the concept of India emerging as a stronger power in the South Asian region in the near future. However, despite the important beginning made in the Indo-US defence and strategic cooperation through the signing of the 1985 MOU, issues like India's non-adherence to the NPT, CTBT, MTCR and draft FMCT seriously affected their relations because of

[80] *The Hindu*, 9 and 10 December 2006.

their divergent approaches on vexed issues. Even though the Cold War had ended, the two countries continued to have serious differences over issues that had existed between them for several decades, like the nuclear cooperation issue. Even on the Kashmir issue they were not on the same platform, and it definitely cast a serious shadow in their bilateral relationship. The beginning made after the 1985 MOU came to a complete halt when India conducted a nuclear explosion in 1998. It can be concluded that continued differences over Kashmir, nuclear proliferation and a host of other issues did not allow the successes achieved during the 1980–1992 period to be institutionalized and carried further in a big way.

The chapter highlighted that the USA also assumed a very harsh attitude in the early 1990s towards India keeping its nuclear option open, which brought it into direct conflict with India's interests over the nuclear issue. India did not succumb to the US pressure on it to sign the NPT. It rather made it clear to the USA that it could not be coerced to sign treaties that it considered discriminatory and did not work for complete disarmament. India tried to remind the world about its disarmament credentials and reminded the international community of a previously presented proposal at the UN SSOD in 1988. It suggested carrying forward the then-proposed negotiations for total disarmament. Thus, India always expressed its commitment to international efforts towards achieving the goals of nuclear disarmament. This had been India's principled stand on the NPT issue in an unambiguous manner.

The chapter clarified India's differences with the USA on the NPT and nuclear proliferation issues in a detailed manner. It investigated the change in India's position on the issues of the NPT and CTBT. India's views on disarmament—the total elimination of nuclear weapons—which had guided its policies on the nuclear issue, gradually changed over a period of time, and later, the nuclear question got linked with the question of the country's security. This added a new dimension to India's ongoing controversy with the USA in the aftermath of the indefinite extension of the NPT in 1995. The issue of security had assumed importance among Indian policymakers, and

India's stand on the CTBT was a result of this new policy view. The ferocious debate that took place in India over the CTBT resulted in the closing of India's nuclear option after it carried out nuclear explosions in May 1998. India declared itself to be a state with nuclear weapons. It also presented its nuclear doctrine to the world.

Undoubtedly, India's decision of going nuclear helped it in elevating its status and prestige at the international level. After President Clinton's visit to India in March 2000, almost all the important leaders of the world visited India, and it helped break India's seclusion after the May 1998 nuclear explosions that had led to the imposition of sanctions on it by many countries. It also helped Indo-US relations get institutionalized during President Bush's tenure in many ways. The NSSP and the enhanced level of military cooperation between the two countries were very significant. This process continued during President Bush's second term in the White House. During the visit of US State Secretary Condoleezza Rice to India in March 2005, he stated that both countries were keen to maintain the momentum of strategic partnership that had been formalized post the 9/11 terrorist attack on the World Trade Center.

The amount of euphoria that had been generated because of the 18 July 2005 and 2 March 2006 joint statements during the visit of President Bush (Jr.) to India about the formalization of the Indo-US nuclear deal did once again raise serious doubts about the intentions of India and the USA towards each other. There remained much misunderstanding over the issue of separation of the civilian nuclear reactors from the military ones and the acceptance of full safeguards by India under the IAEA. Even though the bill was passed jointly by the two houses of the US Congress and the nuclear deal of 2005 was subsumed under the 123 Nuclear Agreement of 2008, there remained several unanswered questions about the fate of the visualized cooperation between the two countries, thereby substantiating the hypothesis that the relation of India and the USA were guided more by politico-strategic factors and less by any other factors. The next chapter carries forward the discussion on the post-2008 developments.

Energy Security Dynamics

4

One of the aims of the Nuclear Cooperation Agreement of 2008 was for the USA to help India in achieving the latter's 'energy security' goals through the nuclear mode. Hence, energy security dynamics emerged as the fulcrum of the Indo-US strategic partnership in the 21st century. As discussed in Chapter 3, many hurdles still persisted in the path of the operationalization of the Indo-US Civil Nuclear Cooperation Agreement 2008. This chapter primarily deals with the developments leading to its operationalization under the UPA and NDA governments, which had implications for India's energy security. It provides a background of India's efforts towards energy security through the nuclear mode. It highlights the current status of the implementation of the agreement and its impact on India's energy security goals. The chapter analyses dynamics of US help to India in the latter's resumption of nuclear trade with the rest of the world, the role of the bill regarding India's nuclear liability in delaying the sale of nuclear reactors to India and the setting up of nuclear parks in India. It analyses the intricacies of the foreign policies of the two largest democracies of the world getting intertwined with their overall security policies. At last, it focuses on challenges that have emerged for India's energy security goals in the post-Fukushima period demanding fresh policy interventions and reduced dependence of India on nuclear energy.

INTRODUCTION

Globally, countries are facing challenges regarding ever-depleting resources of energy for meeting the aspirations of their people. India, in the past few decades, has been grappling with problems of a global nature. Its ability to meet all such challenges today is under test, as it has only 2.3 per cent of the total land mass with one-sixth of the population of the world to support for a decent living. Despite all the achievements of India, locally and globally, a fact that erodes its success story is its remaining at the 129th rank, as per the UN Development Programme (UNDP) Report (2018–2019),[1] in terms of the Human Development Index, even after seven decades of its independence. Any strategies regarding India succeeding in enhancing its energy security in the 21st century must factor in this fact. Thus, India's future energy consumption is expected to be driven by its economic growth and demographic trends.

Policymakers in India are expected to initiate appropriate policies for meeting the excessive energy demands and work for achieving the goals of energy security in the near future. The demands of big, emerging economies, such as Brazil, Russia, China, South Africa and many other nations, for energy resources are likely to constrain the ability of countries like India to enhance their energy security, either indigenously or through imports. It is against this backdrop that the role of the USA has been all-important in enabling India to continue on its path to becoming a major power without facing a threat on its energy security front.

One of the hallmarks of Indian foreign policy in recent decades has been to focus on enhancing the energy security goals of the country through diplomatic efforts. The foreign policies of the UPA government led by PM Manmohan Singh (2004–2014) and the NDA government led by PM Narendra Modi (2014–2020), to a very large extent, have remained intertwined with the economic policies of the country for ensuring constant energy supplies in a changing international security scenario. Maintaining consistent economic growth for a country of India's size requires a well-defined energy security policy in the 21st century.

The Modi government has set a target of taking India's GDP to US$5 trillion by 2025. India's future energy consumption is expected to be driven by its economic growth and demographic trends. India

---

[1] UNDP HDI Report 2018–19.

was expected to maintain an economic growth of around 6–7 per cent under the Twelfth Five-Year Plan[2] (2012–2017) despite the downturn in its economy. For India, the security scenario in the Middle East and West Asia since 2011 raised uncertainties in the international energy market because of Israel's ongoing war in Gaza, the Islamic State of Iraq and Syria (ISIS)-led war in Iraq and the continuing war in Syria and Yemen, which had raised crude oil prices in the international market. Any instability in this region is known to exert immense pressure on the economies of developing countries like India. Following in the footsteps of PM Manmohan Singh and his government's energy security policy, PM Narendra Modi's government, since May 2014, also has been keen to push nuclear trade and commerce with the USA in the direction of attaining energy security goals, which was strongly evident during US State Secretary Kerry's visit to India in 2014. It must be mentioned here that Bush and Manmohan Singh readied the legislative framework for the final signatures on the nuclear agreement in 2008 and the resumption of India's nuclear trade with the rest of the world after seeking necessary waivers from the international nuclear regimes. However, it was Obama and Modi who got the nuclear agreement fully operationalized and got contracts awarded to companies for the sale of nuclear reactors and setting up of nuclear parks in India.

PM Narendra Modi's government took several measures for reversing the downturn in the Indian economy so that the projected growth rate of 7–8 per cent could be sustained. It is expected to work in tune with the USA, which in the 2010s has shown extra interest in enabling India to achieve its green and clean energy goals. The volatility in crude oil prices in the international market has compelled the Indian government to continue working for boosting its energy security programme. For a developing country like India, energy security refers to its ability to minimize vulnerability to supply interruptions in oil–gas–uranium reactors, ensure the opening up of sea routes round the year and ensure stability in the price of energy resources and the smooth transfer of technologies. India knows for sure that the USA is the world leader

---

[2] After the substitution of the Planning Commission with the NITI Aayog (National Institution for Transforming India), the practice of Five-Year Plans has been discontinued on a permanent basis.

in energy-related technologies and exercises considerable influence on the oil and nuclear energy market on a worldwide basis.

The Indo-US Civil Nuclear Cooperation Agreement[3] signed in 2008 is also known as the '123 Nuclear Agreement'. It finally got operationalized under PM Narendra Modi's government in India and President Barack Obama's administration in the USA in 2015–2016. While India and the USA were still busy in establishing the necessary framework for the operationalization of the Indo-US Civil Nuclear Cooperation Agreement of 2008, the world was completely shaken up by the Fukushima nuclear disaster in Japan in March 2011. Despite the nuclear disaster, the Indian government has stuck to its plan of raising nuclear energy production up to 20,000 MWe by 2020 and 63,000 MWe by 2032. PM Narendra Modi's visit to the USA in October 2014 and the follow-up visit of President Barack Obama to India in January 2015 gave a big boost to Indo-US energy cooperation in general and nuclear cooperation in particular, which cleared all pending obstacles on account of India's 'Civil Liability for Nuclear Damage Act, 2010',[4] also known as the 'Nuclear Liability Act', allegedly blamed for preventing full operationalization of the nuclear agreement since 2010.

ENERGY SECURITY THROUGH THE NUCLEAR MODE: A BACKGROUND

Harnessing nuclear technology for the generation of electrical energy had always been on the agenda of PM Nehru's government. All successive governments in India have consistently worked for achieving

---

[3] The Indo-US Civil Nuclear Cooperation Agreement is also known as the '123 Nuclear Agreement', because it was Section 123 of the US domestic legislation of US NNPA 1978 that was amended through a bill initiated by Congressman Henry J. Hyde for the enactment of the 'US and India Peaceful for Atomic Energy Act', which allowed any US president to sign a nuclear cooperation agreement with a country that was not a signatory to the Nuclear Non-Proliferation Treaty (NPT) of 1968. https://www.congress.gov/bill/109th-congress/house-bill/5682.

[4] The Civil Liability for Nuclear Damage Bill, 2010, seeks to create a mechanism for compensating victims of nuclear damage arising from a nuclear incident. It caps the liability of the operator at ₹5,000 million. http://www.prsindia.org/billtrack/the-civil-liability-for-nuclear-damage-bill-2010-1042.

this goal indigenously. India's nuclear energy programme had to be navigated through the building of indigenous capabilities without being overly dependent on foreign help. India was expected to develop the art of manoeuvring through networks of nuclear regimes created by those industrialized countries that enjoyed a monopoly over key technologies. It needed to overcome all such hurdles from time to time.

Realizing the potential of nuclear energy, India, under Nehru, has been laying a strong foundation for its nuclear programme since its independence. Nehru emphasized that a developing country like India has more uses for nuclear energy, as its power resources are limited, than any advanced country of the world.[5] It is noteworthy here that successes achieved in the nuclear sector by India are largely attributed to the vision of Nehru that resulted in the beginning of a nuclear programme by the Indian scientific community led by Homi Bhabha and others soon after India's independence. The crux of India's nuclear energy programme was achieving self-reliance in this technological area. Continuity and bipartisan support to the nuclear programme by the political class have been the hallmarks of India's nuclear energy programme since its inception. India's nuclear energy programme has received complete support from Nehru's successors, L. B. Shastri, Indira Gandhi, Rajiv Gandhi, H. D. Deve Gowda, P. V. Narasimha Rao, Atal Bihari Vajpayee, Manmohan Singh and the incumbent PM Narendra Modi, who all played a very important role in turning India into a legitimate nuclear power at the international level.

As discussed in Chapter 3, one of the benchmarks of India's nuclear policy soon after the passing of the Atomic Energy Act in 1948 was to start the country's three-stage plan for establishing nuclear power under the Department of Atomic Energy, which was created in 1954. It is important to underline here once again that the Indian nuclear power programme was based on the strategy to use the limited available uranium and vast thorium resources. The leadership envisioned a three-stage nuclear programme for ensuring India's emergence as a self-reliant nuclear power. The first stage is based on setting up pressurized heavy-water reactors (PHWRs) using indigenously available

[5] Nehru, 'Apsara', 255.

natural uranium producing electricity and plutonium, which falls under the commercial domain. This is followed by the second stage, in which plutonium fuels fast breeder reactors (FBRs) producing electricity, an additional quantity of plutonium and uranium-233 from thorium. The third stage is based on the thorium–uranium-233 cycle.[6] India's civil nuclear energy strategy has always been directed at attaining complete independence in the nuclear fuel cycle, for which India most recently compelled the US administration in 2008 to allow full rights to the country under the nuclear agreement. India insisted diplomatically on being given all necessary waivers despite being a non-signatory to the NPT.[7] It has been fighting against multiple organizations over the past several decades seeking complete strategic autonomy in its nuclear programme. Nuclear power generation in India over the past decades has not been very easy because of the tight control of international nuclear regimes such as the NPT, CTBT, MTCR, NSG, London Group, Wassenaar Group, Australia Group and IAEA over proliferation of nuclear technologies. All such regimes were led by the USA, as they pursued policies that were completely inconsistent with India's nuclear policy of keeping its nuclear programme completely immune from any external interference. The techniques of controlling trade in high-end/dual-use technologies by all these international nuclear-cum-missiles regimes is discussed in Chapter 6.

As discussed in Chapter 3, India had been suffering stagnation in its nuclear programme after the end of the 1971 India–Pakistan war and its first nuclear explosion in May 1974 that ended the monopoly of the Western world in maintaining nuclear supremacy at the international level. It is important to mention here that the 1974 nuclear explosion had to later be designated as a 'PNE' so as to reduce the international pressure on India's nuclear programme. India, then onwards, preferred pursuing its civilian-cum-military nuclear programme in an ambiguous manner under the policy of keeping its 'nuclear option open' in the ensuing years, until it 'closed its nuclear option' and became a nuclear weapon state in 1998. India's nuclear

---

[6] Government of India, *National Report to The Convention on Nuclear Safety*, 6.

[7] Kumar, 'Emerging Indo-US Strategic Partnership and the China Factor', xxxii–xxxiii.

programme underwent transformations during the 1980s and 1990s[8] because of the prevailing security scenario then, amidst fears of the USA's and China's nuclear cooperation with Pakistan in providing a design of a nuclear weapon and also carrying out Pakistan's first nuclear weapons test on Chinese soil itself.[9]

PM P. V. Narasimha Rao's government, in order to keep pace with the ongoing neoliberal economic policies and security considerations, maintained continuity in the country's nuclear programme. Amidst the ongoing slugfest with the USA over the NPT's revision and CTBT discussions inside the UNGA, the Rao government moved a step ahead of its predecessors and decided to carry out another nuclear explosion, but it was made to abandon the idea because of pressure from the USA, whose satellites picked up pictures of unusual movement near the Pokhran firing range. PMs H. D. Deve Gowda and I. K. Gujral also withstood US and international pressure on India's stand on the NPT during the NPT Review and Extension Conference in 1995 and the finalization of the CTBT in 1996. In light of the country's nuclear energy policy commensurate with energy security, India decided not to succumb to international pressure and not to sign the NPT and the CTBT. This decision did help PM Vajpayee's government go ahead with carrying out nuclear explosions in May 1998 and declare India a nuclear state. PM Vajpayee's government also prepared India's nuclear doctrine and declared it to the rest of the world so as to enable the latter to know about India's do's and don'ts regarding the use of its nuclear arsenal under certain conditions.

Maintaining continuity in its nuclear energy policy over the last two decades, India needed to end its isolation regarding nuclear commerce and trade because of the discriminatory policies of nuclear regimes such as the IAEA, NSG, London Group, MTCR, Wassenaar Group, Australia Group and others. India, which found itself technologically in a position to exploit nuclear energy in a bigger way but was constrained in doing so because of the above-mentioned nuclear regimes, could not access nuclear fuel or reactor plants from abroad. As discussed in Chapter 3, PM Manmohan Singh's government signed the historic nuclear deal in

---

[8] Kumar, *Indo-U.S. Politico Strategic Relations*.

[9] M. Nallapat's story that appeared in *The Sunday Guardian* on 3 August 2014.

2005 and nuclear agreement in 2008 with the USA, which ended India's isolation over the past three decades, and it was expected that India's nuclear programme would grow by leaps and bounds.[10] Over a period of time, the Indian nuclear programme has attained self-sufficiency, extending from uranium exploration and mining, through fuel fabrication, heavy-water production and reactor design and construction, to reprocessing of used fuel and waste management. However, the long delay in the implementation of the three-stage nuclear programme has been a matter of concern. The significance of the 2008 agreement with the USA for the resumption of India's nuclear trade is expected to pave the way for its receiving crucial technology for the completion of its three-stage nuclear energy programme.

In the last decade and a half (post the nuclear agreement of 2008), GOI has decided to continue increasing the proportion of nuclear energy in the total generation of electricity in the country through thermal, hydro and other modes. For India, energy security refers to its ability to minimize vulnerability to oil–gas supply interruptions and ensure the opening up of sea routes round the year and stability in the price of energy resources. Nuclear power has a significant role to play in meeting the demand for secure energy supply, offering several advantages—it is an important alternative to the expensive oil and natural gas. Nuclear energy is seen as a viable alternative for reducing carbon dioxide emissions, which is necessary to mitigate climate change. Concerns around energy security and climate change have made nuclear energy very important today. Nuclear energy has immense potential for reducing India's ever-increasing dependence on imported gas and petroleum. It also saves much-needed foreign exchange reserves and reduces the country's current account deficit. The Modi government has taken several steps for overcoming the current account deficit, along with stopping the depreciation of the Indian rupee vis-à-vis the US dollar, which has imposed heavy burdens on India's gas and oil import bills.[11]

---

[10] Kumar and Singh, 'Dynamics of Indo-US Nuclear Deal and Its Strategic Implications'.

[11] India's crude oil import bill was around US$88 billion in 2017–2018, which increased by 42 per cent to US$125 billion in 2018–2019. https://www.google.com/amp/s/energy.economictimes.indiatimes.com/amp/news/oil-and-gas/indias-crude-oil-import-bill-to -peak-at-record-125-billion-in-current-fiscal-oil-ministry/66319124.

Several reports of national and international agencies have been focusing on the GOI preparations underway for opening up India's nuclear energy sector for attracting FDIs to set up nuclear parks in the country. According to GOI[12] sources, India's nuclear energy production will reach 20,000 MWe by 2020 and 63,000 MWe by 2032. Currently, India has an installed capacity of 4,560 MWe of nuclear power. According to the Nuclear Power Corporation of India Limited (NPCIL), there are currently seven new nuclear reactors under construction. There are two 1,000 MWe reactors already built and commissioned in Kudankulam, which have been operational since September 2010 and March 2011.[13] Post Fukushima, these nuclear power plant sites have witnessed many protests by local people regarding safety concerns, leading to a delay in the final commissioning of the plants in 2013.

According to another report, by 2022, the total generation of nuclear energy is expected to increase by eight times, catering to around 10 per cent of India's electricity needs. In addition, by 2052, the generation of atomic energy is expected to increase 70-fold, contributing nearly 26 per cent of India's total electricity requirements. Therefore, the reliance on nuclear energy to satisfy the power needs of the world's second fastest-growing economy is poised to record quantum progress.[14] Though there exists a large reserve of uranium in the world, tight controls maintained by international nuclear regimes have been casting a shadow over the supply of nuclear reactors, as well as nuclear fuel, that is, uranium,[15] thereby severely affecting the nuclear programmes of countries in general and that of India in particular. However, the scenario in India underwent a paradigm shift after the culmination of the Indo-US Nuclear Agreement in 2008. The following sections highlight the UPA and NDA governments' cooperation with the USA in the direction of achieving nuclear energy security after the 2008 signing.

---

[12] Government of India, *A strategy for the Growth of Electrical Energy in India*.

[13] NPCIL, *Plants in Operation*.

[14] IDSA Task Force Report, *Development of Nuclear Energy Sector in India*, 5.

[15] For details please see, Kumar, *Indo-U.S. Politico Strategic Relations*.

ENERGY COOPERATION: UPA GOVERNMENT (2004–2014)

It was the UPA-I government (2004–2009) led by PM Manmohan Singh that achieved India's most important deal with the USA. It has proved to be a watershed agreement as far as the Indian nuclear energy programme, which received a massive boost after remaining stuck because of the denial of international technology regimes, is concerned.[16] For the USA, an important reason for having a nuclear deal with India in July 2005 was its concerns regarding climate change and helping countries like India reduce their dependence on fossil fuels for maintaining the economic growth above 8 per cent. For India, concerns regarding energy security brought it close to the USA. An assessment of the Indo-US Civil Nuclear Cooperation Agreement suggests that nuclear energy had been highly prioritized by the then UPA government. The deal ended India's isolation regarding nuclear trade and enabled the country to conclude civilian nuclear agreements for the import of reactors and fuel from countries like France, Russia, Mongolia, Kazakhstan, Namibia, Australia, Canada and South Korea. India is also about to finish an agreement with Japan.

As a result of the culmination of the 123 Agreement between India and the USA in 2008 and after the necessary waivers from the IAEA and NSG, it became easier for India to import some 12 1,000 MW light-water reactors (LWRs) from Russia, France and the USA. Additionally, it is supposed to build 12 indigenously designed 700 MW reactors. This will support the generation of some 25,000 MW of nuclear power by 2020, which could go up to 50,000 MW by 2030.[17] While intensifying the search for uranium domestically—there have been recent successes in Meghalaya and Andhra Pradesh—India could obtain uranium from overseas. It may explore participation in uranium enrichment if its capacity in enriched uranium reactors is significant. Of course, in parallel, India should pursue the FBR programme vigorously and begin thorium utilization as early as it is practically and economically possible.

---

[16] Kumar, 'South Asia and Future of the Nuclear Non-Proliferation Regime in the 21st Century'.

[17] http://www.npcil.nic.in/main/AllProjectOperationDisplay.aspx.

India's manufacturing base for nuclear power equipment is well developed for heavy-water reactors; it is also being developed for FBRs. Similarly, Indian industries can be inducted in producing equipment for LWRs, which may also be imported from Russia, France, the USA or elsewhere. With the change in domestic laws, participation of the private sector is on the rise, and in a few years, India will be in a position to export a heavy-water reactor power plant as a whole. There will be big opportunities for Indian companies and Indian technical personnel to service a resurgent global nuclear industry, in an era when the world as a whole looks for non-carbon energy sources. Simultaneously, India has also been continuing discussions for achieving the goals of a 'nuclear weapon-free world'. PM Manmohan Singh's 26–27 September 2013 visit to the USA[18] had cleared the hurdles in setting up six nuclear reactors in the Indian state of Gujarat by US companies and thereby ended the delay in the operationalization of the nuclear agreement on account of India's Nuclear Liability Act. S. K. Jain[19], Chairman of the NPCIL, considers that nuclear power is already economically competitive with thermal coal away from coal pitheads. 'But, with increase in unit capacity size, reduction in project gestation periods and safe and higher operation levels, it is our endeavour to make it competitive with coal-thermal even at coal pithead'. It is also implied that nuclear power will emerge as one of the cheapest sources of electricity in regions that are far away from coal belts. The improved economics, environmental benefits and safe record of nuclear energy will reinforce its position as the number one choice for electricity generation.

The Indian government repeatedly identified energy supply as a crucial security need. Following his election in 2004 as PM, Manmohan Singh argued that 'energy security is second only in our scheme of things to food security'. The Common Minimum Programme stated that its aim was to 'put in place policies to enhance the country's energy security particularly in the area of oil'.[20] During the Eleventh

---

[18] Transcript of the statement to the media by PM Manmohan Singh after meeting President Obama. https://mea.gov.in-focus-article.htm?22264/Transcript.

[19] Jain, 'Nuclear Power in India', 17.

[20] Planning Commission, *Tenth Five Year Plan*, Chapter 7.3, Sect. 2.

Table 4.1 *India's Nuclear Power Reactors (under the 11th FYP) under Construction or Completed*

Reactor	Type	MWe Net (Each)	Project Control	Commercial Operation	Safeguards Status
Kaiga 4	PHWR	202 MWe	NPCIL	5/2010	
Kudankulam 1	PWR (VVER)	950 MWe	NPCIL	12/2010	Item-specific
Kudankulam 2	PWR (VVER)	950 MWe	NPCIL	Mid-2011	Item-specific
Kalpakkam PFBR	FBR	470 MWe	Bhavini	9/2011 or 2012	–
Total (4)		2572 MWe			

Source: Adapted from WNA Reactor Table: Rajasthan/RAPS, also known as Rawatbhata.[21]

Five-Year Plan (2007–2012); see Table 4.1, a new generation capacity of nearly 55,000 MW was created, yet there continued to be an overall energy deficit of 8.7 per cent and peak shortage of 9.0 per cent.[22] The Twelfth Five-Year Plan (2012–2017) also laid special emphasis on the development of energy infrastructure with an investment of ₹56.3 lakh crore (approximately US$1 trillion), which was nearly double the allocation made by the Eleventh Five-Year Plan.[23]

To increase India's nuclear power generation capacity, the UPA-I government approached many international vendors to start investing in India subsequent to the culmination of the Indo-US Civil Nuclear Agreement 2008. For instance, Russia's Atomstroy agreed to build six more light-water-pressurized reactors in Kudankulam by 2017 and four in Haripur after 2017. French company Areva signed an MOU with NPCIL to build a total of six European pressurized reactors (EPR). GE Hitachi Nuclear Energy signed agreements with NPCIL and Bharat

[21] World Nuclear Association. *Nuclear Power in India*. London: World Nuclear Association, 2009, 6–7. Available at http://www.world-nuclear.org/info/inf53.html (accessed on 1 October 2020).

[22] Government of India, *Economic Survey 2011–12*, 260–261.

[23] Government of India, *Economic Survey 2012–13*, 231–232.

Heavy Electricals Limited (BHEL) to build a multi-unit power plant using 1,350 MWe advanced boiling water reactors (ABWRs). Many other companies, such as Atomic Energy of Canada Limited and Korean Electric Power Corporation, also signed similar agreements with India regarding servicing India's existing PHWRs.[24]

The UPA-II government (2009–2014) was blamed for not paying much attention to increasing India's nuclear power because of its enactment of the controversial 'Nuclear Liability Act 2010' that did not allow the export of nuclear reactors to India by companies of foreign origin, especially US companies. Failures on many economic and social fronts resulted in the big defeat of the UPA government in the general elections of 2014, and it brought the BJP-led NDA government headed by PM Narendra Modi into office.

'Civil Liability for Nuclear Damage Act, 2010' (Nuclear Liability Act)

The opposition parties, led by the BJP, played a very negative role in getting the sum of compensation fixed at ₹5 billion within the 'Civil Liability for Nuclear Damage Act, 2010', thereby making contracts less lucrative for all suppliers of nuclear reactors, including US companies, that had entered into contracts with NPCIL for the sale of their reactors to India. The adoption of this controversial clause was sufficient for slowing down the operationalization of the Indo-US nuclear agreement of 2008.

The Civil Liability for Nuclear Damage Act,[25] 2010 fixed liability for nuclear damage and specified procedures for compensating victims. The country had not forgotten the Bhopal gas tragedy of 1984 that had killed several thousand people in India. Taking a cue from that

---

[24] World Nuclear Association, *Nuclear Power in India*, March 2010.

[25] The Civil Liability for Nuclear Damage Bill, 2010 seeks to create a mechanism for compensating victims of nuclear damage arising from a nuclear incident. It caps the liability of the operator at ₹5,000 million. http://www.prsindia.org/billtrack/the-civil-liability-for-nuclear-damage-bill-2010-1042.

accident, the Act capped the liability of the nuclear operator at ₹5 billion. In case of damage exceeding ₹5 billion and up to 300 million SDR, the federal government was to be liable for paying compensation. All operators except the federal government needed to take insurance or provide financial security to cover their liability. For facilities owned by the government, the entire liability up to 300 million SDR was to be borne by the government. The Act specified who could claim compensation and the authorities who would assess and award compensation for nuclear damage. There was also a provision for penalizing a company or operator in the case of non-compliance with the provisions.

The Act delayed the award of contracts to companies because of their fear of ₹5 billion, which was a very big amount for the operators and would have made the companies' business financially unviable in case of any accidents or terrorist attacks on a nuclear power plant constructed by them. Many nuclear reactor suppliers of US origin were faced with financial problems domestically, as the nuclear industry had not been doing so well over the past years. There were several cases of bankruptcies and acquisitions and mergers leading to litigations regarding non-payment of past financial liabilities. The problems got further aggravated when the Fukushima nuclear power plant disaster occurred on 19 March 2011.

It led to the bankruptcy of big companies like General Electric (GE), Westinghouse and Toshiba, as they lost several billion dollars on account of paying compensation to the affected people and the Japanese government and incurring unforeseen expenditures on the clearing of radioactive garbage from the area around the disaster, which continued for several months after the accident. It also led to the beginning of a heated debate across the world regarding the safety of nuclear power plants in case of natural or man-made disasters. Many countries, such as Germany, Japan and France, took the lead in announcing the shutting down of their nuclear power plants and reducing the generation of electricity through the nuclear mode. All these developments had serious implications for India, as it had been making euphoric projections about increasing the contribution of nuclear-generated electricity to 26 per cent of the total electricity produced by 2030.

NUCLEAR INDUSTRY DEVELOPMENTS IN INDIA
(POST THE IAEA AND NSG WAIVERS)

The USA has played a commendable role in getting the roadblock removed for the resumption of nuclear trade between India and the rest of the world after facilitating India's entry into the IAEA, MTCR and London Group and helping India to get a special waiver from the NSG despite its pending membership of the NSG. Many diplomatic and theoretical framework aspects of this facilitation by US officials have already been discussed in detail in Chapter 3, and this chapter primarily deals with the operationalization part of the nuclear agreement. The IAEA[26] was created in 1957 with the objective of promoting safe, secure and peaceful technologies, besides preventing countries from using their nuclear technologies for military purposes. It was on 1 August 2008 that the IAEA approved the Indian draft on the safeguards agreement. The NSG[27] was formed in 1974 and has 48 member countries. It works to further limit nuclear trade among countries, especially that with non-nuclear nations.

India received a special waiver from NSG guidelines on 6 September 2008. It was a major victory for India, as the NSG had specifically been created just after India's nuclear explosion in 1974. The waiver enabled India's getting access to dual-use technology and items mentioned in the 'trigger list'.[28] It was only after the NSG waiver that India concluded agreements with French company Areva and with Russia for the purchase of nuclear reactors under the new arrangement. Following the NSG agreement in September 2008, India signed agreements with the USA, Russia, France, UK and Canada, as well as Argentina, Kazakhstan, Mongolia and Namibia. The USA was hopeful that the facilitation of India's access to all international nuclear regimes would increase nuclear trade between India and US companies and that the award of fresh contracts would provide the USA new economic sustainability.

---

[26] https://www.iaea.org/about.

[27] Hibbs, *The Future of the Nuclear Suppliers Group*, 5.

[28] *The Economic Times*, 'Indo-US Nuclear Deal: India Gets NSG Waiver', 6 September 2008.

The Russian pressurized water reactors (PWRs) were an appendage to India's three-stage plan for nuclear power and were simply to increase the generation capacity more rapidly. As mentioned earlier, plans for eight 1,000 MWe units at the Kudankulam site are underway. There are confirmed reports that Russian companies have shown interest in building 18 nuclear reactors of different types in India. According to a World Nuclear Association (WNA) report, ROSATOM has announced that it expects to build no less than 18 reactors in India. In December 2014, another high-level nuclear cooperation agreement was signed with Russia for building 20 more reactors, apart from cooperation in the development of Russian-designed nuclear power plants in Third World countires, uranium mining, production of nuclear fuel and waste management. India was also to confirm a second location for a Russian plant, with Haripur in West Bengal being engulfed in doubt. Most of the new units are expected to be the larger 1,200 MWe AES-2006 designs.[29] *The Times of India*[30] (New Delhi), on 7 November 2019, reported that Russian atomic energy corporation ROSATOM had expressed interest in collaborating with Indian companies not only for building large nuclear power plants but also for the joint development of medium- and small-sized nuclear power reactors, including floating nuclear reactors. The construction of nuclear power plants with the help of Russian companies is to be completed in four phases in India.

As discussed earlier, Russian companies were the largest beneficiaries of the opening up of nuclear trade and commerce with India from 2008 onwards. It is interesting to note here that India has used pragmatism in its diplomacy and tried to find a balance between Russia and the USA for having strategic cooperation with both. It has taken bold diplomatic steps for having closer cooperation with Russia and the USA both, for the sake of maintaining strategic autonomy in its foreign and security affairs. India has shown to the world that if Russia can work with China and have closer defence and strategic cooperation with it, India too can adopt a similar approach towards the USA. ROSATOM has won contracts for making investments in India's newly

---

[29] World Nuclear Association, *Nuclear Power in India*, March 2020.

[30] *The Times of India*, 7 November 2019.

proposed nuclear parks where companies like GE, Westinghouse and Toshiba could not make much inroads. It is important to mention here that the USA had been sincere in its approach to facilitate the access of India to various international nuclear and missiles regimes and getting nuclear trade with India started. Undoubtedly, the resumption of nuclear trade between India and rest of the world was a very important diplomatic victory, expediting the achievement of energy security goals for two reasons: it enabled India's purchase of nuclear reactors and its purchase of uranium from any part of the world.

INDIAN CONTRACTS FOR COMPANIES OF THE USA AND THE WEST

It is important to mention that when the Indo-US Civilian Nuclear Agreement 2008 was signed, the US administration expected that most of the contracts for the construction of new nuclear power plants in India and sale of nuclear reactors would be given by the Indian government to companies of US and Western origin only. Unfortunately, almost a decade and a half after the agreement, the way things have unfolded so far makes it clear that India has used this opportunity for leveraging its foreign policy and other economic interests by awarding contracts to companies of different countries. In simpler words, India has shown pragmatism in its approach by diversifying the sources for the purchase of nuclear reactors and award of contracts for the construction of nuclear power plants, in tune with its overall policy of multi-alignment with the world. The net result has been that Areva from France; ROSATOM from Russia; Westinghouse, GE and GE Hitachi from the USA; Toshiba from Japan; and companies from the UK and Canada were chosen. Further, for advancing the goal of achieving self-reliance through the promotion of indigenous companies, PSUs like NTPC and BHEL and Indian private companies like Tata Group, GVK, GMR Group, Mahindra Group and Reliance Power were also given contracts and allowed to float companies on a joint collaboration basis. India also threw open its nuclear industry for investments from private companies, both Indian and foreign, and it invited private investments in the setting up of nuclear parks in different parts of the country.

·   According to the WNA report of March 2020,[31] India signed a nuclear cooperation agreement with the UK in November 2015 with 'a comprehensive package' of collaboration on energy and climate change matters involving £3.2 billion (US$4.9 billion) in programmes and initiatives related to energy security and energy access. India also signed a preliminary agreement with GE Hitachi and Westinghouse in December 2015 and, after several years of negotiations, a full nuclear cooperation agreement was signed by India and Japan in November 2016.

The nuclear capacity target is part of the national energy policy. NPCIL held meetings and technical discussions with three major nuclear reactor suppliers—Areva of France and GE Hitachi and Westinghouse Electric Corporation of the USA—over the supply of reactors for its projects and for new units in Kaiga. These resulted in more formal agreements with each reactor supplier as early as 2009. Now, in 2020, their work is already in advanced stages. Similarly, in late 2008 itself, the flag-bearing company of nuclear operations in India, NPCIL,[32] had announced that as part of the Eleventh Five-Year Plan (2007–2012), it had started site work for 12 reactors, including the eight PHWRs of 700 MWe each, three or four FBRs and one 300 MWe advanced heavy-water reactor in 2009. Now, in 2020, many of these projects are on the verge of completion.

INDIGENIZATION UNDER NPCIL

NPCIL has been trying to fulfil all the promises it announced way back in 2009 after the finalization of the 123 Nuclear Agreement with the USA. It had said that 'India is now focusing on capacity addition through indigenisation' with progressively higher local content for imported designs, up to 80 per cent. Looking ahead, its augmentation plan includes the construction of 25–30 LWRs of at least 1,000 MWe by 2030.[33] Early in 2012, NPCIL projected the following additions to the 10.08 GWe reactor anticipated in 2017 as 'possible': a 4.2 GWe

---

[31] World Nuclear Association, *Nuclear Power in India*, March 2020.

[32] World Nuclear Association, *Nuclear Power in India*, December 2009.

[33] Ibid.

PHWR, 7.0 GWe PHWR (based on recycled U), 40 GWe LWR and 2.0 GWe FBR.

Not all projections made by NPCIL have materialized, because the finalization of contract for the construction of nuclear power plants and the sale of nuclear reactors involves several technicalities and have to take place at the global level. In recent years, there has been a slowing down of nuclear power generation in India because of several global and local factors. Despite euphoric projections, global factors, such as the Fukushima nuclear power plant disaster of 2011, climate change and global warming, besides local factors, such as inadequate legislative framework, non-availability of land for the setting up of nuclear power plants in many states of India, protests/agitations because of the higher level of people's awareness post the Fukushima disaster and threats of displacement and non-rehabilitation, have made the task of the Indian government as well as suppliers very difficult. These have resulted in long delays and economically non-profitable ventures for several companies, having a bad effect on their financial health. Many companies of the USA lost contracts on these accounts.

In June 2012, NPCIL announced four new sites for twin PHWR units: at Gorakhpur/Kumhariya near Fatehabad district in Haryana, at Banswara in Rajasthan, at Chutka in Mandla district and at Bhimpur, the last two being in Madhya Pradesh. Initially, these plants would add 2,800 MWe, followed by a further 2,800 MWe. Site work has started at Gorakhpur with the Haryana state government's support.[34]

In mid-2015, NPCIL confirmed plans of 700 MWe PHWR units for Kaiga 5 and 6, costing about ₹6,000 crore. In September 2019, India's Ministry of Environment, Forest and Climate Change (MoEF) approved NPCIL's plans. NPCIL is also planning to build an indigenous 900 MWe PWR, an Indian pressurized water reactor (IPWR) designed by BARC in connection with its work on submarine power plants. A site for the first plant is being sought, a uranium enrichment plant is planned, the reactor pressure vessel's forging will be carried

[34] World Nuclear Association, *Nuclear Power in India*, March 2020

out by Larsen & Toubro (L&T) and NPCIL's new joint venture plant at Hazira, and the turbine will come from BHEL. Meanwhile, NPCIL offered both 220 MWe and 540 MWe PHWRs for export, in markets requiring small- and medium-sized reactors and approval in principle, modified in 2017 and later in 2018.[35]

There will be a significant jump in the total number of nuclear reactors that are likely to come up, which points to the fact that GOI has no chance of slowing down its nuclear energy programme despite the closure of several nuclear power plants in countries like Germany, France and Japan in the aftermath of the Fukushima accident of March 2011. It is reported that nuclear parks would have a capacity of 8,000–10,000 MW at a single location. The last section of this chapter carries a table showing the nuclear parks that are coming up in different parts of the country.

NUCLEAR ENERGY PARKS

As stated earlier, NPCIL is known for treading the path of self-reliance in India's core sector of nuclear energy security, which is also evident from its claim that 'it will be in position to export 220 and 540 MWe PHWRs to countries needing small-to medium sized reactors'. Had India not taken a principled stand during the 1960s–1990s at all possible international forums on nuclear proliferation, the NPT, CTBT and MTCR issues, and had it succumbed to the USA-led international nuclear technology regimes' pressures, it would not have ever reached the stage where it is today. It is because of this reason that no Indian government across the political spectrum of the country has ever deviated from the nuclear energy policy that was laid way back in the 1950s, soon after India's independence in 1947.

India's three-stage nuclear programme is in progress. The only interesting major departure in India's nuclear energy sector that is noticeable today has been the permission given to private companies of India, such as Reliance Power, GVK, GMR Group, Mahindra Group and Tata Group, to float joint sectors with existing power PSUs such as

---

[35] Ibid; see Table 4.2.

Table 4.2 New Nuclear Power Reactors (under the 12th FYP) Planned or Firmly Proposed

Reactor	State	Type	MWe Gross (Each)	Project Control	Starting Year of Construction
Gorakhpur 1 and 2	Haryana (Fatehabad district)	PHWR × 2	700	NPCIL	2020
Gorakhpur 3 and 4	Haryana (Fatehabad district)	PHWR × 2	700	NPCIL	–
Chutka 1 and 2	Madhya Pradesh (Mandla)	PHWR × 2	700	NPCIL	2020
Mahi Banswara 1 and 2	Rajasthan	PHWR × 2	700	NPCIL	2020
Mahi Banswara 3 and 4	Rajasthan	PHWR × 2	700	NPCIL	2021
Kaiga 5 and 6	Karnataka	PHWR × 2	700	NPCIL	2020?
Kudankulam 5 and 6	Tamil Nadu	AES-92 × 2	1,050	NPCIL	2020?
Subtotal planned					
(TFYXII plan 2012)					

Reactor	State	Type	MWe Gross (Each)	Project Control
Tarapur	Maharashtra	AHWR	300	NPCIL
Haripur 1 and 2	West Bengal (but likely to be relocated to Kovvada or another site in Andhra Pradesh)	AES-2006	1,200	NPCIL
Kalpakkam 2 and 3	Tamil Nadu	FBR × 2	600	Bhavini
Kudankulam 7 and 8	Tamil Nadu	AES-2006	1,200	NPCIL

Kudankulam 9–12	Andhra Pradesh	AES-2006	1,200	NPCIL
Bhimpur 1–4	Madhya Pradesh	PHWR	700	NPCIL
Chutka 3 and 4	Madhya Pradesh	PHWR	700	BHEL–NPCIL–GE
Rajouli, Nawada 1 and 2	Bihar	PHWR	700	NPCIL
		PWR × 2	1,000	NPCIL/NTPC
Jaitapur 1 and 2	Ratnagiri, Maharashtra	PWR–EPR	1,700	NPCIL
Jaitapur 3 and 4	Ratnagiri, Maharashtra	PWR–EPR	1,700	NPCIL
Jaitapur 5 and 6	Ratnagiri, Maharashtra	PWR–EPR	1,700	NPCIL
Markandi (Pati Sonapur)	Orissa	PWR	6,000	NPCIL
Kovvada 1 and 2	Srikakulam, Andhra Pradesh	AP1000	1,250	NPCIL
Kovvada 3 and 4	Srikakulam, Andhra Pradesh	AP1000	1,250	NPCIL

Source: Adapted from WNA Reactor Table.[36]

[36] World Nuclear Association. *Nuclear Power in India*. London: World Nuclear Association, 2020. Available at http://www.world-nuclear.org/information-library/country-profiles/countries-g-n/india.aspx (accessed on 1 October 2020).

NPCIL, NTPC and others. This policy is in tune with the overall policy of GOI to work towards making India a hub for heavy machinery in the Indo-Pacific region. Another development that has taken place in India's nuclear energy sector is the opening of this crucial sector to foreign private companies, whereas secrecy and monopoly of government departments/PSUs had been the norm for several decades. GOI is moving forward with its policy of inviting foreign investments in the nuclear energy sector too. The idea of dedicated parks similar to software parks has crept into the nuclear sector too. Accordingly, the process of allowing foreign companies to make investments in exclusive nuclear parks is underway in the country. Of course, nuclear parks would be financed by foreign companies and operated by NPCIL for a particular time period, patterned on other infrastructure projects under a combination of public–private partnership (PPP) and build–operate–transfer (BOT) models.

In line with the construction of previous nuclear power plants, such as 8-units at Rajasthan nuclear plant, NPCIL intends to set up five further 'nuclear energy parks', each with a capacity of up to eight new generation reactors of 1,000 MWe each, six reactors of 1,600 MWe each or simply one 10,000 MWe reactor. By 2032, 40–45 GWe would be generated by these five reactors. NPCIL confirmed that it had started work since 2012 on four new reactors at all four sites designated for imported plants. The new energy parks are to be built in: *Kudankulam* in Tamil Nadu, with three more pairs of Russian water-water energetic reactor (VVER) units that would generate 9,200 MWe—environmental approval has been procured for the first four; *Jaitapur* in Maharashtra—work has started on six Areva's EPR reactors that would generate 9,600 MWe, and environmental approval has also been procured for these; *Mithi Virdi* (or Chayamithi Virdi) in Gujarat, set to host US technology (Westinghouse AP1000); and *Kovvada* in Andhra Pradesh, set to host US technology (GE Hitachi ESBWR). GE Hitachi confirmed that it had signed a contract in 2010 to supply six economic simplified boiling-water reactors (ESBWRs) to NPCIL, to be set up in: *Haripur* in West Bengal, set to host four further Russian VVER-1200 units that would generate 4,800 MWe; *Kumharia* in Fatehabad district of Haryana—though earmarked for four indigenous

700 MWe PHWR unit, the AEC had approved the state's proposal for a 2,800 MWe nuclear power plant; and **Bargi** in Madhya Pradesh, designated for two indigenous 700 MWe PHWR units. NPCIL stated that it had initiated pre-project activities at all the above-mentioned places. At **Markandi** (Pati Sonapur) in Orissa, there are plans for up to 6,000 MWe of PWR capacity. Major industrial developments are planned in the area, and Orissa was the first Indian state to privatize electricity generation and transmission. The AEC also mentioned the possibility of new nuclear power plants in Bihar and Jharkhand.[37] The Indian government has continued to advance its civilian nuclear programme despite the fact that grave concerns regarding the dependence on nuclear energy and related safety aspects have been expressed from different quarters after the Fukushima nuclear power plant accident.[38] People's protests at Kudankulam, a nuclear power plant site in the state of Tamil Nadu, could only be ended after the intervention of Supreme Court of India.

ENERGY COOPERATION: NDA GOVERNMENT UNDER PM MODI (2014–2020)

PM Modi hails from the state of Gujarat, which has the potential of emerging as an energy hub of the country. The presence of Reliance Power's refinery, along with that of Essar and Cairn, in Gujarat and Rajasthan has an important role to play in the achievement of the country's energy security goals. PM Modi has been dealing with energy-related issues since he was the chief minister of Gujarat. The BJP's determination to get the new Land Acquisition Bill passed by the Indian Parliament in Budget Session 2013 itself showed the urgency of making land available for upcoming nuclear and thermal power projects in a hassle-free manner. PM Narendra Modi's government presented its second budget on 28 February 2015, and the day before, it had also released *Economic Survey 2014–15*, which had emphasized India's ambitious solar power generation to the tune of 100,000 MW by 2022. *Economic Survey 2014–15* projected that India would likely

---

[37] World Nuclear Association, *Nuclear Power in India*, December 2009.

[38] For details of India's preparedness in the aftermath of the March 2011 Fukushima accident, please see Gopalakrishnan, A Nuclear Regulator Without Teeth.

grow at 8.1–8.5 per cent in 2015–2016, making it the world's fastest growing major economy, outpacing China.[39]

According to Chanda Kochhar, the budget for 2015–2016 had given a strong push towards catalysing a revival of the investment cycle through fiscal spend, public sector investment and the proposed national investment fund. This would clearly meet the immediate imperative of rebooting the infrastructure sector. At the same time, it laid the foundations of an institutional framework for sustainable private sector participation in the energy sector through the 'plug-and-play' model for Ultra Mega Power Projects (UMPPs), which could be extended to roads, where all the necessary enablers would be in place before a project was actually awarded.[40] The Ministry of Power has already launched an initiative for the development of coal-based supercritical UMPPs of about 4,000 MW capacity each. Four UMPPs, in Sasan in Madhya Pradesh, Mundra in Gujarat, Krishnapatnam in Andhra Pradesh and Tilaiya in Jharkhand, have already been transferred to the identified developers and are at different stages of implementation. The Mundra UMPP units (5 × 800 MW) have been fully commissioned and are generating electricity. Three units of the Sasan UMPP (3 x 660 MW) have been commissioned so far. The remaining units of Sasan and the other awarded UMPPs are expected to come up in the Twelfth Plan (except the last unit of the Tilaiya UMPP, which is likely to come up in the Thirteenth Plan).[41]

Economic Survey 2013–14 stated that in the previous four decades, that is, from 1970–1971 to 2011–2012, the compound annual growth rates (CAGRs) of production of the primary sources of conventional energy, namely coal, lignite, crude petroleum, natural gas and electricity (hydro and nuclear) generation, had been 4.9, 6.2, 4.2, 8.7 and 4.3 per cent, respectively. In the same period, the consumption of coal, lignite, crude oil, in terms of refinery throughput, natural gas (off-take) and electricity (thermal, hydro and nuclear) had increased at CAGRs of 4.9, 6.2, 6.0, 10.7 and 7.1 per cent,

---

[39] *The Hindustan Times*, 28 February 2015, p. 9.

[40] Kochhar, 'A Spring in the Economy's Step', 12.

[41] Government of India, *Economic Survey*, 195.

respectively.[42] *Economic Survey 2013–14* highlighted the capacity addition target for the Twelfth Plan period, which was estimated at 88,537 MW, comprising 26,182 MW in the central sector, 15,530 MW in the state sector and 46,825 MW in the private sector. It stated that the capacity addition target for the year 2012–2013 had been 17,956.3 MW, against which a record capacity addition of 20,622.8 MW (20,121.8 MW thermal and 501 MW hydro) had been achieved—the highest ever annual capacity addition. The capacity addition target for the year 2013–2014 was 18,432.3 MW, against which a capacity addition of 17,825.1 MW was achieved.[43]

The Modi government deserves credit for having got the ball rolling domestically; it also took several steps on the diplomatic front internationally, especially with neighbours and the USA, in this direction. Modi, in his visits to Bhutan and Nepal in 2014 and Sri Lanka in 2015, emphasized the harnessing of hydro power in a joint manner with Bhutan and Nepal, and committed to have nuclear energy cooperation with both Sri Lanka and Bangladesh. The Modi government has consistently been pushing ahead nuclear energy cooperation with Russia. It amply proves the rationale behind the elaborate planning for giving a big boost to India's nuclear energy programme. It appears as if India wants to compensate for all the delays and losses from the 1960s till 2005 and maximize its gain after the end of all discriminatory practices by international nuclear and technological regimes like the NSG, IAEA, MTCR, NPT, CTBT, London Group, Wassenaar group, etc.

India also continued to maintain a closer energy cooperation with Russia. PM Modi met President Vladimir Putin during the 2014 BRICS Summit in Brazil. In this Summit, they committed to continuing privileged strategic cooperation with each other. Russia[44] is an important partner in peaceful uses of nuclear energy, and it recognizes India as a country with advanced nuclear technology with an impeccable non-proliferation record. The construction of Kudankulam Nuclear Power Plant (KKNPP) Units 1 and 2 (VVER 1,000 MW units) is an

---

[42] Ibid., 193.

[43] Ibid., 195.

[44] India–Russia Bilateral Documents. https://www.mea.gov.in.

example of the fruitful cooperation between India and Russia. KKNPP Unit 1 became operational in July 2013 and attained full generation capacity on 7 June 2014, while KKNPP Unit 2 is at an advanced stage of construction. India and Russia also have an ongoing cooperation in the field of hydrocarbons and power. Oil and Natural Gas Corporation (ONGC) Videsh Limited has made substantive investments of over US$5 billion in two major oil and gas projects—Sakhlin-1 and Imperial Energy Limited (Tomsk). Russian companies are engaged in several power plant and oil and gas projects in India. In May 2014, ONGC and Rosneft signed an MOU for the exploration of hydrocarbons in the Arctic offshores. Thus, the new government in India, within a span of 2–3 months, had made many diplomatic efforts in engaging the country with the rest of the world on the issue of its energy security. PM Narendra Modi visited the USA in October 2014, and President Barack Obama paid a return visit to India in January 2015, which reflected their strong bilateral determination to continue cooperation in the energy sector, which is very vital for India acquiring the wherewithal to defend and promote its national interest effectively.

RE-ENERGIZING INDO-US ENERGY COOPERATION

Indo-US energy cooperation received a significant boost under the Modi government, which made a commitment to electrify every home in India by 2019. US State Secretary John Kerry visited India in the last week of July 2014 and stated,

> With fewer limits on foreign technology and investment in India's green energy sector, U.S. can help make clean power more cost-effective and more accessible at the same time. U.S. can provide 400 million Indians with power without creating emissions that dirty the air and endanger public health. And by working together to help an entire generation of Indians leapfrog over fossil fuels, it can actually set an example to the world.[45]

India's willingness to work along the USA in the energy sector reflected a big change on the part of GOI.

---

[45] U.S. Department of State, 'U.S.–India Energy and Climate Cooperation'.

A testimony of a senior US assistant secretary for South Asia before the US Senate presented a very optimistic picture. The testimony strongly pointed in the direction of a revival of Indo-US nuclear energy cooperation. The official emphasized,

> We have seen tremendous progress in our energy cooperation since the launch of the U.S.-India Energy Dialogue in 2005. US will be fulfilling the promise of delivering cutting-edge U.S. nuclear energy technology to meet Indian energy needs. These are top priorities for the United States and India.[46]

The USA has been playing a very important role in the 'Make in India' initiative launched by the Indian government to give a boost to manufacturing in India. It has reflected the commitment of the USA to cooperate with India in the nuclear energy and defence technology sectors after the increase in the FDI limit to 49 per cent in the Indian defence sector by the Modi government.

PM MODI'S MEETING WITH PRESIDENT OBAMA IN THE USA IN SEPTEMBER 2014

Modi and Obama extolled the broad strategic and global partnership between the USA and India, which was to continue to generate greater prosperity and security for their citizens and the world. PM Modi emphasized the priority India accorded to its partnership with the USA, a principal partner in the realization of India's rise as a responsible, influential world power. Given the shared values, people-to-people ties and pluralistic traditions, President Obama recognized that India's rise as a friend and partner was in the USA's interest. Modi and Obama together committed to a new mantra for the relationship: *Chalein Saath Saath*: Forward Together We Go'. [47] The issues of economic growth, energy and climate change were high on the agenda of PM Narendra Modi during his visit to the USA in 2014, and agreements were reached there to implement fully the Indo-US Civil Nuclear Cooperation Agreement. They agreed to strengthen and expand the highly successful Indo-US Partnership to Advance Clean Energy (PACE) through a series of priority

[46] Biswal, 'Re-energizing U.S.-India Ties'.

[47] Press release, 30 September 2014. www.usembassynewdelhi.com.

initiatives, including a new Energy Smart Cities Partnership to promote efficient urban energy infrastructure.[48]

Both leaders were committed to working towards a successful outcome in the 2015 Paris conference of the UN Framework Convention on Climate Change (UNFCCC), including the creation of a new global agreement on climate change. The leaders recalled previous bilateral and multilateral statements on the phasing down of hydrofluorocarbons (HFCs). They recognized the need to use the institutions and expertise of the Montreal Protocol to reduce the consumption and production of HFCs. They also launched a new Climate Fellowship Program to build long-term capacity to address climate change–related issues in both countries. President Obama and PM Modi instructed their senior officials to work through the Energy Dialogue, Joint Working Group on Combating Climate Change and other relevant fora to advance these and other initiatives. Finally, an MOU was signed between the Export-Import Bank and the Indian Renewable Energy Development Agency Limited, which was to make up to US$1 billion in financing available to bolster India's efforts to transition to a low-carbon and climate-resilient energy economy.[49]

PRESIDENT OBAMA'S MEETING WITH PM MODI IN INDIA (25–27 JANUARY 2015)

President Obama's visit to India and his meeting with PM Modi in January 2015 put a final stamp on all those issues that the two countries had committed to work towards together in September 2014. The highlights of President Obama's visit to India was the breaking of the logjam in the implementation of the Indo-US Civil Nuclear Agreement (or the '123 Agreement') between India and the USA, which had come into force on 6 December 2008. The agreement had been in limbo following the provisions of supplier liability in the Indian Civil Liability for Nuclear Damage Act (CLNDA) of 2010. This impasse was resolved thanks mainly to the creation of an insurance

[48] Ibid.
[49] Ibid.

pool to cover liability.[50] The Modi government had the difficult task of pushing ahead the Indo-US Nuclear Agreement of 2008 with the USA in a big manner. The Indian government remained committed to increase its nuclear energy production to 20,000 MWe by 2020 and 63,000 MWe by 2032. PM Modi's visit to the USA in September 2014 and President Obama's return visit to India succeeded in ending the stalemate at the beginning of the nuclear commerce and trade talks between India and the USA. Now, India expected receive a big boost in its nuclear power generation and assurance of fullest operationalization of the concluded nuclear deal with the USA.[51] Key to the resolution of the nuclear liability in the Indo-US deal was the coming together of the four big Indian insurance companies to create an insurance pool as a consortium that would provide the necessary cover to both the operator and the suppliers (domestic and foreign). This was the kind of system operating in major nuclear power-producing countries such as the USA, France, Russia and Japan.[52]

As discussed, the two consecutive meetings between PM Modi and President Obama finally led to the operationalization of the Indo-US Civil Nuclear Agreement of 2008 among the companies of the USA and India. Some important reasons underlying the unexpected delay were 'India's Nuclear Liability Act 2010', protests and non-availability of land, delays in environmental licenses, poor financial conditions of US companies on account of acquisitions and mergers (A & M), etc. Democratic countries have often remained prone to delayed decision-making; especially, India and the USA have a long experience of long-delayed negotiations and multidimensional calculations and fears. It must be said that the nuclear energy cooperation, which began in 2005, did bring in a paradigm shift in the two countries' bilateral strategic relationships. Since then, neither country has looked back. There have been some losses on the part of US nuclear reactor supplier companies that did not do big business with India, but these have been balanced through the consolidation of the USA's sale of defence equipment to

[50] Ramachandran, 'Hurdles Ahead', 10–11.

[51] Kumar, 'PM Modi Government's Diplomacy for India's Nuclear Energy Security'.

[52] Ramachandran, 'Hurdles Ahead', 12.

the tune of US$18 billion between 2010 and 2020. This sale speaks volumes about the historical transformation that has taken place in Indo-US energy ties.

NUCLEAR ENERGY AND NUCLEAR DISASTER CONCERNS

The set-up and operation of new nuclear power plants and reprocessing plants is intertwined with developmental and environmental concerns and areas under mega projects being struck by natural calamities, such as floods, earthquakes, tsunamis, man-made accidents or breaches of security, all leading to the threat of nuclear disaster. Dependence on nuclear power, storage and disposal of nuclear waste, safety of areas surrounding reprocessing plants and transportation of nuclear warheads and their safety are highly risky propositions facing the country. The risks remain very high and raise serious questions over the capabilities and responsibilities of the central and state governments in India, which cannot match the state preparedness and disaster planning in Japan and other developed countries of the world. The National Disaster Management Authority (NDMA) guidelines for dealing with nuclear disasters remain, by and large, on paper only. One remains sceptical about India's preparedness in terms of its national and international responsibilities and capabilities in the case of any nuclear disaster taking place in the country.

After the Indo-US nuclear deal, India has embarked on a massive civilian nuclear energy programme, and in the next three–four decades, more than 40 new nuclear reactors are likely to be set up in different parts of the country. Any increase in the number of new nuclear installations would be fraught with fears of coming under attack by terrorist groups. It can only be opined that both India and Pakistan should strengthen the existing international nuclear regimes, such as the NPT, CTBT and FMCT, for meeting such challenges from any corner in the larger interest of the world as well as humanity.

India has also to reduce the delay in fully implementing the three-stage nuclear programme for achieving total nuclear security. Indian diplomacy has also to mobilize international support for dealing with nuclear terrorism that could take several forms, from an attack on nuclear power plants and reactors to the detonation of a nuclear bomb in an urban area. India must work hard for curbing international smuggling of fissile materials, which has doubled since 1996. Reports of the IAEA have recorded more than 550 confirmed incidents of nuclear trafficking since 1993. Even doubts regarding considering nuclear energy as a source of clean energy have been raised in different parts of the world, including within India, and it would be important for India to prepare itself to allay these fears about its nuclear programme. A sense of prudence is needed on the part of India, considering that countries like Germany, France and Japan have decided to slow down/discontinue generation of electricity through the nuclear mode over the next few decades. Undoubtedly, the nuclear disaster in Japan's Fukushima in March 2011 has forced policymakers the world over to rethink the advantages of having civilian nuclear programmes within their countries. It has triggered a fresh debate worldwide regarding whether nuclear energy is an appropriate alternative to fossil fuels.

ENERGY COOPERATION: PRIME MINISTER MODI–PRESIDENT TRUMP

Following his predecessors, President Trump has been supportive of continuing past policies towards India, whereby there has been a complete convergence of the geopolitical interests of the two countries. President Trump's administration has not been harsh on India and allowed US defence and energy exports to continue to India. Though US companies in the nuclear reactor business have not been able to break the ice with India because of their internal bankruptcy laws, the USA, under President Trump, is keen to give a push to big-ticket defence and energy deals with India. US companies in the nuclear sector have lost a lot at the hands of French and Russian companies that managed to secure several contracts for the sale and construction of nuclear reactors in India.

It is because of these reasons that the Trump administration has applied pressure on India under the Countering America's Adversaries

Through Sanctions Act (CAATSA). Several new issues on which US interests do not match with India's global interests have cropped up, such as India's import of S-400 missiles from Russia, import of oil from Iran, exemption given to Pakistan for International Monetary Fund (IMF) bailout package and the deal with Taliban in Afghanistan. US defence companies such as Lockheed Martin, Boeing, Raytheon and Sirkorsky have emerged as the largest US companies supplying critical equipment to India, such as C-17 and C-130J transport aircraft and Apache and Chinook helicopters. The defence deal between the USA and India during 2010–2020 has reached US$18 billion.

CONCLUSION

It can be concluded that India has embarked upon a massive nuclear power programme in the 21st century as part of its military and energy security policy, and it is expected to generate 63,000 MW of electricity through the nuclear mode in the next two to three decades. The generation of electricity through the nuclear mode is set to reach up to 26 per cent of the total electricity generated through all other modes by 2050. India already has 22 operational nuclear reactors, and several new nuclear reactors are coming up in different Indian states. The first tenure of the UPA government created history by getting India's isolation regarding nuclear commerce and trade ended at the international level by finalizing the Indo-US Nuclear Agreement of 2008.

It gave a boost to India's future energy security policy and also brought the UPA government back into power in the year 2009, with Manmohan Singh becoming PM of the country for a second time. However, non-operationalization of the Indo-US nuclear agreement resulted in the UPA government getting blamed by the opposition parties of the country for complete policy paralysis. The slowdown in the Indian economy shattered the aspirations of the middle class, especially the young generation of the country. The disenchantment of the younger generation with the UPA government resulted in its massive defeat and the establishment of PM Modi's government at the centre. The new government, so far, has given positive indications that it would overcome all shortcomings of the previous government and ensure that India bounces back at the international level.

People in the country have great expectations from the leadership of PM Narendra Modi, who is expected to give a new direction to India's foreign policy, which will have important bearings on the country's energy security policy in general and nuclear energy in particular. The new government has shown its commitment to continue nuclear energy cooperation with all those with whom the UPA government had concluded agreements. At the same time, it has also made departures from the past and started refocusing on the South Asian region for removing the trust deficit with SAARC countries, as evident from Modi's visit to Bhutan and Nepal. The government has shown its keenness to change the FDI norms for the defence and insurance sectors so as to increase the participation of foreign companies in the country's economic growth story. One ought to wait for some more time, as only a few months have passed since its second tenure started in May 2019, before finally carrying out an assessment of the Modi government's foreign and energy policy.

Defence Ties

Trajectories in the 21st Century

This chapter analyses India's growing geopolitical–strategic importance in the South Asian region making it imperative for India and the USA to have long-term defence and strategic ties, which had begun with the signing of MOU in 1985, though the two countries exercised restraint towards and had suspicions on each other. Since the 1985 MOU, both the countries have moved 35 years ahead and 75 years in total with bitter and fruitful achievements. India's defence and strategic cooperation with the USA had taken a hit during President Clinton's two tenures (1993–2000), but it picked up after the culmination of the 'Indo-US Strategic Dialogue' by Jaswant Singh and Strobe Talbott. The 9/11 attack on the USA and the announcement of the NSSP in 2004, combined with the nuclear deal in 2005, transformed the Indo-US defence and strategic cooperation and put it back on the highest pedestal. This chapter traces the various global, regional and bilateral factors responsible for ups and downs in the materialization of the substantial Indo-US defence ties since the 1985 MOU, including the NSSP in 2004 and the nuclear deal in 2005. It looks at factors inhibiting India's defence ties to the fullest extent with the USA till the signing of the NSSP in 2004 and the Indo-US nuclear deal in 2005. Contemporary issues like the Logistics Exchange Memorandum of Agreement (LEMOA), Communications Compatibility and Security Agreement (COMCASA), 2+2 Dialogue, Quad and Indo-Pacific cooperation under Indo-US relations are discussed in Chapter 7.

INTRODUCTION

India and the USA held divergent views on security issues in the first 40 years of their post-Second World War relations and hardly ever shared common views on any of the key international security issues.[1] As discussed in the preceding chapters, it is evident that the geopolitical differences and divergence of strategic goals on global and regional issues, to a very large extent, inhibited Indo-US defence and strategic cooperation. Differences in their strategies to deal with security issues were responsible for the very limited defence cooperation between the two countries till the signing of the 1985 MOU.

As analysed in Chapter 1, except for limited cooperation in the 1950s and later in 1962–1963, Indo-US relations of the past remained marred because of the USA's reluctance to transfer technology and know-how of manufacturing armaments to India. Looking at the history of their defence cooperation till the resumption of supply of nuclear fuel in the early 1980s, the USA and India were at odds on several international issues like India's trade agreement with Iran while the US embargo continued, its recognition of the Palestine Liberation Organization (PLO), New Delhi's recognition of the Soviet-backed government in Kampuchea and its signing of a US$1.6 billion arms deal with the Soviet Union that had invaded Afghanistan in 1979, which did not augur well for Indo-US relations.[2] In 1980, India explored the possibility of purchasing an arms package worth US$300 million, comprising some 200 long-range 155 mm Howitzers, 60 TOW launchers and about 4,000 anti-tank missiles, but it did not materialize because of US unwillingness to 'let India make the items under license, or produce the ammunition locally with their technical collaboration, after the initial purchase of these arms'.[3]

For India, any improvement in Indo-US defence cooperation would automatically have led to a corresponding change in Pakistan–USA relations.[4] As discussed in Chapter 2, the signing of the MOU in 1985 triggered changes in Indo-US defence cooperation. The MOU enabled the transfer of dual-use technologies to India and ensured US collaborations with Indian defence projects. Towards the end of the Cold

[1] Mahapatra, *Indo-US Relations*, 92.

[2] Limaye, *US-Indian Relations*, 187.

[3] Reddy, *The Hindu*, 22 May 1983.

[4] *Patriot*, 10 June 1992.

War in 1990, Indo-US relations had started improving, and India too appeared to improve its non-alignment credentials by readjusting its relationship with both the superpowers. For India, overdependence on the Soviet Union for its defence requirements was strategically dangerous. India's keenness on acquiring technology from the West, especially from the USA, was high on its agenda. As a result of PM Indira Gandhi's and PM Rajiv Gandhi's efforts, Indo-US relations had begun to grow stronger 1985 onwards. The Reagan administration too recognized India's capabilities and its growing potential and reciprocated by earning 'India's goodwill and above that, to reduce the leverage the Soviet Union had as India's dominant arms supplier'.[5] The 1985 MOU on the transfer of technology became a basis for defence cooperation between the two countries, and by 1988, it led to the transfer of supercomputer technology to India and the USA's cooperation with India in its Light Combat Aircraft (LCA) project.[6] With the end of the Cold War, the lessening of differences on many global and bilateral issues led to the development of closer military relations between India and the USA.

In the early 1990s, General Kicklighter, the US army commander in the Pacific, brought to India a list of specific proposals for closer relations. This resulted in visits of high-level officers of the two countries, greater attendance at each other's training establishments and stronger getting-to-know-you efforts. In January 1995, US Secretary of Defense William Perry's visit to India provided an opportunity to formalize these military-to-military relations and provided for closer civilian relationship or defence policies and technology. A step in the direction of institutionalizing defence cooperation had begun. It started well, but developments in the 1990s—tensions on Indo-Pak borders, US arms transfers to Pakistan under the Brown Amendment, provocative statements by top US officials on Kashmir and the Clinton administration's nuclear non-proliferation policy and tightened export controls—led to the derailment of the Indo-US defence cooperation.

[5] Mukherjee, 'US Weaponry for India', 596.
[6] Ibid.

THE END OF THE COLD WAR AND THE US-LED NEW WORLD ORDER

In the early 1980s, President Reagan's liberal policy on US arms manu-facturers wishing to make sales to India did not work, as fewer con-straints on arms transfers were intended to benefit only 'other nations with which the United States shared common security interests' alliances and cooperative relationships'.[7] India remained out of the purview of such easing of restrictions on the part of the USA, as it was not a member of any USA-led security alliance. As discussed earlier, the new cold war impinged on the Indian subcontinent because of the USSR's invasion of Afghanistan, presence of a rapid deployment force (RDF) in the Indian Ocean region, revival of the Cold War and US arms transfers to Pakistan, which was considered as the frontline state by US policymakers. The arms transfers to Pakistan, India's strong reaction to US actions and related topics are discussed in the earlier chapters.

During PM Rajiv Gandhi's tenure (1984–1989), India had made major defence purchases from the USSR but none from the USA, despite the fact that India had begun diversifying its sources for arms purchase and had made purchases from the UK, France and Sweden. In order to modernize its defence forces, GOI purchased MiG-23MF aircraft; MiG-27M; AN-32 and IL-76 military transport planes; MI-17, MI-25 and MI-35 helicopters; submarines and T-72 tanks from the Soviet Union. India also purchased Howaldtswerke-Deutsche Werft (HDW) submarines from Germany, Mirage 2000 aircraft from France, Bofors guns from Sweden and Sea Harrier vertical take-off and landing (VTOL) multi-role aircraft from the UK.[8] The Indian navy acquired 12 submarines, a second aircraft carrier, squadrons of Sea Harrier air-craft, TU-142 long-range maritime patrol aircraft and a leased Charlie nuclear submarine.[9]

India's policy of defence modernization and diversification and the more flexible arms transfer policy of the Reagan administration

---

[7] Buckley, 'Arms Transfers and the National Interest', 52.

[8] Smith, *India's Adhoc Arsenal*, 111–112.

[9] Gupta, 'Determining India's Force Structure and Military Doctrine', 448.

remained caught in the past misunderstandings of India and the USA[10] and did not make much impact on their bilateral relations, which continued to be guided, for the most period, by Cold War politics. There were no purchases by India from the USA due to the US legislations prohibiting arms and technology transfer to India. Their differences over the process of such transfers and modalities of co-production and the USA's suspicions that India could become a source of leakage of advanced technologies to the USSR or Russia prevented any major transfer of arms packages or technology transfers to India.

Western experts were of the view that the USA was making a big play to capture significant segments of the Indian defence market, but suspicions still persisted. There had been cases in the past wherein the US intention had been to subvert Indian defence capabilities where the USA could not penetrate, as had happened in the case of the 155 mm Howitzer that India had tried to buy from the USA. While giving India the impression that it was willing to sell the gun to India, the USA delayed negotiations for several years before indicating that it would sell the guns but not the technology for their licensed production. India lost 7 years in acquiring the guns from Sweden.[11] The author, on the basis of his doctoral research findings, has reasons to mention here that the Indo-US defence collaboration for India's LCA project suffered a delay of more than 30 years on account of alleged attempts by the USA to sabotage important defence projects of other countries in order to resist losing ground on the arms market to other countries like India.

Defence Ties under the 1985 MOU: Prospects and Challenges

The post-1985 MOU period witnessed the enormous growth of personal, educational, economic and cultural ties between the USA and India. There was also an ideological transformation in the structure of informed US political thinking about India.[12] The broad transformation

---

[10] Limaye, *US-Indian Relations*, 191.

[11] Victor, *India*, 195.

[12] Cohen, 'The Reagan Administration and India', 142.

in their relations enabled India to make purchases of arms under a new arms transfer policy. The then US deputy assistant secretary of defence for Near Eastern and South Asian affairs said, 'We think we can play a reliable, mutually advantageous role in aiding India to modernise its forces and should do this as a part of more comprehensive, cooperative bilateral relationship'.[13]

It is important to observe that India, in its pursuit of defence modernization, had started diversifying and had no inhibition in seeking US armaments, equipment and technologies. The important thing was that the USA too had no inhibitions in dealing with India's PSUs or GOI departments. It was ready to do business with either of them.

In the light of India's push for modernization of its armed forces and its willingness to cooperate with the USA, the statement of Defence Minister K. C. Pant was significant: 'US has indicated its willingness to give us access to some of their advanced technologies to us. The LCA and Super Computer and other areas of high technology have been specifically identified for such cooperation between India and the United States'.[14] The USA's readiness to acknowledge India's regional interests paved the way for India's willingness to consider US strategic concerns with regard to South Asia and the adjoining areas. The USA expected that India, soothed by US technological support for its defence and other industries, would adopt a more constructive attitude than it had in the past towards US strategic interests around the Indian Ocean and the Persian Gulf.[15] The USA–Iraq war did indicate some convergences in Indian and US policies towards the Persian Gulf region.

There was a view that the US-Pakistani tie could not be shaken unless India moved closer to Washington. One strategist saw India as the emergent regional great power and an ideologically palatable alternative to the China.[16] The changing equations in the region since

---

[13] Cited in Chakrapani, 'US Offers Help to Modernize Defense'.

[14] *Lok Sabha Debates*, Session 10, c. 319 and cc. 330–331.

[15] Mukherjee, 'US Weaponry for India', 601.

[16] Cohen, 'The Reagan Administration and India', 146.

the collapse of the USSR and the USA's recognition of India's key role in the security and stability of Asia, besides National Security Decision Directive (NSDD) 147 and India's handling of the 1987 Sri Lankan crisis and Maldives crisis in 1988, improved the prospects for Indo-US defence cooperation towards the end of the Cold War. The Reagan administration aspired to take advantage of the end of the Cold War and sought to build defence ties with India.[17]

The most significant upswing in Indo-US ties was the signing of the Indo-US MOU in November 1984, which was exchanged in May 1985 when PM Rajiv Gandhi visited the USA. It was the first time that defence technology involving items on the Commerce Control List (CCL) and US Munitions List was going to be sold to India. The 1985 MOU dealt with exports controlled by the US government for national security, as well as non-proliferation and foreign policy, purposes. It also laid down procedures for the sale and transfer of sensitive dual-use equipment and provided a platform in which to address proliferation issues.[18] As an analyst put it, the MOU

> did lead to a surge of technology licenses to Indian companies and Government institutions, but mainly for the items that were below the level of state-of-the-art technology. In the period 1984–88, there was a five-fold increase in the US Government approvals of civilian technology exports to India.[19]

Notwithstanding the cooperation between India and the USA in the areas of arms purchase, technology transfer and licensed production of major conventional weapons, the USSR, France and the UK remained the three largest suppliers of armaments and other defence equipment to India till the end of the 20th century.[20]

---

[17] Mahapatra, *Indo-US Relations into the 21st Century*, 102–103. For similar views also see, Kux, *Estranged Democracies*.

[18] Santhanam and Singh, 'Confidence Resorting Measures for Indo-US Commerce in Controlled Commodities', 324–325.

[19] Chellney, *Nuclear Proliferation*, 102. Also see Gordon, *India's Rise to Power in the Twentieth Century and Beyond*, 76–77.

[20] Thomas, 'Prospects for Indo-US Security Ties', 386.

The 1985 MOU was designed to protect US technology because of India's relationship with the Soviet Union and its advanced nuclear and missile programmes.[21] The growth in US technology transfers to India after 1985 was impressive, as it included sale of the Cray X-MP-14 supercomputer, the advanced 'silicon-on-sapphire' microprocessor chip for India's INSAT-2 satellite and 16 GE F404 engines to Hindustan Aeronautics Limited (HAL) for the development of LCA, which reflected a major leap forward in Indo-US technological cooperation.[22] Although assurances were obtained that the supercomputer's use would be confined to the civilian sector, it nevertheless carried potential technological benefits for the military sector as well.

Light Combat Aircraft and Supercomputer Technology Transfer as a Game Changer

Rajiv Gandhi's visit to the USA in June 1985 led to India to become the first non-aligned developing country to receive high technology for supercomputers and GE F404 engine technology for the indigenous LCA project.[23] India was going to be sold advanced aero-engines for the development of LCA, satellite and booster rocket technology for India's space programme and supercomputers for weather forecasting. The sale of GE F404 engines for LCA was important, as the advanced technology was to be fitted on future US fighter aircraft and was not yet found even on the advanced Soviet Union MiG-29 aircraft and prototype MiG-31s.

Reciprocal visits of officials from both India and the USA continued for the facilitation of technology transfer to India. *The Washington Post* of 15 October 1985 reported that Arunachalam was 'shown a level of US technology never before seen by an Indian Defense specialist'.[24] The news item also reported that Arunachalam was taken around several US aircraft and electronic industry establishments, given a special

[21] Chanda, 'A Thaw with Washington', 21.

[22] Thomas, 'U.S. Transfers of Dual-Use-Technologies to India', 840.

[23] Kumar, *Yearbook on India's Foreign Policy (1984–1985)*, 28.

[24] Cited in Subramaniam, 'Indo-US Security Relations During the Decade 1979–89', 167.

security clearance to visit the GE factory in Lynn, Massachusetts, and provided with classified data on the F404 engine. Shortly after the visit, Talbot Lindstrom led a team to Delhi, India, and sold 10 F404 turbofan engines that were to be used on the initial prototype of the LCA.[25] The LCA were to be eventually fitted with the indigenously developed Kaveri engine. The visit of Talbot paved the way for the first ever visit of a US defence secretary, Casper Weinberger, to India in November 1986. The visit facilitated the release of advanced electronics for the LCA as requested by India and resulted in giving a go-ahead for the expansion of US defence cooperation with India.[26] India was assured all the technical support for the successful development of LCA. Agreements with the USA on defence technology transfer included LCA technology, radar technology, anti-tank weaponry, night vision equipment, Main Battle Tank fire control and transmission systems and ammunition and advanced materials.[27] Frank Carlucci became the second secretary of defence to visit India in 1988, who confirmed the Reagan administration's desire 'to contribute to, and be a part of India's future by supporting India's larger quest for self-reliance'.[28] The process that had started in 1985 finally stood institutionalized after 35 years, in 2020, and the net result was that the US Lockheed Martin entered into an MOU worth US$18 billion dollars with Indian PSU Bharat Electronics (BEL) for the joint industrial production of 114 F-21 fighter aircraft in India.

After the defence secretary's visit, India and the USA also decided to cooperate on: (a) third-generation anti-tank systems and (b) instrumentation test and evaluation and manpower training. The USA made it known that the rationale behind it being a part of India's larger quest for self-reliance in the defence sphere was to strengthen Reagan's strategy of moving India away from the USSR for its military purchases. It was also to build a more substantial cooperation between the two

---

[25] Smith, *India's Adhoc Arsenal*, 173.

[26] Limaye, *US-Indian Relations*, 213 and Mukherjee, 'US Weaponry for India', 605.

[27] LCA Programme Talks Set as USA and India Move Closer, 1089. Also see, Gordon, *India's Rise to Power in the Twentieth Century and Beyond*, 81–84.

[28] Kumar, 'Defence in Indo-US Relations', 38–39.

countries, besides mere technology transfer to India.[29] This is how both the countries tried to remain engaged as far as defence cooperation was concerned. The letter of agreement (LOA) for technical assistance on the LCA project was signed in September 1988. Apart from the LCA project, however, licensed production of major conventional weapons and Indo-US cooperation in the co-production of defence armaments and related equipment did not materialize, which proved that difficulties persisted in the consolidation of defence ties between the two countries.

It needs to be mentioned here that US decisions on technology transfer—cooperation on the LCA radar and the sale of GE F404 engines and the Cray XMP-14 supercomputer—had not been easily forthcoming on account of the USA's fears that India was a Soviet Union conduit for US technology. The USA even feared that India's only aircraft-manufacturing company, HAL, with its division making Soviet MiGs, had the potential of being Moscow's shopping cart.[30] However, the inordinate delay in the production of LCA and its rising cost raised questions inside and outside the country about the likely success of the LCA project. Thus, the 1980s witnessed a large number of high-level political and military official exchanges and the signing of very important agreements. From the USA's side, two defence secretaries, a chief of US Army Staff and an assistant secretary, undertook visits to India. From the Indian side, PM Rajiv Gandhi, Defence Minister K. C. Pant and other officials visited the USA. This period clearly witnessed a high level of defence cooperation between the two countries, which had not ever been seen in the past.

Defence Cooperation During the US–Iraq War of 1990–1991

The situation towards the end of the Cold War in early 1990 had been changing fast, and the collapse of the USSR had resulted in the dawn of a new world order under the sole superpower, the USA. Accordingly,

---

[29] Limaye, *US-Indian Relations*, 214–215.

[30] Cohen, 'The Reagan Administration and India', 141.

India was also expected to adjust its policies. It was time for India to help the USA in its war with Iraq. India supported all the UNSC resolutions against Iraq and complied with it strictly as never before. Towards the end of 1990, PM V. P. Singh's government allowed the refuelling of US military aircraft on Indian soil during their supply runs from the Philippines to the Persian Gulf. This helped the US Air Force (USAF) to operate its military transport aircraft with full pay-load capacity. The issue of allowing US aircraft to have overflight and refuelling facility in India turned out to be a big embarrassment for PM Chandra Shekhar, who had just taken over after the fall of V. P. Singh's government, once news of the same broke out.[31] A big hue and cry was raised all over the country over the fact that India had colluded with the USA against a Muslim country. Inside Parliament, members raised serious doubts over GOI's decision to give such per-mission to the USAF.[32] MPs considered that the government, in the name of neutrality, had taken the decision of appeasing, supporting and approving all naked crimes of US imperialism on a small coun-try like Iraq. All political parties, including the largest, the Congress party, were of the view that 'this is something India was moving away from its policy of non-alignment'.[33] MPs were critical about the Indian government's blanket permission to the USAF to have an air corridor through India during its overflights without even halting, thus denying the Indian government its sovereign right to examine those planes. The free air corridor was an open sanction to the US military build-up.[34] I. K. Gujral, a minister of GOI, conveyed to the US administration India's decision to stop the overflight and refuelling facility provided to USAF aircraft. He also assured the Parliament that the policy of non-alignment was still relevant. India did not want any single power to take the responsibility of restoring peace in a particular region.[35] It could be inferred from the above that a close defence cooperation with the USA was not possible during any crisis in a nearby or distant

---

[31] *The Times of India*, 21 February 1991.

[32] *Lok Sabha Debates*, cc. 464–590.

[33] Ibid., c. 469.

[34] Ibid., c. 483.

[35] Ibid., c. 569.

region, especially against any of the developing nations or non-aligned countries. It also appeared that the decision of allowing US warplanes access to refuelling facilities was generally considered as abject surrender to US imperialism. This was seen as a policy of appeasement of US imperialism, destroying India's policy of non-alignment. The role of the then largest opposition party, the BJP, had been very controversial in early 1990. It never supported the Indian government on close Indo-US defence cooperation. However, after almost three decades and a half since 1985, the same BJP party is in power in India under PM Narendra Modi has taken Indo-US defence–strategic cooperation to its peak by signing the LEMOA and COMCASA agreements with the USA on 7 September 2018 during the 2+2 Dialogue (annual meeting of external affairs and defence ministers).

Although cooperation with the USAF in allowing US warplanes to refuel in India was viewed as an indication of an increased level of defence cooperation, Muchkund Dubey, the then foreign secretary of India, contradicted such views. On being asked whether the permission given by GOI was part of a broader understanding on defence cooperation, he was very emphatic in stating that such permission was given purely on humanitarian grounds.[36] He further stated,

> it was a kind of help to the US administration in taking man and material to the Gulf countries. The moment opposition parties in India raised hue and cry about the Government of India's decision, US administration was told about the Indian government's inability to allow US aircraft refueling in India. The US government was convinced about India's position and did not pressurise India for allowing such facilities any longer.[37]

It is noteworthy that the USA, after invading Iraq in 2003, wanted Indian forces to participate there in restoring peace after the end of the war, but PM Vajpayee's government refused to send forces there. Once again, the USA wanted Indian forces to participate in its Afghanistan war, but it did not receive support from India. It can be said that pure defence ties with the USA involving soldiers was not

[36] An interview with Professor Muchkund Dubey, Former Foreign Secretary, GOI.
[37] Ibid.

possible in those years, and they had to remain confined to the holding of military exercises together or the sending of soldiers to each other's country for training. Such thinking was expected to impinge on future Indo-US defence cooperation too. India preferred US help in the modernization of its military hardware, transfer of technology and joint productions only.

Defence Cooperation: Lt General Kicklighter's Proposal

As discussed in the preceding sections, the visits of high-level military flag officials of India and the USA to each other's countries culminated in an agreement for enhancing service-to-service contacts and exchanges between the military establishments under the famous proposal of Lt. General Kicklighter.[38] Despite major differences over the nuclear issue, cooperation between the armed forces of the two countries substantially increased. India had resumed its participation in the IMET program run by the USA. The importance of the programme was evident from the fact that four Indians service chiefs attended it. A high-level dialogue between the two armies, with representatives meeting with increasing frequency, was also set in motion.[39] Kicklighter's proposal led to the visit of successive Indian army chiefs to the USA and reciprocal visits of US flag officers to India. The 'Kicklighter proposal' envisaged expanded cooperation and partnership between the militaries of the two countries.[40] Consequently, an army Executive Steering Group (ESG) was set up in January 1992, followed by those for the navy and air force in March 1992 and August 1993, respectively.[41] An upswing in strategic understanding between India and the USA was evident when a joint steering committee of the two armies worked out the number of army officers from the Indian Army and US Army Training and Doctrinal Command (TRADOC) who would jointly study and exchange information about their respective tactical, doctrinal, operational and

[38] Government of India, Ministry of External Affairs, *Annual Report 1990–91*, 3.

[39] GOI, Report no. 41, 50–51.

[40] Mahapatra, *Indo-US Relations*, 105.

[41] Kumar, 'Defence in Indo-US Relations', 44–45.

logistical concepts.[42] The cooperation under Kicklighter's proposal led to the conduct of the first ever military-to-military exercises between the two countries' forces on a regular scale.[43] Thus, in February 1992, Indian army and US Army and Air Force paratroopers held their first ever joint training exercise, named Teak Iroquois, followed by a second one in October 1993. The two navies held three rounds of the first ever joint naval exercises—Malabar I, II and III. While the first round had been preliminary and explanatory in nature, the second and third rounds of the Malabar exercises were three-dimensional, involving maritime reconnaissance aircraft, surface ships and submarines.[44] Such cooperation between the two navies was definitely guided by the US desire to forge a cooperative relationship with the Indian navy, taking into consideration the strategic importance of the Indian Ocean.

Since 1991, the two countries had been conducting joint military exercises on an annual basis. They also started holding joint naval exercises, and the USA fielded its two nuclear-powered submarines in naval exercises in 1995. The USA was also interested in having an agreement with India for US naval ships' repairs to be undertaken at Mazagon docks and making Goa and Cochin permanent ports of call for the US Navy, which was refused by India.[45] It was only after the signing of LEMOA and COMCASA in 2018 that it became possible for US ships to dock at Indian ports. The circle has moved complete one cycle. According to Indian defence experts, India benefitted from such joint naval exercises. The Indian navy could fine-tune its tactics to detect nuclear-powered submarines, two of which were fielded by the USA. However, the Indian defence experts were apprehensive of such cooperation in future too, because of non-expansion of the defence agenda between the two countries.[46] The strong foundation laid during the earlier decades have helped India and the USA in institutionalizing their defence and strategic cooperation in the 21st century.

[42] Mahapatra, 'Indo-US Dialogue', 118–119.

[43] Government of India, Ministry of Defense, *Annual Report 1992–93*, 8.

[44] Government of India, *Annual Report, 1992–93*, 78.

[45] Vinod, 'India-United States Relations in a Changing World', 446–447.

[46] Aneja, 'Limits to Defence Ties'.

It has enabled them in experiencing a new height in their defence cooperation, which has unfolded under the annual '2+2 Dialogue' meetings held alternatively in the two countries' capitals and involving their foreign affairs and defence ministers/secretaries. In 1996, US army officials, for the first time, attended a low-intensity conflict (LIC) course in India. It offered them insights about fighting terrorist groups, which helped US forces later when they attacked Afghanistan in 2001 and Iraq in 2003 after the 9/11 attack.

Another first was US army officers attending the Junior Command Course at the College of Combat, the Engineers Commanders Course and also a commando course in 1995. In 1995, the IAF and USAF for the first time exchanged combat pilots' instructors at their air force academies. The two armies also began exchanging medical officers for short capsule courses. The Indian army's sustained involvement in high-altitude warfare (in Siachen glaciers and the Sino-Indian border in the Northeast) and counter-insurgency warfare was of special interest to the US army. Similarly, the Indian army, which set up a nuclear, biological and chemical warfare directorate at the army headquarters, expressed its interest in having its officers attend chemical and biological warfare courses at Aberdeen.[47] On the whole, Indo-US cooperation remained confined to the institutional level only.

Defence Ties under the Agreed Minutes on Defense Cooperation 1995

On 12 January 1995, India and the USA signed the 'Agreed Minutes on Defense Cooperation' during the US Defense Secretary William J. Perry's visit to India. This became the umbrella arrangement for the 1985 MOU and the Kicklighter joint-exercise proposal. Under the agreed minutes, cooperation expanded between the different structures under the defence departments of the two countries.[48] *The Hindustan Times*,[49]

[47] Kumar, 'Defence in Indo-US Relations', 54.

[48] Sidhu, 'Enhancing Indo-US Strategic Cooperation', 57.

[49] *The Hindustan Times*, 15 January 1995.

a national daily, reported that US pressure on the question of signing the NPT and MTCR had relented; Washington supported bilateralism in Indo-Pak differences over Kashmir. It was pointed out that India, which had been showing keenness to develop military cooperation with the USA since the end of the Cold War, felt that opportunities would now be available for technologically upgrading the weaponry of the armed forces and their fighting skills. It should be noted that the growth of bilateral defence relations in new areas was to be evolutionary and related to the convergence of global and regional issues. This left room for dialogue, constant interaction and harmonization of differing perceptions.

The 1995 agreement asked for periodic consultations among civilian officials and military officials of India and the USA from their respective defence ministries.[50] It asked for cooperation with the UN peacekeeping mission and the sharing of mutual concerns on the emergence of new threats to international security. The document called for future cooperation to focus on more frequent high-level exchanges, the presence of observers at each other's military exercises and joint training exercises at progressively higher scales and higher levels of sophistication.[51] It also emphasized deeper defence ties in research and production areas, which were to be monitored at the joint technical group (JTG) level.[52] It is noteworthy that the USA signed this agreement with India at the same time it sold Pakistan the promised F-16s worth US$368 million as part of an arms package under the Brown Amendment.[53] India was expected to make certain accommodations towards the USA as their global interests demanded cooperation with Pakistan. The policy of accommodation of certain interests has helped both India and the USA in moving forward in leaps and bounds. Ultimately, it has also led to the de-hyphenation between India and Pakistan.

---

[50] For details on the Agreed Minutes of Defence Cooperation, see United States Information Service (USIS), *Press Release* (New Delhi), 12 January 1995.

[51] USIS, *Press Release*.

[52] USIS, *Press Release*, 12 January 1995.

[53] *Deccan Herald*, 18 January 1995.

NUCLEAR EXPLOSION 1998: DEFENCE TIES
COME TO A COMPLETE HALT

The developments towards the end of the 20th century and beginning of the 21st century witnessed a change in India's tone that had become less aggressive against Washington. Likewise, Washington also showed greater flexibility and accommodation to Indian views, even though certain basic differences persisted.[54] India was being pressurized by the USA on the NPT, CTBT and nuclear proliferation issues under President Clinton. The issue of Kashmir also had become a bone of contention because of the statements of US officials like Robin Raphel and others. These controversies have been discussed in earlier chapters. The two countries' continued differences on matters important to both from the viewpoint of their national security and a clear clash of interests in their global and regional policies were reflected in India's Ministry of Defence *Annual Report* for the year 1994–1995, which clearly accused the Western powers of jeopardizing India's quest for self-reliance for national security and defence preparedness. It was because of US pressures that India had postponed the user trials of the indigenously developed Prithvi surface-to-surface missiles (SSMs) to avoid annoying US sensibilities on the eve of P. V. Narasimha Rao's visit to Washington, DC, in 1994.[55]

It was evident that notwithstanding the improvement in Indo-US bilateral defence relations, differences over India's non-adherence to various international regimes such as the MTCR, NPT, CTBT, NSG and possibly even the FMCT placed further restrictions on how much further the USA would go with regard to the sale of defence technology to India. Thus, it seemed that there were inherent limitations to how far the USA would be willing to go in terms of arms sales to India. On balance, one could say that any kind of defence and strategic cooperation between them that had witnessed an upswing during the Rajiv–Reagan Regime could not be sustained, especially during the Clinton administration's tenure. The defence and strategic cooperation could not take off; rather, it was grounded because of the divergence

[54] Government of India, Ministry of Defense, *Annual Report 1994–95*, 2–3.

[55] Ibid.

of interests. There was hardly any evidence of any institutionalization of Indo-US defence and strategic cooperation taking place during the mid-1980s.

The developments of May 1998, when both India and Pakistan conducted several nuclear explosions, resulted in heightened tension in the South Asian region. This development raised US concerns over nuclear proliferation and the outbreak of a war between India and Pakistan over Kashmir resulting in the possible use of nuclear weapons. India faced the lowest point of its relationship with the USA because of the latter's decision to impose economic sanctions against India for it having conducted the nuclear explosions. Possibilities of defence cooperation then seemed to be remote because of the US decision to impose sanctions against around 500 Indian companies, government as well as private companies, which it considered to be associated directly or indirectly with India's nuclear programme. Thus, talks of transfer of technology in defence-related areas came to a grinding halt.

Notwithstanding the developments of May 1998, several rounds of talks took place between Jaswant Singh, Minister of External Affairs, and Strobe Talbott, US Assistant Secretary of State, as part of a Strategic Dialogue between India and the USA. Though the contents of the Strategic Dialogue were never disclosed, it definitely led to an increased level of understanding between the two countries. India could clarify to the US administration the changed security environment in and around the country that had led it to carry out explosions and declare itself to be a state with nuclear weapons. It explained to the USA during these talks that India would in no way create obstacles for the CTBT coming into force in September 1999 as well as in no way allow any kind of proliferation of nuclear technology on its part. It was after much efforts and convincing exercises undertaken by both the sides on several of the contentious issues and many assurances given by both to each other to take each other's concerns into consideration and to continue consultations in future too. It was under these changed circumstances that the USA relented on the issues of the NPT, CTBT and missile development programme. Then, the historic visit of the then PM Vajpayee to Pakistan resulted in the Lahore declaration, defusing tensions between the two nuclearized neighbours. However, this process received a serious setback because of the Kargil crisis that started in May–June 1999.

India and the USA succeeded in breaking the deadlock that had emerged in the post-May 1998 period, after a gap of more than two decades, when US President Clinton visited India during March 2000. His visit to India raised a lot of hopes that the USA would accommodate India's viewpoint about its security concerns and would lift the sanctions against India because of which all joint projects had been affected, as the cooperation between the agencies of the two countries had come to a complete halt. Indo-US cooperation in trade and economic areas, especially in the software area, increased substantially. However, the sanctions continued to remain in force despite the assurance provided by US officials that they would be lifted soon.

CLINTON'S VISIT TO INDIA IN 2000: RESUMPTION OF DEFENCE TIES

President Clinton's visit to India in March 2000 symbolized a new level of maturity in the relationship between the world's two largest democracies. It indicated to the beginning of a new era in Indo-US defence and strategic cooperation. PM Vajpayee's return visit in the same year formalized the commitment. The signing of the 'Vision Document' was definitely a defining moment in Indo-US relations, as it took place in the aftermath of India's nuclear explosions in 1998, the Lahore visit of Vajpayee and the Kargil conflict. It also led to India becoming an important destination for leaders of most of the important countries, such as Russia, the UK, Japan and Germany, which helped India in building its image that had suffered considerably after the boycott of Conference on Disarmament (COD) on the issues of the CTBT, the May 1998 nuclear explosions and the Kargil conflict in 1999. It raised further the possibility of institutionalization of Indo-US relations in the area of defence and security. There was a realization on the part of the USA that India could be an important country that might share some of the responsibilities, in the Gulf, Indian Ocean region and Southeast Asian region, along with the USA in the new world order.

Jaswant Singh's visit to the USA in April 2001, just after President Clinton's visit to India, resulted in the revival of dialogue on defence cooperation. This visit was reciprocated by US Joint Chief of Staff, General Henry Shelton's visit to India in the same month, which led to the revival of the dormant institution-level dialogue between the officials of the two countries. Both countries once again committed to expand the nature of defence cooperation when Indian PM Vajpayee visited the USA in November 2001.[56] As a result of the series of visits of officials and leaders to each other's country, the third meeting of the Defence Policy Group (DPG) was resumed in December 2001. A beginning was made to expedite the defence cooperation in areas such as the Acquisition and Cross-Servicing Agreement (ACSA), foreign military sales, joint military exercises and cyber security coopera-tion. The fifth DPG meeting was held in the USA in August 2003 and resulted in both countries agreeing to establish high-level dialogue on defence technology issues.[57]

All these high-profile visits helped India and the USA in prepar-ing the ground for the announcement of the NSSP in 2004. The two countries also resumed joint military exercises like Balance Iroquois in Agra in May 2002. The Malabar series of naval exercises was also held in Kochi in October 2002. It was followed by *Vajra Prahar* and *Yudh Abhyas* in Mizoram in April 2003 and 2004, respectively. One of the biggest exercises involving air force and navy personnel, Cope Thunder, was held in Alaska in July 2004, and Malabar 4 was held in Kerala in October 2004. All joint exercises focused on interoperability and promotion of security cooperation between the two countries.[58] The most important thing about all such ties was that these steps were taken in the aftermath of the heinous 9/11 terrorist attack against the USA in 2001. It must be mentioned here that the 9/11 attack did changed the perceptions of India and the USA and became the trig-gering factor that helped both countries strengthen their defence and security ties in their GWOT.

[56] USIS, *Factsheet*, 20 April 2001.

[57] www.usembassynd.com

[58] Ibid.

Against the backdrop of the developments of the early 21st century, it was time to watch whether Indo-US defence and strategic relations would still remain tied to US-Pak relations or if they would assume an independent status, free of US-Pak ties. The post-9/11 period provided both countries an important opportunity to get their defence and security cooperation expanded and moved to a higher level, factoring global perspectives, especially in the Indian Ocean region and the Asia-Pacific, later combined as the Indo-Pacific region, for meeting the challenges of the 21st century. Successes on the part of India's relations with ASEAN countries and Japan amply proved that Indo-US relations in the early 21st century were steady and more stable than any time in the past seven decades and a half. A US expert[59] believed that as long as the world remained unipolar, New Delhi had a much greater stake than Washington in maintaining a closer relationship. A noticeable point is that there was a distinct departure from the traditional viewpoint on the part of Indian policymakers of seeing the USA as a strategic threat and joining with other countries in balancing the sole superpower, the USA. Now, in 2020, it is the other way round, with India ready to embrace the USA, Japan and others against China in the post-COVID-19 era in light of the changing world order and the recent border skirmishes near the India–China LAC in March–April 2020.

Both the USA and India were to factor in the idea of 'natural alliance' between the two but, at times, India has continued to emphasize its policies of 'strategic autonomy' in its foreign and strategic policies and maintaining close ties with Russia, France and Israel in recent years, though this has not created doubts in the minds of US policymakers as to whether India could be relied upon or not. It was this dilemma that both needed to overcome for giving a big push to their ongoing defence ties in the 21st century.[60] However, the finalization of the NSSP in 2004 and the Indo-US nuclear deal in 2005 dispelled all past fears on the part of the Indian strategic community. The historic turnaround in Indo-US defence and strategic cooperation has become a reality only because of the strong convergence of interests

[59] Cohen, *India*, 306–308.

[60] Ibid., 307.

of the two countries, which was supported by their intellectual and middle-class communities.

DEFENCE TIES AFTER THE 9/11 ATTACK

Al Qaeda's attack on New York's World Trade Center and the Pentagon on 11 September 2001 dramatically changed the security scenario at the international level, in general, and that in India and the USA, in particular. Both countries were bound to use this opportunity for fighting the war on global terrorism together. India came forward in providing unconditional support to the USA in the war against terrorism immediately after the 9/11 attack, which sent a positive message to the USA, and it was bound to have positive impact on Indo-US defence ties. PM Vajpayee went ahead and endorsed the National Missile Defense Program launched by the Bush administration in May 2001. It augured well for US policymakers. The realities of the post-9/11 world order demanded that both countries move beyond the format of only holding annual joint military exercises and start expanding areas of their bilateral defence and strategic cooperation. It was time for both to focus on developing joint capabilities and enhancing confidence, jointly confront multilateral security issues, factor in issues like protection of energy supplies and sea lanes, conduct peacekeeping missions and combat terrorism in their ongoing defence ties. It was in these areas that the Indo-US defence ties were likely to grow stronger in the 21st century world order.

Notwithstanding past difficulties, very important engagements between their defence forces were evident from 2001 onwards on a regular basis. For instance, the Indian navy relieved on the US navy in the Strait of Malacca against pirates during the 'Operation Enduring Freedom' in April 2002, and both conducted joint naval exercises involving their maritime reconnaissance aircraft, in the largest ever USA–India military exercises held in 2002 and again in 2003. It was the turn of air force aircrafts of all type fighters, transport, bombers, and reconnaissance participating in joint air-force exercise in February 2004.[61] The joint military-naval exercises were followed by

[61] CISIS, *Indo-US Relations*, 42.

the high-profile visits of their top flag staff officers which included all three Indian chiefs and US Joint Chief of Staff, General Myers and US army chief between 2002 and 2003. The successes of the high-profile visits resulted in the announcement of the NSSP in 2004 by President George W. Bush, which also paved the way for the signing of the historic Indo-US nuclear deal in July 2005, leading to a complete transformation in Indo-US 21st century relations.

Carrying forward the ongoing defence cooperation, the USA sold 12 AN-TPQ-37 Firefinder counterbattery radars and two interim radars to India in 2002, besides the GE F404 engines for the LCA that had already been transferred to India.[62] There was a new dynamism and substance evident in Indo-US bilateral defence ties in the post-9/11 period. New areas such as border management under a 'complete border management system' had emerged on the agenda of their ongoing cooperation. An Indian team visited the Sandia National Laboratories in New Mexico to explore a sensor system used by the USA along its border with Mexico. A new mechanism for sharing of information between India's Integrated Defence Staff (IDS) and the US Joint Staff Office had been established. Indian experience in peacekeeping was another area where Indian and US troops joined forces in holding a joint peacekeeping exercise, 'Shantipath', involving computer war-gaming simulation, which was held in New Delhi in early 2003. From the discussions made, it appeared that the Indo-US defence relationship during this period had grown to a stage where it could be inferred that the two militaries could work in unison to combat the regional and global challenges of terrorism, administer peacekeeping and humanitarian action, keep the high seas safe for the proliferation of weapons of mass destruction and be a force of stability in Asia.

Next Steps in Strategic Partnership, 2004

Another hallmark of this period was seen during PM Vajpayee's visit to the USA in September 2004, when the two countries' leaders announced the NSSP. As part of the NSSP, three crucial areas assumed

---

[62] Ibid., 44.

the centre stage of future Indo-US defence ties: easing of restrictions on India on the export of dual-use technology goods; increase in civilian nuclear and civilian space cooperation; and missile defence.[63] President Bush (Jr.) confirmed it through his statement made in January 2005 emphasizing cooperation in the three areas, justifying the expanding nature of Indo-US defence ties henceforth. US Secretary Ken Juster hailed this agreement as a 'major milestone in the U.S.-India relationship',[64] and Secretary Condoleezza Rice stated that the goal of US policy 'is to help India become a major world power in the 21st century'.[65] Secretary Rice's visit to India in March 2005 laid the road map for future Indo-US strategic partnership:[66] India and the USA were to initiate a senior-level strategic dialogue and hold a discussion on 'Convention Production'; they were to begin a high-level energy dialogue to include energy security, civil nuclear energy and clean energy, and they were also to begin an economic dialogue. The consolidation of Indo-US defence ties under NSSP 2004 moved them to another higher level; the New Framework for the USA–India Defence Relationship in 2005 is discussed in the following section.

New Framework for the US–India Defence Relationship, 2005

Just before the nuclear deal announcement in July 2005, Defence Minister Pranab Mukherjee and his counterpart Donald Rumsfeld signed the 'New Framework for the USA–India Defence Relationship' for the next 10 years in Washington on 28 June 2005.[67] The agreement was different from past agreements, as it emphasized that defence transactions would not be seen as 'ends' alone but would act as a means to strengthen Indo-US bilateral security, reinforce their strategic partnership, enhance greater interaction between their armed forces and

---

[63] Kronstadt, 'India–U.S. Relations'. Also see, *Washington File*, 8–15.

[64] Kronstadt, 'India–U.S. Relations'.

[65] Chaudhri, 'American Indian Century'.

[66] *The Times of India*, 31 March 2005.

[67] *The Hindu*, 30 June 2005.

promote better understanding between their defence establishments.[68] The agreement also focused on holding joint exercises and regular exchanges; participating in common-interest multinational operations; developing military capabilities against terrorism; combatting proliferation of weapons of mass destruction; and encouraging collaboration in missile defence. Both nations also agreed to work under the guidance of the DPG and a new Defense Procurement and Production Group for setting the tone and tenor of Indo-US 21st century strategic ties.[69] Thus, under NSSP 2004, a landmark strategic agreement having far-reaching consequences for India, the Indo-US nuclear deal, was signed by the leaderships of the two nations in Washington on 18 July 2005. It scripted a new history of Indo-US ties, and the two countries are about to complete 75 years of their diplomatic relationship in the next few years. This nuclear cooperation agreement is discussed in detail in the preceding chapters.

DEFENCE TIES: POST THE NUCLEAR AGREEMENT OF 2008

As discussed in the preceding paragraphs, India and the USA lacked a strong formal strategic alliance between them till the culmination of the Indo-US nuclear deal of July 2005. There was better realization now on the USA's part about India's role in the Indian Ocean, Asia-Pacific and Gulf regions. The USA also was appreciative of India as a valuable contributor to the UN peacekeeping process and saw India as one of the biggest economies of the world with which it would like to continue working. After the signing of NSSP 2004 and the Indo-US nuclear deal in 2005, a greater convergence of Indian and US interests on global and other geopolitical issues could be seen. The changes in Indo-US defence ties were magnificent and were expected to bear positive results for both countries in the 21st century's evolving world order. The idea that India may be cultivated as a possible counterbalance to China tarted gaining strength, and the China factor has compelled India and the USA to cement their ties further in the

[68] The Tribune, 30 June 2005.

[69] Ibid.

Indo-Pacific region and with respect to the challenges that have emerged in the post-COVID-19 changing world order. The actions of the leaders of both countries continue to show that they have no hesitation in accepting each other as 'Natural Allies' and work together to formulate policies that would enhance the bilateral and multilateral interests of both. This aspect of Indo-US ties has been analysed in detail by the author in his other works.[70]

A significant feature of the revamped and upgraded Indo-US defence ties in the 21st century is the sale of high-end defence equipment and weapons systems to India by successive US administrations. Big-ticket sales include that of 10 C-17 heavy-lift aircraft worth US$4.1 billion, the sale of eight Boeing P-8I aircraft to the Indian Navy in March 2009, the sale of six Lockheed Martin C-130J Super Hercules transport planes worth US$1 billion in January 2008 and the sale of the USS Trenton, a naval vessel worth US$48 million, in 2007.[71] Most recently, India also received Chinook and Apache military helicopters from the US Boeing company worth US$43 billion. The list is growing longer every year. The period between 2008 and 2020 has seen the USA selling arms worth US$18 billion to India, besides the new contracts won by Lockheed Martin for the joint production of multi-role fighter aircrafts under the 'Make-in India' programme.

Things have turned around for US companies, and the sky has opened up for doing their business in India after the decision of the Indian government to raise the limit of FDI in the defence sector to 49 per cent. Under the completely new economic and security architecture, US companies can play a very vital role in the modernization of India's defence sector and achieve the goal of replacing Russia as the largest supplier of military hardware to India, a goal that was set way back in 1995 as one of the bases for future Indo-US strategic cooperation. The results of all such changes are visible from the fact that the USA has sold defence weapons and equipment worth US$18 billion dollars[72] to India between 2008 and 2020.

---

[70] Kumar, 'US and South Asia in the New Millennium', 42.

[71] Desilva-Ranasinghe, *South and West Asia Research Programme*.

[72] Mallick, *2+2 Dialogue and Indo-US Relations*.

Experts suggest that India is expected to place orders of advanced military hardware worth US$30 billion over the next 5 years. The author is in a position to make an assessment that the beginning of the recent India–China crisis along the LAC in Ladakh in March 2020 will push the entire procurement process onto the fast-track mode. The early trends have started emerging as this book was going to press for publication. Although Russia and Israel remain India's two leading defence suppliers, arms sales from the USA are set to grow exponentially over the coming years. Both India and the USA have already made projections that their overall trade and economic relations are likely to touch the mark of US$500 billion in the next decade. The author has a feeling that it might go further higher, as the India–China annual trade worth US$109 billion in 2019 is going to get badly affected in light of India's recent clashes with China on the Indian border in March 2019 and the post-COVID-19 changing world order turning against China. India might see several US companies shifting their production bases to India in the post-COVID-19 era.

Against the backdrop of all such changes, it is expected that Indo-US bilateral relations will soar to new heights in the energy sector, civil nuclear sector, defence sector and 5G sector. One is sure to witness a fundamental change in India's policy through the country befriending the USA openly and embarrassing China more frequently on issues of Quad, enhancing Indo-US cooperation in the Indo-Pacific region and cooperating with the USA in the UNSC and various other forums. India will open up more to the idea of joining the USA in the 'containment of China', for which US policymakers have been waiting for decades. The USA will also have to be more forthcoming in meeting India's aspirations of building its military capabilities to face the challenges emerging from China. The USA also knows that if any country comes close to checking China militarily, it is India. In light of the fast-changing security scenario, the future is very ripe for closer Indo-US defence ties. India has a historic opportunity to occupy the centre stage of global order. The prospects for stronger Indo-US defence ties also lie in the fact that Russia, because of its close defence ties with China in recent decades, has not been finding favour with India; at the same time, Russia is not ready to accommodate India's security concerns regarding its latest sale of arms to China. The limitations in

India–Russia defence ties make for a win-win situation for the USA and its companies.

'Signing of the New Framework for Defense Cooperation in 2005 and 2012 and renewed in 2015, U.S. Defense Technology and Trade Initiative (DTII), provided a 'flexible mechanism to ensure that senior leaders are involved in finding opportunities for science and technology cooperation (to include co-production) and moving away from the tradittonal buyer-seller dynamic'.[73] Technology transfers, as well as co-production and co-development arrangements, should be fast-tracked. India has already gone ahead with placing an order for 32 USA-manufactured MK-54 lightweight torpedoes, in a deal worth US$86 million.[74] Groundbreaking agreements have been reached between India and the USA. One needs to wait and see to what extent these agreements can be turned into realities on the ground and whether the two countries will succeed in breaking the 'buyer–seller' model.

Challenges to Deeper Defence Ties

The problem that prohibits stronger Indo-US defence ties has been beautifully explained by former US Ambassador to India, Karl Inderfurth, who sees India's foreign policy of maintaining 'strategic autonomy' and pursuing the path of multi-alignment as largely responsible for preventing the USA's coupling with India in the defence and strategic arena. India, in the past, has also been reluctant to assume additional responsibilities in the Indo-Pacific region away from its immediate maritime boundaries, raising a doubt in the minds of US policymakers as to whether India would ever get ready to assume bigger responsibilities in areas that were likely to witness contests between rising powers, like China, and the existing power, the USA.[75] It is essential for India to not always pursue a defensive policy; at times, India also needs to be offensive, like China. It ought to accept a larger, more proactive role in the Indo-Pacific region along with

[73] Ibid.

[74] Desilva-Ranasinghe, *South and West Asia Research Programme*.

[75] Inderfurth and Latif, 'U.S.–India Military Engagement'.

the USA, Japan and Australia. India also needs to pay more attention to financial and legislative constraints. It also needs to pay attention to introducing reforms for training its bureaucracy that is less prone to change and more willing to live in the past and take less risks. There are other issues that have the potential of casting a shadow upon stronger Indo-US defence ties: the current status of USA–Pakistan ties; India's internal instabilities; the India–China border row; India seeing the USA as reliable military partner; and India's willingness to absorb US technologies. After the easing of FDI norms for companies of US origin in the defence and space sectors by the Modi government, one needs to watch whether US companies choose India as their destination. A similar euphoria was raised after the nuclear agreement of 2008, and it was felt that US companies would be the largest beneficiaries of making investments in India through selling nuclear reactors for India's nuclear power plants; however, in reality, it turned out to be different. In this context, one can say that both countries are faced with immense opportunities for tapping into each other's potential and maximizing gains. India needs technology and equipment, whereas US companies need buyers like India with deep pockets. The two countries need to move beyond technology transfer and licensed production to co-development and co-production in their defence, missiles, nuclear and energy and 5-G related projects.

DEFENCE TIES IN THE CONTEMPORARY PERIOD

Ties under PM Narendra Modi's Government (2014–2020)

After PM Modi's visit to the USA in 2015, many scholars in India and the USA are upbeat about future Indo-US ties. They are all very optimistic about the huge impact Modi's visit has had upon US policymakers. The role of the Indian diaspora in shaping Indo-US ties has become very important under PM Modi's government. Never has any Indian PM in the past connected with the diaspora in stadiums the way PM Modi has done in the last few years in New York and Houston. With the kind of lift and speed PM Modi provided to the consolidation of Indo-US defence, economic, strategic, energy and counterterrorism cooperation, it seemed as if he was in a hurry to achieve everything during his first term itself. PM Modi has taken a lot of interest in removing all kinds of bottlenecks in Indo-US strategic relations. History has already been made in that PM Modi has undertaken around 80 visits of different countries in the past 6 years of his tenure (2014–2020). It was PM Modi who got the Indo-US Nuclear Agreement of 2008 operationalized after getting India's Nuclear Liability Act 2010 improved so as to accommodate the interests of US nuclear reactor suppliers so that they could resume their operations in India.

Analyst Ashley Tellis[76] in 2012 suggested four trends that continue to hold ground and provide a road map for Indo-US ties and their future trends: (a) the relationship has moved beyond 'parallel actions' to convergence and independence on regional and global matters; (b) there has been a greater understanding between the political leadership in the two countries; (c) the ties have moved beyond transactional to creating dependency/complementarity; and (d) the Pentagon has begun to 'own and guide' the India relationship. These old views of the American expert aptly outline the road map ahead for Indo-US relations. Because of the historic turnaround in Indo-US relations, President Trump visited India in February 2020. The personal chemistry between PM Modi and President Trump has been enough to send a very strong message to US and Indian policymakers and policy implementers.

'Make in India' has been one of the flagship programmes of the incumbent Modi government, which moves from everyday needs to the needs of the Indian military. India, one of the world's biggest defence importers, would like to turn into a noteworthy defence exporter with US support. India has the aspiration of emerging as a hub for the manufacture of defence equipment and important weapons systems, which will enable it to take the status of exporter instead of net importer. PM Modi has been moving in the direction of making India a defence exporter and has contacted defence companies for technological help. With India hoping to purchase in excess of 100 military aircraft, an arrangement that would be worth around US$15 billion,

[76] https://www.thehindu.com/opinion/op-ed/Looking-beyond.

US companies Boeing and Lockheed Martin are keen to win contracts for some of its biggest defence projects. India is pushing for developing a complete ecosystem such that external defence companies come to India and join forces with Indian companies to manufacture parts and items in India, advancing the Make in India venture. A long list is there, like nuclear cooperation, sale of military hardware, joint military exercises under defence–strategic cooperation and energy sector cooperation where Indian and US companies can join each other under 'Make in India' venture. More than 30 JTGs are functional between India and the USA, covering every single aspect of their relations. The unexpected prolonged trade war between the USA and China and the emergence of the COVID-19 crisis have further deepened the wedge between the USA and China, and there always remains a possibility of many US companies shifting base from China to India. The involvement of the USA would be comprehensive in making India a developed nation.

The USA has also been keen to see India emerge as an industrial hub in the Indo-Pacific region, as US companies feel disenchanted with their business operations in China. India has the potential to offer US companies a very important alternative, and the USA is of the view that there remains much scope for both countries to expand their economic and trade links. Most recently, PM Modi's government initiated several legislative measures for enabling the arrival of US MNCs to India because of the ongoing USA–China trade war. The assertiveness and aggressiveness in China's policy towards its neighbours Taiwan and Hong Kong have alerted the countries of the world. Of course, no USA–India trade deal could be finalized during President Trump's visit to India in February 2020. Stronger Indo-US defence ties in the 21st century have provided a bulwark to the Indian government in preparing for the emerging threats to India from the China–Pakistan nexus in areas ranging from the Strait of Malacca to Gulf of Aden, which India considers to be regions of its own security architecture. The change in US approach towards India with respect to Quad meetings, Indo-Pacific cooperation, 2+2 Dialogue, etc. has certainly been the result of hard work put in by the leaderships and officials of both sides in the last 35 years. One can say that on the completion of 75 years of Indo-US bilateral relationship, there will be many things to cheer despite the several ups and downs of the past.

Ties under President Donald Trump's Administration (2016–2020)

There have been several important developments at the global and regional levels during PM Modi's and President Trump's tenures which have helped both countries not deviate from each other. Both have strongly favoured the continuation of the bonhomie established by their predecessors. One of the high points of Indo-US cooperation today is the seeking of peace and security in the Indo-Pacific region. Another pillar of Indo-US relations is defence and counterterrorism cooperation. An important area is military hardware and transfer of key technologies to India. The decision of the Trump administration to sell Sea Guardian UAV to India has been a remarkable one, as India is the first non-NATO partner country to which this technology is being transferred. As India stands designated as the major defence partner of the USA, it is likely to be sold technologies for: intelligence, surveillance and reconnaissance; fifth-generation fighter aircraft production; and Future Vertical Lift system or advanced-technology Ground Combat Vehicles. On several occasions, high officials of the USA have expressed the sentiments of their government to help India overcome its defence and security concerns by enabling it to produce things jointly with the USA. President Trump's visit to India in February 2019 ensured the ongoing level of cooperation with India. A noteworthy development before President's Trump visit was the culmination of the COMCASA and LEMOA agreements between India and the USA in July 2018, according to which forces of both countries are expected to share information, learn each other's military doctrine and give topmost priority to the interoperability of each other's armed forces in hours of emergency. The detailed provisions and outcomes of the COMCASA and LEMOA agreements are discussed in Chapter 7. The launch of the first-ever USA–India Counterterrorism Designations Dialogue has been a very important outcome of the two countries' closer cooperation, as it has helped India exert international pressure on Pakistan, which poses a serious threat to India's unity and territorial integrity.

Today, Indo-US relations cover almost every sector of India's growth story. At the global level, the USA, on a number of occasions, has supported India's membership to the UNSC, NSG, IAEA, MTCR and other multilateral organizations in the 21st century. Indo-US cooperation under Quad and in the Indo-Pacific region has become very important, as both countries have common concerns arising on account of the assertive policies of China in the Indian Ocean region, South China Sea region, East China Sea region and Yellow Sea region. Both countries share common concerns on China's ambitious Border Road Initiative (BRI), a worldwide connectivity project through which China plans to establish direct connectivity running from Europe to Africa through road and sea routes.

Following his predecessors, President Trump has been supportive of continuing past policies towards India, whereby there has been a complete convergence of the geopolitical interests of both countries. The Trump administration has not been harsh on India and has allowed US defence and energy exports to India to continue. Though US companies in the nuclear reactor business have not been able to break the ice with India because of their internal bankruptcy laws, the USA, under President Trump, is keen to give a push to big-ticket defence and energy deals with India. US companies in the nuclear sector have lost a lot at the hands of French and Russian companies that have managed to secure several contracts for the sale and construction of nuclear reactors in India. It is because of this reason that the Trump administration has applied pressure on India under the CAATSA. There are still several issues on which US interests do not match with India's global interests, such as India's import of S-400 missiles from Russia, its import of oil from Iran, the US exemption given to Pakistan for IMF bailout package and the USA's deal with Taliban in Afghanistan.

CONCLUSION

The steps taken by President Clinton during his second term and his 2000 visit to India did break the ice in bitterness in Indo-US relations that had been ongoing over the past several decades, except for the limited achievements of the 1985 MOU. His visit resulted in the release of the Vision Document and the mellowing of US tones in the aftermath of India's May 1998 nuclear explosions. President Bush

(Jr.) gave to India the famous NSSP, and one of the cornerstones of the NSSP had been the Indo-US nuclear deal of 2005, which later became the Indo-US Nuclear Agreement of 2008. Since then, neither country has looked back. It has been an extraordinary achievement for India that since 2000, every single US president has visited India. Since NSSP 2004, Indo-US defence ties have grown stronger. Visits of military officials at the highest level have become a regular feature. Holding of joint army, naval and air force exercises has become an annual feature. Both countries have been working together for ensuring security in the Indo-Pacific region in light of China's assertive and aggressive policies in the South China Sea, East China Sea, Yellow Sea and Indian Ocean region.

Overall, Indo-US defence ties have been the high point of Indo-US relations since the signing of the 1985 MOU. As on today in April 2020, it is going to be completion of 35 years that both the countries have succeeded in raising their bilateral relationship at its peak. The journey has been arduous, reflecting amply that democracies do not take decisions very fast. The inhibitions shown by earlier governments in India in having stronger defence and strategic cooperation with the USA are almost over. All four US presidents in the 21st century have strongly supported the idea of moving ahead with India. Indian policymakers have also realized that with US cooperation, India's interests are served better, and slowly, India has managed to emerge high on the global table. It has succeeded in emerging as a 'giver' at the global level rather than being a 'taker'. India has emerged as an agenda setter at the global level regarding counterterrorism measures, climate change issues, peace and stability issues, multilateralism under the WTO, IMF, G-20, BRICS, Brazil, South Africa, India and China (BASIC), etc. A few important aspects of the strong Indo-US defence ties are also discussed in Chapter 7. US defence companies such as Lockheed Martin, Boeing, Raytheon and Sirkorsky have emerged as the largest suppliers of critical equipment to India, such as C-17 and C-130J transport aircraft and Apache and Chinook helicopters. If not for their closer defence ties, it would have been difficult to ever imagine that the defence deal between the USA and India during 2010–2020 would reach US$18 billion.

Transfer of Technology

6

This chapter discusses the theoretical and operational aspects of technology, which has been a major instrument of social change for humankind. One of the bases for stronger Indo-US relationship was the USA helping India by transferring some key technologies in the industrial and defence sectors, which has been crucial for the attainment of self-reliance goals for a country of India's stature. The chapter discusses the 'dual-use' technology transfers with regard to theory, practice and trends. It highlights the pangs and pains of dual-use technology transfers between the USA and India in the last seven and half decades of their diplomatic relationship. The differences emerging in Indo-US technological cooperation because of the tightened US export control regimes have also been dealt with in this chapter. Deterioration in their bilateral relations because of technology transfer being linked with US nuclear non-proliferation and other global concerns and its implications for India's space and missile development projects have also been addressed. The chapter deals with the transfer of technology only at the government-to-government level. No cases of transfer of technology involving private players are discussed.

INTRODUCTION

Major technological changes have led to fundamental socio-economic, political and cultural transformations. However, technological advancement has also been accompanied by a huge imbalance in the technological capacities of nations. The imbalance has become so marked and significant that developing countries have become synonymous with technological 'have-nots'. K. K. Subrahmanian,[1] an Indian

---

[1] Subrahmanian, 'Technology Transfer', 308.

defence analyst, defines technology as not just an abstract knowledge but rather a combination of equipment, skill and knowledge. It comprises all kinds of skills and all kinds of information, including information about information.

Access to technology can be achieved through various channels, namely joint venture agreements, sale purchase agreements, know-how agreements, licence/patent agreements, trademarks agreements and turnkey contracts.[2] Transfer of technology is the term used for a whole range of forms through which technological knowledge is transmitted from suppliers to recipients through the licensing and transmission of technical know-how and trade secrets; the supply of technical information through plans, diagrams, instructions and training of personnel; the provision of engineering and other services for the erection and commissioning of industrial plants; and the provision of technical assistance and services for the operation and management of business enterprises.[3]

Transfer of technology also takes place through multilateral cooperation agreements involving government institutions and relating to infrastructure projects. Historically, the technological backwardness of developing nations has its origin in their colonial past. There has been a profound disparity between developed and developing nations in terms of research and development expenditure, science and technology, institutional infrastructure, manpower, trade in technology, goods and services, etc. This imbalance is aggravated because of the severe technological dependence of developing nations on developed countries.[4] In the literature of international relations, controversies related to the backwardness of developing nations because of poor research and development facilities leading to their complete dependency on the developed world is dealt with under the topic of North–South divide. The case of the asymmetric relationship between the USA and India is also analysed within the North–South gap framework.

---

[2] Jegathesan, 'Factors Affecting Access to Technology Through Joint Ventures', 101.

[3] Adeoba, 'Technology Transfer and Joint Ventures', 107–108.

[4] Ibid.

The term 'dual-use' applies to the application of technology rather than its conception. There are three categories of technology, namely technology that is exclusive to the military, technology that has no significant application for the military and technology having both military and civil uses. It is difficult to draw a distinction between these categories. For example, a fighting platform in its application is exclusive to the military, but its discrete equipment may have multiple uses; likewise, a C3I (Command, Control, Communication and Intelligence) system may be unique to the services, but its assemblies and sub-assemblies and components may have across-the-board application. Unquestionably, the two facets of technology, military and industry–commercial, reflect a common conception—it is their purposive divergence that underscores the term and therefore the debate.[5]

It is in this context that the chapter helps us in comprehending the problems and prospects of technology transfer that the developing nations have grappled with, particularly India vis-à-vis the USA since its independence, having limited success under the MOU signed in 1985 and the Indo-US nuclear deal in 2005. India has been a victim of denial of 'dual-use' technology transfers from anywhere in the world because of the discriminatory policies followed by USA-led international nuclear and missile regimes. India, under different governments, has pursued a policy of diversifying its sources of high-end technologies, but every time, India's flagship programmes in space, missile and nuclear technology have suffered because of the denial of international nuclear and technology regimes. This has always acted as a bone of contention in Indo-US relations. India has been careful in its dealings with the USA, making it clear that no strategic cooperation with the USA is possible unless the latter enables the transfer of technologies to India for its flagship nuclear, defence, space and missile programmes. India also has been leading the struggle against discriminatory international regimes enjoying US patronage. It took almost 60 years of India's diplomatic efforts at different levels for the USA to finally sign the historic nuclear deal with India in 2005, which facilitated India's entry into nuclear and missiles regimes like the IAEA

---

[5] Deva, 'Dual Use Information Technology Criticalities and Denial', 133. Also see Thomas, 'US Transfers of "Dual-Use" Technologies to India', 826–828.

and MTCR and helped it avail an NSG waiver that allowed technology transfer to India. India's efforts also led to the resumption of nuclear and missiles technology trade with the country, despite it being a non-signatory to the NPT and CTBT. The subsequent sections traverse through the different phases of Indo-US technological cooperation.

THE EARLY DECADES

For a variety of reasons, technology transfers take place from the developed 'North' to the developing 'South', and these may be political, economic or sometimes even military. At the general level, transfer of technology also comprises a component of foreign policy on the part of the supplier country. Until the late 1970s, problems relating chiefly to the terms and conditions of transfer transactions remained on the main agenda of the UN Conference on Trade and Development (UNCTAD) and the UN Commission on Science, Technology and Development (UNCSTD). The negotiations at UNCTAD finally culminated in the creation of an International Code of Conduct on the Transfer of Technology. From 1995 onwards, the code has been part of the Agreement on Trade-Related Aspects of Intellectual Property Rights (TRIPS) under the World Trade Organization (WTO).

India is one of the few major countries among the developing nations that have made a quantum jump in the fields of atomic energy, biotechnology, space, electronics, solar energy, agriculture, automobiles and missiles technology. The role of foreign collaborators has been significant in the successful transplant of imported technology for India's development, industrial modernization and self-reliance. Since 1947, India's science and technology policy was largely oriented towards the development of agriculture and modern industry. India's interest in procuring technology from the USA was evident from Nehru's visit to the USA in October 1949 during which, while laying stress on India's requirements, he said that the USA was one of the few countries that had such people of experience and training at their disposal.[6] Science and technology has been on top of India's priority in its development plans during the last several

---

[6] Rehman and Sondhi, 'United States India Co-operation in S&T', 285.

decades. The 1958 Scientific Policy Resolution was significant for the creation of a sound institutional base for science and technology. India's keenness to have US technical assistance, under President Truman's Point Four Program of technological assistance, however, got enmeshed with the USA's containment policy.[7]

India's actions and decisions at the international level were determined by its own interests, needs and requirements, as well as its beliefs and its own reading of the situation. It was not willing to be commanded and dictated by other powers and countries. India had been playing a critical role in the enhancement of peace and stability in the South Asian region and in the world as a whole. During the Cold War, India's leadership of the NAM had been its hallmark, besides its key role in issues of disarmament, apartheid and North–South dialogue. No doubt, India strove hard for positioning itself as a dominant power in the South Asian region and an emerging major power in the world. Until the late 1960s, India's need for active and massive economic–technological assistance from the USA often came into conflict with its security, strategic goals and promotion of trade, commerce and technology. India's goal of attainment of self-reliance has often been marred by the inevitable linking of forthcoming technological exports and assistance from the USA with the economic, political and strategic objectives of the latter's domestic and foreign policy.

India's relations with the USA came into conflict for the first time over the issue of technology when the USA did not meet India's demand of setting up a steel plant[8] with an Indian PSU because of its perceived differences over India's socialistic pattern of economy. This brought the Soviet Union into the picture, which agreed to collaborate with the PSU. For India, self-reliance in the industrial sector was high on its priority, and it was interested in the development of heavy industries as well as infrastructure, which was in contradiction with the conditions of US economic aid and assistance. India's emphasis had been on its policy of getting technological assistance from both the East and the West.

[7] Ibid.

[8] Ibid., 292.

The policy statement of the US State Department in 1950 admitted that divergences in US and Indian views towards China and Indo-China issues were a matter of serious foreign policy conflict that blocked closer understanding with India.[9] After the India–China war in 1962, India started laying more stress on its defence industries. India, for the first time, received US support and cooperation, receiving know-how and technical assistance for long-term defence production. However, the cooperation did not last long, as the USA continued to have certain reservations regarding the co-production of weapons and also wanted India to settle the Kashmir issue with Pakistan. The setting up of TAPS with US help in 1963[10] was in keeping with India's own desire to establish strategic ties with the USA to ward off further Chinese threat to its security.

As discussed earlier, India's security perspectives were shaped by the India–Pakistan wars of 1965 and 1971 and the emergence of the US-Sino-Pakistani axis in the 1970s. This also led to India's signing of a treaty of friendship and cooperation with the Soviet Union in 1971. The Soviet link allowed India to received aircraft, tanks and ships and modernize the inventories of its armed forces on extremely favourable terms that had never been forthcoming from any of the Western countries. The Soviet Union not only transferred the technologies but also assisted the Indian defence industry in undertaking licensed production, which helped India develop an indigenous military capability to withstand external pressures. It was on this issue that India and the USA were to differ most of the time when India asked for any technology assistance from the USA. Notwithstanding US pressure on it to sign the NPT, India's assertion of its ambition of being a dominant power in the South Asian region became more explicit after it carried out a nuclear explosion in May 1974. India did not like being equated at par with Pakistan as a result of US Cold War politics in the region during 1970s–1980s, especially after the Soviet invasion of Afghanistan in 1979.

GOI's Technology Policy Statement (TPS) of 1983 emphasized support for domestic technology development with technological

---

[9] Ibid., 288.

[10] Bose, 'Nuclear Proliferation', 34.

self-reliance and the reduction of dependence on foreign inputs.[11] The TPS, aimed at protecting domestic technology, permitted import of technology on a selective basis. It further outlined a commitment to promote the absorption, adaptation and subsequent development of imported know-how through adequate investment in R&D.[12] It was in this context that India needed advanced technology for its defence sector's indigenous development programmes of LCA, Integrated Guided Missile Development Programme (IGMDP) and space launch vehicles (SLVs). Over the years, the Indian Defence Research and Development Organisation (DRDO) has grown to comprise, at present, 50 laboratories/establishments and about 15 airworthiness certification centres, spread throughout the country. DRDO, which is responsible for the diffusion of all kinds of technologies for its various programmes, has also launched a major self-reliance plan for defence and defence industrial base. This 10-year plan, publicly announced in April 1994, primarily concerns self-reliance in high-technology weapons systems and equipment required by the armed forces in the near future.[13] The policy continues even today, as India is on the verge of becoming a developed-cum-industrialized country of the world. As on date, India has gained diplomatic experience in navigating through all hurdles placed by international technology denial regimes. It is this experience that finally helped India to compel the USA to sign a nuclear deal with it in 2005 and enable it in seeking waivers from NSG, IAEA and MTCR for the resumption of nuclear trade with countries of the world as a non-signatory to the NPT and CTBT.

THE COLD WAR PERIOD

India Diversifies Technology Procurements

India's need for advanced technology was directly proportional to the ongoing developments in the neighbouring countries, which had a direct bearing on India's internal as well as external security. China's

---

[11] Lok Sabha Debates, c. 267.

[12] UNCTAD/ITD/TECHNOLOGY/10, 6–7.

[13] Chaudhary, 'India's Security Policy', 190–191.

developmental and modernization programmes,[14] along with Pakistan undertaking manufacturing of high-technology items and its quest for a technological edge over India through acquiring sophisticated weapons and US arms package[15] worth \$4.02 billion during the period 1987–1993, had its impact on India's decision of modernizing its defence forces and equipment. The nuclearization of Pakistan[16] qualitatively created a new security situation for India. The need for acquiring technologies from the USA had also become imperative because of the Sino-Soviet rapprochement.

Towards the mid-1980s, the relationship between India and the USA was also a reflection of the contemporary international situation and the recognition by the USA of India as an emerging power. India's actions during the mid-1980s were consistent with its emerging as a major power after its successful intervention in Sri Lanka in 1987 and the Maldives in 1988. It is necessary to mention here that the USA–Iraq war in 1991, the failure of the Soviet technologies of electronic warfare during the Gulf War of 1991 and the collapse of the Soviet Union were important factors in shaping of future Indo-US science and technology cooperation.

India was inclined to seek certain technologies that were part of the US administration's licensing and clearance and which were to be transferred only on a government-to-government basis. India needed US capital and technology, whereas it provided the USA with vast Indian markets. However, the US technologies to India were not transferred freely because of the USA's domestic laws and its effort to link the technology transfer with its foreign policy objectives, including its nuclear non-proliferation goals.

India sought advanced technology mainly for domestic economic development purposes. However, such advanced technology had relevance for the defence sector too. India's negotiations with the industrialized West for technology transfer were primarily in the

---

[14] Singh, 'Security Environment in South-Asia', 177. Such concerns were also expressed in Government of India, Ministry of Defence, *Annual Report 1985–86*, 2 and 3.

[15] Government of India, *Annual Report 1987–88*, 2.

[16] Government of India, *Annual Report 1991–92*, 4.

context of 'North–South' economic relations. On the other hand, because of US perceptions of India's closer relations with the Soviet Union, it often got embroiled in the context of 'East–West' conflict relations. Another fear on part of the US administration was of India's diversion of US civilian technology for military purposes.[17] Seeking to avoid overdependence on either of the superpowers, India, in the 1980s, began diversifying its procurement of military equipment and started production under licence agreements. It purchased Jaguar bombers from Britain, HDW submarines from West Germany and Mirage 2000 aircraft from France.[18]

India is known for having enjoyed a long period of technological cooperation with the former USSR in the setting up of heavy machinery industries, including steel plants, besides joint production of defence weapons and equipment under licensed production agreements. Indian armed forces are known to have depended on the former USSR for almost 70 per cent of their weapons systems and fighter and transport aircraft. The former USSR always facilitated transfers of technologies for the manufacture of crucial weapons, transports, heavy vehicles and other equipment within its ordnance factories. India expected similar cooperation with the USA. The Soviet factor always created suspicions among US policymakers. As Richard P. Cronin[19] stated, 'To date, India's purchase of western military hardware has been motivated primarily by a desire to obtain specific capabilities or technology not available from Moscow, not to reduce significantly or end the Soviet Union connection'. Still, the US administration saw the relatively minor signs of Indian defence diversification and modernization efforts as an opportunity to increase its own sales to India, thereby reducing Indo-Soviet ties in this crucial area, and perhaps garner, over the long term, greater security and strategic understanding with India. The official added, 'Though they still secure 80 percent of their military equipment of the Soviet Union. But we have an interest in encouraging that diversification process

[17] Thomas, 'US Transfer of "Dual-Use" Technologies to India', 826.

[18] Kux, *Estranged Democracies*, 382.

[19] Cronin, 'Policy Alert', CRS-6.

and increasing Indian independence through their capacity to produce indigenously defence equipment'.[20]

Realizing the limits of Soviet technology, India recognized that good relations with the USA would give it greater access to the more advanced technology of the USA in defence as well as in the economic sector. Better ties with the USA would also influence it to continue a positive attitude towards India in international financial institutions and to take greater account of India in its dealings with Pakistan. The 1982 visit of Indira Gandhi[21] to the USA brought three major achievements: first, the settlement of the Tarapur nuclear fuel issue, as France had replaced the USA as the chief fuel supplier; second, the signing of the Science and Technology Initiative (STI) by President Reagan and Indira Gandhi; and third, the declaration of year 1985 as 'the year of India', during which a mammoth Indian art and cultural exhibition was held in the USA. An eminent foreign policy analyst stated, 'Indira Gandhi pressed the door a little open, Rajiv Gandhi pushed this door further and made a determined effort to put this relationship on a new basis of matured understanding of similarities and differences'.[22] The Rajiv Gandhi government brought India closer to the USA and other advanced Western nations going into the 21st century. The liberalization of the Indian economy under him facilitated technology import through FDIs. India's desire for a better relationship with the USA, as expressed by Rajiv Gandhi, also was more enthusiastically reciprocated by Washington.[23] The years of marred relationship between India and the USA gave way to a new way of thinking after the finalization and signing of the MOU[24] in May 1985 between the two countries, which became an important basis for US technology export to India in the future. The objective of the MOU was to establish a mechanism for India without jeopardizing the USA's national security and its nuclear non-proliferation interests.

---

[20] Limaye, *U.S.-Indian Relations*, 197.

[21] Ibid., 168–169.

[22] Dutt, *India and the World*, 84.

[23] Dutt, *Foreign Policy of India*, 124.

[24] Government of India, Ministry of External Affairs, *Annual Report 1985–86*, 32.

The US Technology Policy: Geopolitics and Geo-economics

The USA used strategic exports and arms sales as levers to advance its national interests by coupling export decisions with security assistance and foreign military sales to developing countries and cementing relations with other countries. The USA's decision to sell or otherwise transfer weapons or technologies is most often based on mutual security interests and is designed to affect the world or regional geopolitical balance in favour of the USA. US transfer of weapons or technologies is also viewed as a 'penetration mechanism' that advances US foreign policy interests by tying the recipient state to the USA for spare parts, training programmes and even long-term loans. Strategic exports and arms sales strengthen the national economy by increasing domestic production, earning foreign exchange and reducing the unit cost of weapons systems to the USA and its security assistance recipients through economies of sale.[25] A US expert on South Asia said that Washington had three major regional objectives in the 1980s: to contain Soviet power; to encourage Indian strategic autonomy (defined as a lessening of Indian dependence on the Soviet Union); and to prevent nuclear proliferation.[26] India also saw rapprochement with the USA as a counterpoise to the USA–Pakistan strategic relationship, which had emerged following the Soviet intervention in Afghanistan and was perceived as a way to alleviate adversarial Indo-US relations. Thus, as a result of the convergence of their political and technological interests, India and the USA embarked on high-technology cooperation during the 1980s.[27]

As discussed earlier, these changes in the attitude of both countries were a result of the US recognition of India's pre-eminent role as an Asian regional power and as a growing middle power on the global scene. This was also endorsed by NSDD 147, which underlined to

[25] Wortzel, 'US Technology Transfer Policies and the Modernization of China's Armed Forces', 615–616.

[26] Cohen, 'The Reagan Administration and India', 141.

[27] Sidhu, 'Enhancing Indo-US Strategic Cooperation', 40–41.

all concerned agencies the importance of building a better relationship with India, particularly through accommodating its request for
sophisticated technology subject to expert controls.[28] It underlined to
all concerned agencies the importance of building a better relationship with India, particularly by accommodating India's requests for
sophisticated technology subject export controls.[29] The document's
relevance to increasing defence cooperation was profound.

The changes at the US policy level were also reinforced by commercial motives. The USA had become one of the biggest debtor
countries in the 1980s, and experts attributed it to the US export policies of high technologies that had been detrimental to the country's
economy. These needed the administration's urgent attention. The
Export Administration Amendments Act of 1985 advocated a balanced technology control policy that would give equal consideration
to economic and security interests.[30] As a result, technology controls
were reduced and the administration's trade bill of 19 February 1987
provided for, among other things, shortening of the control lists, faster
processing of export application and administrative strengthening of
the commerce department.[31] The prospects of US-Indian technological cooperation reflected a positive trend in their bilateral relations.[32]

THE INDO-US MEMORANDUM OF
UNDERSTANDING, 1985

Against the backdrop of emerging complementarities on both sides,
GOI and the USA concluded in November 1984 an MOU on technology transfer to India, which became operational in May 1985.[33]

---

[28] Mukherjee, 'US Weaponry for India', 601, and Gordon, *India's Rise to Power in the Twentieth Century and Beyond*, 77–90.

[29] Mukherjee, 'US Weaponry for India', 601.

[30] Boltersdorf, 'The Reagan Administration's Policy on Technology Controls', 172.

[31] Ibid., 173.

[32] Limaye, *U.S.-Indian Relations*, 19.

[33] The minister of state for external affairs told the house in an answer to question no. 1214 on 27 March 1985, quoted in *Lok Sabha Debates*, cc. 97–98.

The MOU was crucial for two reasons. First, it related purely to defence technology, including dual technology, which, according to India, referred to items on the Commodities Control List (CCL),[34] administered by the Department of Commerce, and the Munitions List,[35] administered by the Department of State. Both lists dealt with exports controlled by the US administration for national security as well as non-proliferation and foreign policy purposes. Second, the MOU process, particularly the insistence on item-specific end uses, especially for sensitive dual-use equipment, provided a forum in which to address proliferation issues.[36] The MOU indicated the US willingness to support India's weapons procurement strategies, but only in return for assurances that the advanced technology transferred would be protected from leaks and used only for agreed purposes.

The MOU of 1985 introduced substantial changes in Indo-US relations in the areas of defence cooperation and sale of military and dual-use equipment and technology, and it resulted in the immediate release of a large number of technologically advanced exports. The MOU was followed by another significant agreement that set up 'mission areas discussions' between the defence establishments of the USA and India with the goal of increasing military cooperation and sales of military equipment and technology.[37] The importance of the mission areas approach was to identify relatively precise projects and parameters of defence cooperation that could be isolated from other aspects of bilateral political relations. This offered additional protection to US technology. This also led to the creation of a Blue Book, in April 1987, which laid the guidelines for military-related technology transfers to be used by US industries.[38]

---

[34] For CCL, see US Department of Commerce, 9; *Export Administration Regulation*, 15 C.F.R. 399.1, Supplement 1, 1 October 1982 and *Defence Daily*, 22 April 1987.

[35] For Munition list, see *Federal Register*, '22 Code of Federal Regulations', 47686–9.

[36] Santhanam and Singh, 'Confidence Resorting Measures for Indo-US Commerce in Controlled Commodities', 319–333.

[37] US Department of Defence, *The Technology Security Programme*, 135.

[38] Limaye, *U.S.–Indian Relations*, 212–213.

As per the provisions of the MOU, India agreed: to only import items and not redirect them or any part of them to another destination before its arrival in India; to provide, if asked, verification of possession of items; not to re-export items without the written approval of the Import Certificate Issuing Authorities (ICIA) in India; and not to transfer within India the items specified in this certificate without the written approval of the ICIA.[39] In essence, the MOU was designed to reconcile India's weapons procurement policies with US technology transfer conditions and thereby expand Indo-US military links. It also provided the bureaucratic basis for the USA implementing the decision to expand cooperation with India.

Technology Transfer: Case of Supercomputer Programme

Despite the signing of the MOU, differences were bound to grow over its technical interpretation. The immediate impact of the MOU was the increase in export licences approved for India. The US technology transfers to India after 1985 consisted of items that had previously never been sold outside the Western alliance. In particular, the sales of Cray XMP-14 supercomputers for the Indian Meteorological Department (IMD), advanced 'silicon-on-sapphire' microprocessor chips for India's INSAT-2 satellite and 16 GE F404 engines to HAL for the development of LCA constituted a major leap forward in Indo-US technological cooperation.[40] Although assurances were obtained that the supercomputer's use would be confined to the civilian sector, it nevertheless carried potential technological benefits for the military sector as well. The transfer of supercomputers took place, but it resulted in the creation of a huge controversy regarding the supercomputers' use and their security implications, which is discussed in a subsequent section. The important thing about the MOU was that it facilitated over 6,000 purchases or collaborations in high technology worth $1 billion

[39] Government of India, Ministry of External Affairs, New Delhi, Import Certificates Procedure Under the Indo-US Memorandum of Understanding on Technology Transfer, 2. Cited in Sidhu, Enhancing Indo-US Strategic Cooperation, 42–43.

[40] Thomas, 'US Transfers of Dual-Use-Technologies to India', 840.

till 1988, which required prior approval by the US authorities.[41] In January and March 1988, the workings of the MOU were reviewed by the two sides and procedures simplified, with expectations of even faster and smoother processing.

The transfer of dual-use and military technologies from the USA was accompanied by the reiteration of India's pre-eminent position in the South Asian region. In 1988, the US Department of Defence in its annual report stated that 'India seems determined to achieve a dominant position in the Indian Ocean commensurate with its overwhelming preponderance in population, resources and economic strength'. The report stated that India was building what would be 'a potent power-projection force by end of this century, backed by carrier air power, and increasingly effective surface and submarine forces'.[42] US readiness to acknowledge India's regional interests paved the way for India's willingness to take into account US strategic concerns with regard to South Asia and adjoining areas.

Before 1985, often the US Department of Defence asked for a political price for the ongoing US technological cooperation, namely a compensatory reduction in India's technological and military ties with the Soviet Union. This attitude was extended to the transfer of advanced civilian technology as well. However, after the 1985 MOU, there was an increasing recognition in the USA of the long-term security benefits of civilian technology transfers to India and the promotion of economic interdependence among the nations of the South Asian region based on their economic and technological ties with the USA.[43] The USA had also in principle approved the transfer of International Telephone and Telegraph night-vision manufacturing technology and shipboard data multiplex system and a licence for the assembly and manufacture of 600 Control Data Corporation computers for use in the civil and military

---

[41] According to US figures, 3,461 items worth $853,614 were approved under the Memorandum of Understanding (MOU) and other items worth $600,000 outside the MOU. Only 32 requests were denied and 486 not acted upon, as cited in Kumar, *Yearbook on India's Foreign Policy*, 176.

[42] *The Hindustan Times*, 21 January 1989.

[43] Thomas, 'US Transfers of Dual-Use-Technologies to India', 831.

sectors, valued at US $500 million. India also obtained a license to manufacture semiconductors using US technology.[44]

Indo-US technological dialogue between 1986 and 1989 involved three main items: advanced aero-engines for the development of LCA; satellite and booster rocket technology for India's space programme; and supercomputers for weather forecasting. This was important because GE F404 engines for LCA and advanced technology that were to be fitted on future US fighter aircraft were not yet available on the advanced Soviet Union MiG-29 aircraft and prototype MiG-31s. While space technology and supercomputers (Cray XMP-14) had relevance for India's satellite telecommunications and weather-forecasting needs, they also carried relevance for India's potential missile warheads delivery systems and early warning systems.[45] India's emphasis on seeking US technology got further reinforced during the second US visit of PM Rajiv Gandhi in October 1987.[46] In a way, the MOU of 1985 had become the basis for transfer of technology from the USA to India.

The significance of Frank Carlucci's visit was precisely in the fact that it marked a milestone in the progressively closer defence relationship between India under Rajiv Gandhi and the USA. The contract for the purchase by India of Cray XMP-14 was eventually signed in May 1988, after protracted negotiations over 3 years. The STI was extended once again for a period of 3 years in October 1988. The Cray XMP-14 super-computer was received by India in October 1988 and was installed at the National Centre for Medium Range Weather Forecasting (NCMRWF) on the premises of the IMD in New Delhi. GOI also applied for an export licence for another supercomputer, the Cray YMP-132, for the Indian Institute of Science, Bangalore;[47] however, this supercomputer was never transferred to India on different pretexts.

[44] Chanda, 'Hi-Technological Diplomacy', 37.

[45] Thomas, 'US Transfers of Dual-Use-Technologies to India', 825–827.

[46] Text of PM Rajiv Gandhi's statement at the White House, after lunch with President Ronald Reagan on 20 October 1987, cited in Government of India, *Foreign Affairs Record*, 339.

[47] Government of India, Ministry of External Affairs, *Annual Report 1988–89*, 43.

There were criticisms that India was paying a heavy price for its growing defence ties with the USA, as it was a mark of gradual dilution or minimization of India's criticism of US policies and actions around the world, thereby making a difference to the quality of its non-alignment.[48] The cost of the supercomputer was $8.107 billion. The 6-foot supercomputer was to be used for weather forecasting and agrometeorological services and was installed in the IMD complex in New Delhi. Its operation was supposed to be in Indian hands, but its maintenance was to be looked after by US scientists.[49]

The controversy continued as India was denied access to Cray for military purposes. India was denied a second Cray as it wanted US to provide further access to supercomputer; this led India's Center for Development of Advanced Computing (CDAC) to manufacture much cheaper successful machine later, known as PARAM and ANUPAM in 1990s.[50] The supply of supercomputers remained embroiled in controversies on one or the other pretext. The USA felt that the Cray XMP-24 supercomputer with parallel processors could be put to use by India in its nuclear weapons programme, design of ballistic missiles or intelligence-related defence research, such as analysis of satellite images.[51]

India, on the other hand, had declared that the facility would be primarily used for agrometeorological applications and monsoon studies and, in fact, had also given an undertaking that the supercomputer would not be put to use in nuclear development. However, it was unable to put to rest the US anxieties, as it did not agree with the concept of limited sovereignty, which the USA's NATO allies readily accepted. Because of such reasons, some critics were of view that the MOU was a cleverly worded US Export Administration Act 0f 1979 (EAA) and a formalized but indirect instrument of imposing the NPT. Its demand for in situ inspection of supercomputer uses indeed was the NPT's backdoor enforcement.[52] Another US concern was the proximity of the Soviets to

[48] Kumar, *Yearbook on India's Foreign Policy 1988–89*, 12.

[49] Ibid., 61.

[50] Gordon, *India's Rise to Power in the Twentieth Century and Beyond*, 36–37.

[51] Raj, 'US Hi-Tech Diplomacy and the Supercomputer Deal', 742–743.

[52] Ibid., 744.

the Indian supercomputer facility.[53] Thus, the supercomputer deal, the first major venture of the Indo-US trade, became a victim of the highly contradictory and wishful hi-tech diplomacy practised by the USA.

Technology Transfer: Case of the Light Combat Aircraft Project

In 1985, the US government decided to release GE's F404 engine for India's LCA programme, and subsequently, a report prepared by Talbot Lindstrom became the basis for the evolution of the MOU, which identified three areas for Indo-US defence cooperation. These were aeronautics and aircraft technology, in general, and the LCA, in particular; third-generation anti-tank systems; and instrumentation and training for the National Test Range (NTR).[54] The visits of two successive US defence secretaries, Caspar Weinberger in 1986 and Frank Carlucci in 1988, to India were very crucial, as they facilitated crucial progress on the LCA collaboration through the release of advanced electronics requested by India.[55]

Frank Carlucci's visit was also significant, confirming the Reagan administration's desire to 'contribute to, and be a part of, India's future by supporting with our defence relationship India's larger quest for self-reliance'.[56] Carlucci also announced that the USA wanted to be 'a part of India's larger quest for self-reliance' in the defence sphere as part of its strategy to wean India away from its heavy dependence on Soviet military purchases and establish a more substantial nature of cooperation besides simple technology transfer. Collaboration on the LCA did indeed reach this level.[57] In September 1988, a letter of offer and acceptance (LOA) was signed between the US and Indian

---

[53] Ibid., 745.

[54] Santhanam and Singh, 'Confidence Resorting Measures for Indo-US Commerce in Controlled Commodities', 319–333.

[55] Mansingh, 'New Directions in Indo-US Relations', 209.

[56] Weisman, 'India Gets O.K. to Use US Gyroscope in a Jet Fighter', cited in Limaye, US-Indian Relations, 214.

[57] Limaye, U.S.–Indian Relations, 214–215.

air forces, through the Wright-Patterson Air Force Base, for technical assistance on the LCA.

This agreement allowed Indian technicians access to the four Air Force Wright Aeronautical Laboratories. This opened the way for collaboration and participation of the US industry in the project. The transfer of technology envisaged was unprecedented and covered avionics and flight controls, fly-by-wire systems, flight actuators and carbon composite materials.[58] Amidst cheers and laud applause, the smallest combat fighter in the world, India's own LCA, rolled out on 17 November 1994. Witnessing the roll-out, the then PM P. V. Narasimha Rao affirmed that the entire programme would be completed 3 years in advance of the scheduled year (2005) of its induction into the IAF.[59]

However, the delay in production and cost escalation raised doubts in the minds of some experts from the country as well as abroad. By mid-1991, the LCA was to be much more a hybrid of foreign technologies than ever imagined, with the inclusion of a US engine, Swedish avionics, a US or French fly-by-wire avionics system and an airframe whose main input had come from foreign consultants. From the original estimate of ₹5.60 billion, the cost had risen to ₹16.70 billion, and the production date remained uncertain.[60] As per the GOI report of 1995, the cost of the LCA project had gone up to ₹21.88 billion, and its likely induction into the IAF was to take place by the year 2003 only.[61] The mass production and complete induction of LCA into the IAF is still awaited in 2020. This delay of more than 35 years needs critical appraisal of joint ventures with countries like the USA.

A GOI report[62] attributed the delay to difficulties in the indigenous Kaveri engine's development and resource constraints during 1988–1992 resulting in cost escalations. The report added that two prototypes of the aircraft would be ready by June 1996 and cleared for production

[58] *MILAVNEWS* (October 1988), 19, quoted in Smith, *India's Ad hoc Arsenal: Direction or Drift in Defence Policy?*, 174.

[59] *The Hindustan Times*, 17 November 1994.

[60] Chadha, 'Time for Introspection', cited in Smith, *India's Ad Hoc Arsenal*, 175.

[61] Government of India, *DRDO Major Projects,* paras. 4.22 and 4.23.

[62] Government of India, *DRDO Major Projects*, paras. 4.19, 4.27 and 4.33.

by 2002 and that a sufficient number of engines would be produced by HAL. It openly acknowledged that the project had already suffered tremendous slippages both in time and cost estimates. The Indian Parliamentary Standing Committee on Defence also desired that after the completion of prototype trials, the LCA project should be reviewed. Thus, a shadow was cast over the successful completion of the LCA project because of several rounds of cost escalation and indefinite delay in the LCA's production, raising a big question mark over the ongoing Indo-US cooperation in the ambitious project.

It is noteworthy that the lack of full US cooperation allegedly was a strategic move on the part of the US administration to get involved with Indian companies in order to assist them in this mega project and then withdraw midway or slow down the assistance,[63] allowing the project's cost to escalate and finally abandoning it after reviewing it, or for the achievement of its broader objectives of achieving non-proliferation goals or controlling MTCR violations. All this might have been planned by the USA so as not to allow India to emerge as a militarily powerful country and to deny the country access to the most lucrative arms market of the world while continuing to maintain its own monopoly over the arms market. This argument had some truth in it, as despite important landmarks between both countries being witnessed, contentious issues impeded the flow of dual-use technology to India. The various international nuclear and missiles regimes led by the USA, such as the NSG and MTCR, under the guise of promotion of non-proliferation policies, had been founded on a strategy of preventing Third World development of technologies that might impinge on Western powers' military and economic interests.[64]

Nuclear Suppliers Group. This body came into being in 1974 and has 45 member countries in 2020. It saw that the NPT could not stop proliferation of technologies,[65] as a country like India had succeeded in carrying out its first nuclear explosion in May 1974. The very purpose

[63] An interview with one of the US Scholars (who never wanted to be quoted) during the Regional Center for Strategic Studies (RCSS) Summer Workshop held in Shanghai, China, 20–29 September 1998.

[64] Chellaney, 'Non-Proliferation', 441.

[65] Ibid.

of this body was to further limit the nuclear trade among countries, especially among non-nuclear nations. Since all advanced technologies were dual-use in purpose, these technology control regimes were in a position to effectively curtail the flow of technology to the civilian sphere. India has also been at the receiving end of these technology control regimes because of its competence in nuclear technology and in manufacturing IRBMs.[66] The dubious role of the NSG in India's affairs finally ended after the signing of the Indo-US nuclear deal/agreement in 2005/2008 when India was granted an NSG waiver after it signed a safeguards agreement with IAEA in 2008.

THE END OF THE COLD WAR: NEW WORLD ORDER

Technology Transfer Slows Down: Case of India's Missile Programme

The US policy towards South Asia during the Cold War and post-Cold War period remained putting curbs on India's and Pakistan's ongoing missile programmes. The USA considered India's Agni missile programme as destabilizing the military balance in South Asia. It continued exerting pressure on India to halt its Agni missiles programme by denying it crucial technologies like the combined acceleration and vibration climatic test system (CAVCTS) in 1989. Despite US pressure, India went ahead and test-fired Agni, claiming that it was only a technology demonstration and declaring that a system was not going to be developed. A new US policy became evident when the USA tried to impinge on India's technology transfers through third countries too. ISRO of India had signed an agreement with Russia's Glavkosmos for the sale of three cryogenic engines to it, but US pressure led to the complete cancellation of the contract, which was a very distressing trend emerging in the ongoing Indo-US technology transfers under the 1985 MOU.[67] Many Indians had had a lurking suspicion that the USA did not want to see India emerge as a strong military power that could play an autonomous role at both the regional and global levels,

---

[66] Zuberi and Kalyanaramnan, 'Science and Technology for Development', 1432.

[67] Shrivastava, 'Indo-American Relations', 218.

and the US action lent credence to the suspicion. It was clear to many Indian analysts that the USA might welcome India as part of the global power structure commanded by itself, but it did not want anyone to enjoy autonomy outside that structure.[68]

The main emphasis of India's space programme, which had started in the 1960s, was on satellite launch and the development of communication capability. The aim was to use satellites for mass communication and education. However, it is important to note that most of the technologies used in the space programme were dual in use and thus could be used in manufacturing missiles too. Thus, the Indian programme had a built-in missile dimension. The USA and India had been cooperating in space activities for over 20 years.[69] Both countries recognized the value and importance of international space cooperation and continued to seek joint endeavours in space science, space flight and the practical application of space systems and technologies. However, cooperation in this area too was marred by US concerns centred on the military dimension of India's space research programme. Experts in the USA[70] were of the view that India had made significant progress in rocket and satellite technology, and despite India's denial that it did not intend to translate rocket technology into military capability, they confirmed that India's accomplishments had direct military applicability.

India justified its space research programme on the basis that it needed a missile-based defence capability because of its perception of threats to its security emanating from the regional and global environment. India perceived China's missile capability as a threat to its national security. The scenario had become complicated because of Chinese efforts to provide help to Pakistan in the latter's missile as well as nuclear programme. China had provided covert nuclear and missile assistance to Pakistan as an apparent strategy to build a countervailing power to tie down India.[71] The GOI report in August 1995 stated, 'China has been rapidly modernising its armed forces and

[68] Ibid., 219.

[69] Lok Sabha Debates, cc. 121–122.

[70] Wirsing, 'The Arms Race in South-Asia', 315–342.

[71] Chellaney, 'Non-Proliferation', 439.

equipping itself with sophisticated aircraft, air defence weapons and enhancing its blue water capabilities, China also continued to carry out nuclear tests'. 'Pakistan continues to maintain close ties with China. The latter is major source of weapons, particularly of combat aircraft, missiles and tanks. The sale to Pakistan of M-11 missiles and allied technology by China is a cause of concern'.[72] All these developments in the region were sufficient for India to go ahead with its own missile programme despite the US pressure on curbing nuclear proliferation in South Asia, especially under President Clinton's government. The GOI report underlined that India's missile development programme was necessary in the light of China's IRBM and ICBM programmes. Reacting to India's Agni test in 1989, a US official pointed out that the USA had always been concerned regarding the spread of ballistic missiles throughout the world and that the USA felt that the Agni test did not add to stability within various regions.[73]

The USA's concern over India's development of the Agni and Prithvi ballistic missiles had three levels: first, the USA was concerned over the proliferation of advanced weaponry and ballistic missiles and its impact on force projection capacities; second, it looked at the impact of the emerging Indian missile potential in the Indian Ocean region; and third, it was concerned about future Indian capacity to graduate from a demonstrated IRBM power to a nuclear-capable ICBM power.[74] In short, the USA perceived India as 'part of the problem' of missile pro-liferation and 'not as a partner' in its solution. Washington perceived any attempt by New Delhi to deploy the Prithvi missile as a watershed in the South Asian strategic environment. Hence, it saw the MTCR as a key instrument in the battle against missile proliferation.[75] It is noteworthy that when India conducted its first nuclear explosion in 1974, the USA created the NSG the same year, and when India later started testing its Agni and Prithvi missiles, the USA created the MTCR

[72] Government of India, *DRDO Major Projects*, Paras. 4.10, 4.11 and 4.12.

[73] Joshi, 'Dousing the Fire?', 567.

[74] Singh, 'Effects of MTCR and Multilateral Politics of North South Technology Transfers', 301.

[75] Vinod, 'India-United States Relations in a Changing World', 445.

in 1987. The controversial role of the NSG is discussed in Chapters 3 and 4. The role of the MTCR is discussed in the next section. It is important to note that US pressures on India continued even when the reality was that China had already deployed its missiles more than two decades ago and that the Chinese supplied 2,700-km-range IRBMs to Saudi Arabia in 1988. ICBMs and other missiles continued to be deployed in Central Asia. More than 500 ballistic missiles were estimated to still exist in Afghanistan. Pakistan had already demonstrated the 300-km-range Hatf-2 missile in 1989 and since then has been developing the 600-km-range Hatf-3.[76]

India, time and again, tried to ward off US pressure on it to accept the MTCR norms. An Indian official, on 8 March 1993, blamed the US laws and international regimes' role in retarding India's missile programme and slowing down its acquisition of strategic US technologies. He also underlined that the USA and the regimes could not divert a country like India while national capabilities in some other areas were fairly advanced. Ironically, the international technology denial regimes had spurred indigenous development of capabilities and not prevented countries like Iraq and Pakistan from acquiring technologies through subterfuge.[77]

The 1993 Carnegie Report[78] openly stated that the USA should continue to deny licences for the sale of US technology that would contribute directly to any Indian efforts to develop missiles capable of delivering nuclear weapons. The Agni and Prithvi missile programmes were far advanced. India's export of such missiles or manufacturing technology to hostile or potentially hostile states in order to earn foreign exchange would clearly be damaging to US interests. It showed not only the USA's geopolitical but also its geo-economic considerations when it came to dealing with India's missile programme. It was being proved that the USA was trying to block India in all those areas where it had leverage at the international level, such as in India's nuclear, space and missiles programmes. The Carnegie Report added

---

[76] Singh, 'Ballistic Missiles'.

[77] The text of the speech was published in *Strategic Digest*, 754.

[78] Harrison and Kemp, 'India and America after the Cold War', 37–38.

that Indian efforts to develop an ICBM out of the Polar Satellite Launch Vehicle (PSLV) capable of reaching the continental USA would introduce new strains in the Indo-US relationship, and hence, the USA should make every effort in the years ahead to forestall an Indian ICBM programme. Thus, the USA should limit help to the Indian space programme in non-launcher-related activities.[79] From the arguments, it was clear that the USA, under President Clinton in the 1990s, was not going to relent on India's nuclear and missile proliferation and wanted India to sign the NPT and the proposed CTBT. This aspect of Indo-US relations is discussed in Chapter 3 in a detailed manner. It became explicit that the US technology transfer policy would not make any compromises on its security-cum-proliferation concerns. The USA also had apprehensions that the Indian missile Agni, with its 2,500-km-range, could potentially threaten US economic and political interests in the Persian Gulf. It could hit targets in the southern part of the erstwhile Soviet Union, Pakistan, Afghanistan, Iran, most Gulf states, large parts of China and much of Southeast Asia. Therefore, a key objective of the US non-proliferation strategy was to prevent the deployment of Agni. India's satellite programmes, such as the PSLV and Geosynchronous Satellite Launch Vehicle (GSLV) ones, were also viewed with deep concern in Washington. India thus remained on top of the MTCR list of troublesome countries.

Technology Transfer and the Role of Regimes: The MTCR, NPT and CTBT

The Indo-US cooperation in the area of high technology has over time suffered over different issues, including leakage of technology transfer or maintenance of exclusive control over the area where the technology was to be used. This was because of the USA's export controls and its support to the various international regimes of technology control, besides its policy to relate Indo-Pak nuclear issues with their military aid and assistance programmes, which was never acceptable to India. India's opposition to such US moves always remained very vehement.

---

[79] Ibid.

The very purpose of creating the **MTCR in 1987** by the Group of Seven (G-7) countries was to limit the transfer of technology used in making nuclear weapons delivery systems and counter missile proliferation. The aim of the MTCR[80] was to limit the missile test programmes of countries like South Korea, India, Pakistan and Iran, prominently. On 2 December 1987, India protested against the USA's adoption of a legislation by the US Senate that sought to condition the transfer of high technology to India and Pakistan and the two South Asian countries entering into an agreement on nuclear safeguards.[81] PM Rajiv Gandhi, in a letter addressed to the US president, on 4 December 1987, conveyed India's strong objection to the move of linking the transfer of technology and safeguards for India's nuclear programme.[82] The opposition to this move was so severe in India that MPs of the upper house wanted India to call back its ambassador from the USA.[83] Under India's pressure, the US Senate reversed a controversial amendment to the US Foreign Assistance Act that would have made an Indo-Pak agreement on nuclear non-proliferation a precondition for continued US aid to India. This move paved the way for the continuation of high-technology transfer and defence sales to India.[84] It could be argued that the USA always tried to serve its strategic interests before any sale or transfer of technology to countries like India.

The US concerns on nuclear and missile proliferation impeded the trade in high-technology items.[85] The process that had begun well during President Reagan's and PM Rajiv Gandhi's tenure started facing rough weather under the administrations of President Bush (Sr.) tenure and his successor President Clinton. The USA feared that India would be in possession of 'rocket capability powerful enough for an ICBM' that could threaten the continental USA. The USA, therefore, opposed

---

[80] https://www.nti.org/learn/traties-and-regimes/missiles-technology-control-regime-mtcr/

[81] Kumar, *Yearbook on India's Foreign Policy*, 72.

[82] Ibid.

[83] Ibid.

[84] Ibid.

[85] Government of India, Ministry of External Affairs, *Annual Report 1993–94*, 70.

India's acquisition of such capability.[86] However, it also realized that no government in India would ever give up its nuclear programme. Public opinion in India strongly supported the government decision on India's nuclear programme, and India's ability to stand up to US pressure in the matter was the ultimate test of independence and sovereignty of the country. As an Indian analyst put it, 'Pressure against India is thus going to be counterproductive'.[87] As a direct consequence of the MTCR, soon after the test of Agni, 'the US denied to India a $1.2 million Combined Acceleration Vibration Climatic Test Systems (CAVCTS)'.[88] These technologies were related to space, generation of nuclear energy, communications, informatics and so on. India, on its part, wanted to ensure the formulation and implementation of international rules and procedures in this regard in a fair and just manner.[89]

India continued to defend its right to differ with the USA on the question of the NPT. It believed *the NPT, 1968,* should emphasize the need for tangible progress towards disarmament, a CTBT, a complete freeze on the proliferation of nuclear weapons and the means of delivery and a substantial reduction in the existing stocks.[90] There was not much change in India's stand on the issue of the NPT, as it knew that any compromises on the NPT would force it to make bigger compromises in the proposed CTBT and proposed FMCT discussions inside the UNGA. It has been discussed in greater detail in Chapter 3 that no proposal on nuclear proliferation or arms control was acceptable to India if China was not a party to it. Initiatives like the 5-nation proposal or Pakistan proposed South Asian Nuclear Weapons Free Zone were rejected by India.

India decided to call off any further tests of Agni because of US pressure on the eve of PM P. V. Narasimha Rao's visit to the USA in May 1994. Members viewed that India was being denigrated in the worst manner in the world.[91] George Fernandes stated, 'I would like

[86] Harrison and Kemp, *India and America After the Cold War,* 34.

[87] Shrivastava, 'Indo-American Relations', 219.

[88] Chellney, 'Non-Proliferation', 446.

[89] Government of India, *Annual Report 1992–93,* 10.

[90] Vinod, 'Idealism and Self Interest in Conflict', 222–223.

[91] *Lok Sabha Debates,* Session 10, c. 429.

to urge upon the Prime Minister to postpone his visit to the USA and avoid denigration of the country. Sovereignty of the nation should not be allowed to be suppressed in this way'.[92] Jaswant Singh, another MP, stated, 'Members were not simply agitated because of capping of fissile material production only, rather, US wants India to cap missile programme also'.[93] Later, PM Rao assured members that 'this experiment will certainly be taken up in all its variations according to whatever stages they want or whatever phases they want'.[94] The USA's policy, on the other hand, continued to remain guided by its concerns on nuclear and missile technology proliferation.[95]

The CTBT, 1996,[96] is a comprehensive treaty that prohibits countries from carrying out any kind of nuclear test above ground, underground, under sea or even into space. India was one of the countries, along with the USA, to put forward this resolution inside the UNGA in 1993. In India's view, the USA wanted to close all options for carrying out any kind of nuclear test because it had attained the know-how for conducting sub-critical tests with computers' help inside a laboratory. The CTBT was to come into force in 1996, but because of provisions related to its entry-into-force clause, it is yet to come into force. Though India supported this resolution initially, it later boycotted it and did not sign the CTBT.

Technology Transfer: Case of India's Space Programme

India's space programme continued to remain a major target of USA-led controls. The Bush administration imposed 2-year sanctions against ISRO and the Russian space agency Glavkosmos on 11 May 1992, banning US trade with and technology transfers to them due to their refusal to comply with the USA's requests, and cancelled a deal involving the sale of Russian advanced cryogenic rocket motor technology to India on the ground that it conflicted with the objective of the

---

[92] Ibid., c. 430.

[93] Ibid., c. 433.

[94] *Rajya Sabha Debates*, c. 254.

[95] United States Information Service, *Official Text*.

[96] https://www.armscontrol.org/factsheets/test-ban-treaty-at-a-glance.

US policy of curbing dangerous proliferation of missile technology.[97] By attaining self-reliance in this area, India would have become an important country to compete with in the lucrative international space market. India in the past had remained heavily dependent on foreign launch services for launching its indigenous satellites. Since there was enough content in the INSAT-2 series, the completion of the third and fourth stages was delayed by the US embargo on cooperation between US firms and ISRO.[98]

No doubt, the US action of imposing sanctions was motivated by both commercial and strategic considerations. In the words of an expert,

> the American sanctions against ISRO and Glavkosmos was virtually a kind of war over technology. And it was a war for denial of technology. What Washington desires is non-availability of certain selected technologies to the Third World countries who have the potential to create security problems for the United States.[99]

India reacted strongly to US actions against ISRO. The most important point raised against the US action was that India was not even a member of the MTCR because GOI considered it as a discriminatory regime. The excessive US pressure made India's determination more-stronger for going ahead with its missile and space programme indigenously. The GOI Report[100] of 1995–1996 categorically stated that India's missile programmes would not be adversely affected by the MTCR. Restrictions had been anticipated at the time of sanction of the programme in 1983 itself, and steps were taken to offset the effects.

It is also important to note that the USA, on the one hand, decided to initiate actions against ISRO but, on the other hand, did not take any action when China supplied 30 launchers and over 60 2,700-km-range CSS-2 nuclear-capable missiles to Saudi Arabia.[101] The USA had imposed sanctions on China and Pakistan on 23 June 1991 under

[97] Mahapatra, 'Cryogenic Technology Deal', 312.

[98] Arnett, 'Military Technology', 357.

[99] Mahapatra, 'Cryogenic Technology Deal', 315.

[100] Government of India, DRDO Major Projects, paras. 4.9.

[101] Singh, 'Rocket Deal'.

the MTCR for a 2-year period. However, the sanctions against China were lifted in February 1992 and the sanctions against Pakistan were allowed to lapse at the end of the 2-year period in June 1993.[102] Since then, the USA has chosen to ignore such actions of China and granted it the most-favoured-nation (MFN) status every year to serve its economic interests at the cost of proliferation concerns.

Despite the ban on ISRO, India did test fire in August 1993 its first indigenously designed semi-cryogenic one-ton-thrust engine propelled by liquefied oxygen and gaseous hydrogen, instead of liquid hydrogen fuel as in a cryogenic engine.[103] Because of some snag in the model, it could not be successfully tested. On the whole, the issue of nuclear non-proliferation created a widening chasm between the USA and India under the Clinton administration. The cooperation in the area of high technology was clearly overshadowed by the differences over political and strategic considerations.

Technology Transfer: The Role of Other US-led International Regimes

The political and ideological issues in the post-World War II period, along with the security perceptions and latent economic interests, gave birth to several regimes that controlled the export of various technologies and products. In the nuclear field, examples of such regimes were the *Zangger Committee* and the *NSG*. In the field of 'dual-use' technology, the *Coordinating Committee on Multilateral Export Controls (COCOM), subsumed under the Wassenaar Arrangement*, and the *MTCR* were important regimes. All such groups aimed basically to deny nuclear and dual-use technologies to developing nations on the ostensible ground that they carried the risk of 'proliferation'. These export control regimes had the effect of severely curtailing the flow of technology at the cutting edge of civilian modernization, thereby making it difficult for any Third World country to emerge as a competitor to these regimes' member countries.

---

[102] Ibid.

[103] Goel, 'Propelling a "Cryo"'.

The NSG 1974: This body came into being in 1974, having membership of 45 countries, who saw that the NPT could not stop proliferation of technologies[104] as countries like India succeeded in carrying out its first nuclear explosion in May 1974. The very purpose of this body was to further limit the nuclear trade among the countries, especially the non-nuclear weapon nations. However, the controversial role of the NSG was reversed completely in the post-Indo-US Nuclear Agreement period, as India has been successful in obtaining necessary waivers from the NSG and other regimes having implications for India's nuclear, missile and space programmes. India has made a conventional promise expressing that it will not proliferate nuclear technology or material to other countries and will maintain its intentional ban on testing atomic weapons.

The Zangger Committee, 1971: This committee was established under guidelines for implementing the export control provisions of the NPT (Article III [2]). The committee is credited for drafting a list of items related to countries' nuclear programmes which could be misused by the nations for non-peaceful purposes.[105] Countries, like India in the past, suffered when they pursued programmes outside such bodies. It is pertinent to mention here that the Indo-US Nuclear Agreement of 2008, which is discussed in Chapters 3 and 4, has reduced the scope of all such controversial regimes placing any type of curbs on India's programmes in the 21st century.

COCOM is a mechanism that has controlled about 1,000,000 advanced technologies and industrial items. Besides the international industries' list, COCOM also controls military-relevant items in the IAEA list. It stands subsumed under the Wassenaar Arrangement, which is a 42-member body largely comprising Warsaw Pact countries. *The Wassenaar Arrangement, 1996,* is a body[106] whose main objective is to promote transparency, exchange of views and information, and greater responsibility in transfers of conventional arms and dual-use goods, and it has 42 member countries as on date. It promotes regional

---

[104] Ibid.

[105] Hibbs, *The Future of the Nuclear Suppliers Group*, 5.

[106] https://www.nti.org/learn/traties-and-regimes/wassennar-arrangement/e.

and international security by controlling the transfer of conventional arms and dual-use goods and technology. India's entry into this regime benefitted the country's image at the international level and improved its certifications in the field of non-proliferation without it being a signatory to the NPT.

Since 1995, the issue of security had assumed importance among policymakers, and India's stand on the CTBT in 1996 was a result of this new policy perspective and, later, was a result of the kind of debates that took place in the country over the issue of closure of its nuclear option after it carried out nuclear explosions in May 1998. The USA's ploy that the fear of US economic sanctions and isolation of India at global forums would deter the country from keeping its nuclear option open did not work. On the contrary, defying the CTBT regime, India went ahead and conducted five nuclear explosions in May 1998, leading to worldwide criticism and bringing to a complete halt all ongoing technology-cum-defence cooperation programmes. This action of India made the USA furious, which retaliated through imposing sanctions against more than 500 Indian PSUs. The suspicions of India and the USA about each other came to the fore and exposed severe limitations of Indo-US strategic cooperation.

TECHNOLOGY COOPERATION: THE 21st CENTURY

Technology Transfers: Post Indo-US Civil Nuclear Cooperation Agreement

As analysed earlier, Indo-US technology cooperation suffered a severe setback towards the end of the 20th century under President Clinton's administration because of the difference of opinions between the two countries over the functioning of nuclear and missile technology export control regimes. The USA argued that the diffusion of dual-use missile technologies to developing nations carried a proliferation risk. It was very clear that despite the end of the Cold War, the basic parameters remained largely unchanged. After the May 1998 Pokhran nuclear explosions, the USA realized that it must reconcile with India's views on regional as well as global issues. The change in US policy could be attributed once again to the wavering US global strategic interests, concerns and priorities as opposed to the regional security interests, priorities and concerns of India. The USA realized that even multilateral sanctions would not prevent both India and Pakistan from going nuclear.

It was only after the announcement of NSSP 2004 by President George W. Bush (Jr.) that things started changing on the Indo-US technological front. The signing of the Indo-US nuclear deal in July 2005 was a big occasion for the resumption of technology transfer to India through seeking waivers for allowing nuclear commerce and trade with India from the NSG, Zangger Committee, MTCR and Wassenaar Arrangement and bilateral agreements with countries having advanced technologies or material like uranium. Officials on both sides worked very hard over the next 3 years in removing all kinds of doubts regarding whether any strings were attached with signing the 'nuclear deal' of 2005, or later the 'Hyde Act', and the final signing of the 123 Nuclear Agreement in 2008 as far as transfer of technology was concerned. It was also ensured that no provision of the agreement would impinge on or compromise India's strategic autonomy in any manner. It would be sufficient for satisfying India's demand to have full access to Indian companies so far as transfer of technology on enrichment, processing and use of spent fuel was concerned. The importance of the nuclear deal of 2005 could be gauged from the sheer fact that it ended India's isolation for nuclear trade with rest of the world since the era of the NPT, CTBT, MTCR and NSG. It made it possible for India to conclude civilian nuclear agreements on the import of reactors involving technology transfers and uranium from countries like the USA, the UK, France, Russia, Mongolia, Kazakhstan, Namibia, Australia, Canada and South Korea, and India is about to finish an agreement with Japan.

As a result of the culmination of the 123 Agreement between India and the USA in 2008 and after availing necessary waivers from the IAEA and NSG, it became easier for India to import 12 1,000 MW LWRs from Russia, France and the USA. The transfer of technology by reactor suppliers was to help their Indian counterparts to build 12 indigenously designed 700 MW reactors. This would lead to the generation of about 25,000 MW of nuclear power by 2020 and enable India to take it up to 50,000 MW by 2030.[107] Though India's nuclear industry was well developed for HWRs, it was also being developed for FBRs. The nuclear deal with the USA in 2005 enabled the Indian nuclear industry to manufacture equipment for LWRs, and India was free to import equipment from Russia, France, the USA or elsewhere. With the change in domestic laws, the participation of the private sector was bound to rise and, a few years down the line, India was expected to be in a position to export an HWR power plant as a whole. It was to throw open big opportunities for Indian companies and Indian technical personnel to service a resurgent global nuclear industry. PM Manmohan Singh's 26–27 September 2013 visit to the USA[108] cleared hurdles in the setting up of six nuclear reactors in the Indian state of Gujarat by US companies like Westinghouse, GE Hitachi and Toshiba.

Apprehensions over the Nuclear Agreement with Full Sovereign EPR Rights to India

The nuclear agreement was going to throw open huge opportunities for US companies and help them become suppliers of technologies that were essential for giving a boost to India's civilian nuclear programme. In India, there was also an opinion among the strategic community that if the deal went through and if strategic military cooperation between the two states increased, then the prospects for major military sales to India would become a reality. It is pertinent to mention here that the agreement enabled India to receive defence equipment worth $18 billion between 2008 and 2018. Many of the deals done in this period involved technology transfer and joint development and production.

The nuclear deal received widespread support from the UPA-led Manmohan Singh government in India. However, the scientific community stood divided on the issue of the nuclear deal. Anil Kakodkar openly said that India's nuclear programme would be affected by the separation

---

[107] http://www.npcil.nic.in/main/AllProjectOperationDisplay.aspx.

[108] Transcript of the statement to the media by PM Manmohan Singh after meeting President Obama, available at https://mea.gov.in-focus-article.htm?22264/Transcript.

of civilian and military nuclear installations. He was joined by many other former scientists from government departments in urging GOI to renegotiate the deal considering its serious implications for India's nuclear programme.[109] In order to increase its nuclear power generation capacity, India started attracting investments from many international vendors subsequent to the culmination of the Indo-US Civil Nuclear Agreement 2008. For instance, Russia's Atomstroy agreed to build six more pressurized LWRs in Kudankulam by 2017 and four in Haripur after 2017. The French company Areva signed an MOU with NPCIL to build a total of six European Power Reactors (EPRs). GE Hitachi signed agreements with NPCIL and BHEL to build a multi-unit power plant using 1,350 MWe ABWRs. Many other companies, such as Atomic Energy of Canada Limited and Korea Electric Power Corporation, also signed similar agreements with India regarding servicing India's existing PHWRs.[110]

The debate over allowing India to enjoy complete waivers outside the nuclear regimes continued non-stop till the signing of the 123 Agreement by the USA with India. There was a bigger group of US protagonists of nuclear non-proliferation goals that wanted the USA to abandon the deal with India. Indian scientists had been fearful of US intrusions into the country's nuclear programme. On the other hand, the supporters of the deal, the strategic and scientific community, insisted that 'technology transfer' should be the touchstone of US-Indian relations, as the US records in the past had not been very good. On most occasions, denial of technology had dominated any negotiation between Indian and US officials. Some experts were of the view that the Indo-US nuclear deal would raise the financial and political costs of the Indian nuclear weapons programme, as there was no legal bar on the production of fissile material or the testing of nuclear explosive devices.[111] According to Cohen, a group in the USA believed that strategic autonomy would give India greater leverage over the USA than it had ever had and would, even more importantly, force Pakistan to bend and require China to deal with India as a strategic equal.[112]

---

[109] *Frontline*, 'Cover Story'.

[110] World Nuclear Association, *Nuclear Power in India*.

[111] Vardarajan, 'The Nuclear Deal and "Minimum Deterrence"'.

[112] Cohen, 'Deal Gone too Far'.

The Indo-US nuclear deal of 2005 demanded that India place all its nuclear installations under the supervision of the IAEA by accepting its safeguards and formalizing an India-Specific Safeguards Agreement with it. The IAEA's 35-member Board of Governors, of which India had been a member ever since the establishment of the agency, had to be persuaded to recognize India as 'a responsible state with advanced nuclear technology'.[113] Indian negotiators were expected to overcome another obstacle before their case for membership of the NSG could be approved. The 45 members of the NSG have the role of regulating nuclear trade among them and with countries who are signatories to the NPT.[114] Although India has availed a waiver from the NSG without being a signatory to the NPT, it has not been able to become a member of the NSG because of China's ambivalent stand on India's membership.

Many more issues were raised, like India voting against Iran on the nuclear proliferation issue, leading to the imposition of sanctions against it. There were critiques on both sides. It was because of these reasons that the deal signed in 2005 took another 3 years to become a final agreement in 2008. The developments showed how transfer of technologies has been used by the USA for serving its goals and interests. From the arguments, it is explicit that there seemed to be a major departure from the long-practised policy of the Clinton administration of putting pressure on India to 'cap, roll back, and eliminate' the Indian nuclear programme in the mid-1990s. It was the Bush (Jr.) administration in the aftermath of the 9/11 incident that seemed to accept a modest and stable Indian nuclear force and did not mind seeing India become a major force that would in some way balance out China's nuclear arsenal. The USA, under President Bush (Jr.), actually wanted to see a strong and vibrant India playing a role in the global balance of influence. In the present era, India and the USA have set up a DPG for expediting the process of technology transfer on a case-by-case basis.

Following the NSG's waiver to India in September 2008, the country's scope for availing both reactors and fuel from suppliers in other countries opened up. Civil nuclear cooperation agreements

---

[113] Mohan, 'N-Deal'.

[114] C.R.S. Report, *US Nuclear Cooperation with India*.

were signed by India with more than 10 countries, including the USA. The USA was hopeful that the facilitation of India's access to all international nuclear regimes would increase nuclear trade between India and US companies and result in the award of fresh contracts to them, providing them new economic sustainability. However, companies of US origin could not be awarded contracts in very big numbers because of their weak internal economic and financial positions. US companies like GE, Toshiba and Westinghouse were grappling with post-acquisition/merger effects and liquidation and bankruptcy problems that delayed their participation in the global tendering process undertaken by India. Russian company ROSATOM and Areva from France managed to win most of the contracts for the setting up of nuclear power plants and supply of nuclear reactors to the various proposed nuclear parks. It is noteworthy that India has used pragmatism in its diplomacy and tried to attain a balance between Russia and the USA for maintaining strategic cooperation with both. India has taken bold diplomatic steps in having a closer cooperation with Russia and the USA both, in the name of maintaining strategic autonomy in its foreign and security affairs. In order to allay fears of overdependence upon the USA, and in the light of its policy of maintaining strategic autonomy, India went ahead to give larger contracts to Russia's ROSATOM, allowing the company to make investments in India's proposed nuclear parks where US companies such as GE, Westinghouse and Toshiba could not make inroads.

Looking at places where US and French companies have won contacts for setting up nuclear power plants are as follows: Environmental approval has been procured for the first four; Jaitapur in Maharashtra: Work has started with six of Areva's EPR reactors in view, making 9600 MWe. Environmental approval has also been procured for these; Mithi Virdi (or Chayamithi Virdi) in Gujarat: to host US technology (Westinghouse AP1000); Kovvada in Andhra Pradesh: to host US technology (possibly GE Hitachi ESBWR). GE Hitachi confirmed that it had signed a contract in 2010 to supply six ESBWRs to NPCIL. The AEC also mentioned possible new nuclear power plants in Bihar and Jharkhand.[115]

---

[115] World Nuclear Association, *Nuclear Power in India*, 6–7.

India has stayed a significant market for the USA, particularly as of late. On the eve of Obama's first visit to India in 2010, the USA lifted export tariffs on high-technology gear exports. Ten years later, it has additionally facilitated export tariffs for cutting-edge-item deals with India. This was accomplished through designating India as a Strategic Trade Authorisation-1 (STA-1) nation—the main South Asian country to be on this rundown. The US vision of Asia has, to a great extent, been based on China; however, it is gradually evolving. India's ascent in Asia, combined with the delicacy in USA–China relations, may drive the USA to reconsider its Asia strategy.

The US private defence industry has been in contact with the Trump administration on the issue of technology transfer to India, and the US government has been extremely strong in coordinating efforts with India. Broad discussions have been held between the Indian and US governments on technology transfer. There has been a great deal of progression in US strategy. The Trump administration needs to continue organizing technology transfer to India. The US-India Business Council (USIBC) has bolstered the Modi government's arrangement to guarantee a level playing field for the defence PSUs (DPSUs) and India's private defence industry. This can be helped further through an understanding that permits both India and the USA to impart data to private sector industries.

CONCLUSION

On the whole, much water has flown as far as Indo-US technology transfer cooperation is concerned. The two countries are witnessing the best phase in their bilateral relationship of almost 75 years. The USA has turned out to be the largest exporter of defence equipment, including weapons systems involving technology transfer, to India. Both have established very effective mechanisms for ensuring that high-profile technology projects are cleared on a priority basis. The Indo-US relationship has grown so strong that small pins and pricks do not affect their ongoing technology cooperation at all. The leaders of both countries, in the past 20-plus years, have shown remarkable courage and imagination to make sure that they accommodate each other's aspirations on a long-term basis. The signing of the nuclear deal in 2005 and the nuclear agreement in 2008 has been the turning point defining their strategic relationship in the 21st century. The relationship spans the defence, nuclear, energy, climate change, industrial, space and communications sectors, counterterrorism, Indo-Pacific cooperation, Quad meetings, joint military exercises, the LEMOA, Communication and Information on Security Memorandum of Agreement (Communication and Information on Security Memorandum of Agreement) and PM Modi's dream projects, such as Digital India, Smart City, Make in India, Swachh Bharat Abhiyaan, Stand Up India, Skill India and Atmanirbhar Bharat. In every field, US companies are involved in different capacities. The Indo-US relationship in the 21st century has helped the leaders of the two countries realize the promises they had made to each other in the last 35 years or so.

Things stand completely changed now during President Trump's and PM Modi's tenures, because both India and the USA are very keen on the consolidation of their industrial and technological relations in the years to come. Once again, it is noteworthy that bilateral trade between India and the USA has crossed the mark of $145 billion. As on date, the USA has become the largest trading partner of India, and many of the Indo-US deals involve transfer of technology. Lastly, the US company Lockheed Martin recently entered into a deal with BEL of India worth $18 billion in February 2020 on the eve of President Trump's visit to India for the joint production of 114 F-21 fighter aircraft in India. There have been several cases whereby US companies like Boeing, Microsoft, Bombardier, General Dynamics, Westinghouse and GE have entered into collaborative arrangements for manufacturing their products in collaboration with Indian private companies such as Tata Group, Mahindra Group and Reliance Power, besides Indian PSUs, like NPCIL and National Thermal Power Corporation (NTPC) Limited, for nuclear power projects.

Indo-US Strategic Partnership

The Contemporary Era

This chapter analyses various aspects of the Indo-US strategic relations in the present decade (the 2010s), which has witnessed very important transformations in their bilateral defence–strategic cooperation. It deals with the developments that unfolded after the culmination of their nuclear deal in 2005 and agreement in 2008 and the various stages of the latter's implementation. It analyses the factors that have helped India and the USA get their relations onto a high trajectory. The turnarounds that facilitated them to establish a strategic partnership in the 21st century are examined in this chapter. The dynamics of their strategic relations in the Indo-Pacific region, where the China factor is common to both of them, have also been analysed. This chapter discusses emerging regional and international trends, relating in particular to strategic cooperation, in defence, security and cooperation in high-technology areas of their relationship. It examines the buoyancy in the trajectory of their strategic ties and its impact on US–China relations, which in turn have an impact on India–China security dynamics. The chapter concludes that notwithstanding the institutionalization of the strategic cooperation between India and the USA, Pakistan and China will continue to work together and the USA will continue to look towards these countries for the fulfilment of its own politico-strategic interests in the future too.

INTRODUCTION

A higher level of Indo-US defence and security cooperation, including key technology transfers, has become the centrepiece of their strategic partnership, which is being supported by the top leadership in both countries. For the USA, sooner or later, India will be the country working with whom it may expect a stable balance of power in the Asia-Pacific/ Indo-Pacific region. Despite certain difficulties, the USA has supported policies that have enabled India to emerge as a global power and key balancer in the region. However, for India, close strategic cooperation with the USA should not entail erosion in its policy of strategic autonomy in its foreign policymaking. Under PM Modi, India has tried to revive its relationship with all four powers—the USA, Japan, Russia and China— so as to succeed in its pursuit of maintaining strategic autonomy in its dealings with all of them without aligning with any of them. The USA and India could not sustain the momentum of the strategic partnership that had started building after PM Rajiv Gandhi's visit to the USA in May 1985. The historic 'Indo-US strategic dialogue' between Strobe Talbott and Jaswant Singh resulted in the visit of President Bill Clinton to India in March 2000, which restored this vital strategic partnership in the early 21st century. The changes in the global and regional strategic and security environments were sufficient for scholars to explore perspectives on Indo-US relations further. The factors responsible for changes in their 21st century strategic partnership post the NSSP in 2004 and the nuclear deal in 2005 are explored under the following heads: 'The Contextual Factors in the 21st Century'; 'Convergence of Strategic Interests in the Post-9/11 Era'; 'The NSSP, 2004, Leading to the Indo-US Nuclear Deal, 2005' and 'Strategic Partnership on a High Trajectory Under Prime Minister Modi (2014–2020)'.

THE CONTEXTUAL FACTORS IN THE 21st CENTURY

Looking into the history of India's strategic thinking, C. Raja Mohan[1] says that strategic perspectives are attributed to a country's 'civilizational memory', sense of geography, composite culture and geopolitical relations. At the end of the Cold War, India witnessed a fundamental reorientation in its approach to rediscover its traditional and historical linkages. In the present era, it has been very keen to play an important role not only in the South Asian region but also at the global level.

---

[1] For such views, see Raja Mohan, *The Shaping of India's New Foreign Policy*.

As discussed earlier, India's policy over the last two decades has been to emerge as an important player at the global level, and its defence and foreign policy is to deter aggression, ensuring stability and peace in its neighbourhood, and develop friendly and mutually beneficial ties with countries in and around the region. It has established strategic partnerships with all major powers, such as the USA, EU, Russia, China and Japan. The USA, as the largest economy and military power in the world, could not have ignored the importance of forming strong ties with India, which is one of the fastest growing economies and an emerging global power of the world.

For the USA, three factors were important for the change in its policy towards India in the 21st century. First, India was a big market, with half a billion middle-class buyers for US products. The USA saw that India was a leading power in South Asia. Second, India's interest in maintaining peace and its rising concerns about security issues in Asia coincided with those of the USA, and forming complementarities with India for ensuring peace and stability in Asia was a possibility. The third factor was the emergence of India in the Information and Communication Technology (ITC) and frontier technologies sector, which increased US interests further. Their strategic cooperation had come to a complete halt after India's nuclear tests in May 1998. However, the USA, in 2000, once again decided to continue its strategic partnership with India in areas such as climate change, energy, space, satellite communication and missile defence. For India, it had become imperative to end its isolation at the international level after its 1998 nuclear explosions. India managed to convince the USA about the circumstances that had forced it to go for nuclearization, which helped the country in breaking the stalemate with the USA. India, through a series of nuclear and missile tests, had made its intention clear that it would not succumb to any kind of US or any other international regime's pressure. Its nuclear doctrine emphasized building a minimum credible nuclear deterrence. India and the USA had only two options regarding their relationship: either to make it or to break it. The changed international environment made it imperative on the part of both to pursue the policy of accommodation. The USA was getting used to India's new-found determination to make no compromises on its strategic autonomy. The Kargil crisis of 1999 established the fact that India was on the path to becoming a great power, and the USA took cognizance of India's new capability attained after May 1998. India was ready for assuming larger security responsibilities at the international level, and the USA realized that India could fit into its strategic design better in the 21st century world order. India, in the recent past, on a number of occasions had showed its ability and determination to handle crises to its advantage, such as the crisis with Pakistan in 2001–2002 after the attack on the Indian Parliament and during tsunami relief operations in Southeast Asian countries. As discussed in Chapter 4, the Talbott–Singh dialogue led to President Clinton's visit to India in March 2000 and PM Vajpayee's return visit to the USA in October 2000, where PM Vajpayee declared that the two were 'natural allies'. The USA realized that India could play a vital role in helping secure a stable, peaceful and prosperous Asia.[2] Moreover, the 9/11 attack on the USA in 2001 changed things permanently.

Through the efforts of the Bush (Jr.) administration in the aftermath of the 9/11 attack, Indo-US relations started improving, quelling doubts that had been cast over whether the change in the US presidency would affect the warming of the bilateral relations. The US Congress, through a series of legislative measures, lifted restrictions that had been imposed against India for its carrying out of nuclear explosions, and finally, the Bush administration waived all the remaining sanctions on 28 September 2001.[3] It was an indication of the strengthening of their strategic relations that India, under PM Vajpayee, gave its assurance to President Bush's missile defence proposals (TMD) on 28 September 2001. Another landmark event in their relations happened when sanctions imposed against India after its nuclear tests in 1998 were removed through a series of legislative measures in the US Congress.[4] India's assurance to the USA regarding the latter's proposals for a missile defence programme gave the indications of the rebuilding of their strategic ties. For carrying forward

[2] Talbott, *Engaging India*.

[3] Kronstadt., 'India–US Relations'.

[4] Singh, *A Call to Honour*, 322.

this discussion, US Deputy Secretary of State Richard Armitage visited India in May 2007.[5] India's National Security Advisor Brajesh Mishra paid a return visit to the USA the same year; besides, a number of other high-level visits took place for the discussion of contentious issues like nuclear non-proliferation and the CTBT.[6]

During President Bush's administration, the strategic cooperation comprised handling terrorism and making plans for combatting this danger. In addition, three core areas emerged in view of the security of both countries in the future: a new strategic framework based on the fresh role of nuclear weapons; energy security and joint operations to protect the sea lanes of communication (SLOC) in the Indian Ocean; and the challenges of maintaining strategic stability in the Asia-Pacific (now Indo-Pacific) region over the long term.[7] It is noteworthy that the largest aspect of their strategic cooperation in the present era is ensuring security and stability in the Indo-Pacific region.

India, regarding its defence and security cooperation with the USA, made significant progress after the announcement of the NSSP in 2004. The GOI report of 2006–2007[8] stated that the growth in their relations had been largely incremental, as reflected in the sophistica-tion of exercises and intensity of military-to-military cooperation, and the conclusion of the new framework for their defence relationship on 28 June 2005 resulted in their military cooperation getting insti-tutionalized. The outcomes of the same are discussed in Chapter 4.

THE CONVERGENCE OF STRATEGIC INTERESTS IN THE POST-9/11 ERA

With India charting a new relationship with the USA, strategists and leaders in both countries could foresee the need for a 'natural alliance' between the two. They shared a common view on global matters, such as peace and stability in the Gulf, Indian Ocean, and Southeast

[5] Krishnaswamy, 'Armitage's Visit Reflect Warm Ties'.

[6] Singh, *A Call to Honour*, 327.

[7] US Embassy, *Official Text*, 7.

[8] Government of India, Ministry of External Affairs, *Annual Report 2006–07*, 2–9.

Asian and Pacific regions and China, as a global power, posing challenges to India, the USA and its Asia-Pacific neighbours in the future. Since the late 1980s and early 1990s, the USA had been looking for regional managers in the Gulf and Asia-Pacific regions. It developed a view that India, having demonstrated its military capabilities in the past, could prove to be a useful partner in enhancing and protecting its own interests as part of US global interests. The USA could help India become powerful by transferring more technologies to it and contributing to the modernization of its defence forces for taking care of its security in a better manner that would also be compatible with the USA's overall global concerns. This line of thinking became the basis for all the US presidents in the post-9/11 period deciding on any policy towards India.

Against the backdrop of the developments in South Asia since September 2001, and despite the concurrent US rapprochement with Pakistan, USA–India security cooperation continued to flourish. Many experts and US diplomats rated military cooperation as the most important aspect of the transformed Indo-US bilateral relations. Despite the USA's preoccupation with its wars in Afghanistan, Iraq, Syria, Egypt, Yemen and Ukraine and the host of problems with China, military-to-military ties between India and the USA have been continuing, and today, they form the core of their strategic cooperation.

The Next Steps in Strategic Partnership, 2004

The Indo-US DPG, which had been dormant since India's 1998 nuclear tests and the ensuing US sanctions, was revived in late 2001, and it has been meeting regularly since 2001. The NSPP framework led to the signing of a 10-year defence pact in June 2005, highlighting multifarious joint operations, expanded two-way defence trade involving more technology transfers and co-production, expanded collaboration related to missile defence and the establishment of a bilateral defence procurement and production group. Details on the NSSP are provided in Chapter 4. In April 2007, Tim Keating told a US Senate panel that the Pentagon intended to 'aggressively' pursue expanding military-to-military relations with India in the context of 'Common principles and shared national interest', such as fighting terrorism, preventing weapons proliferation and maintaining regional stability.[9]

The Next Steps in Strategic Partnership, 2004: An Upswing in Indo-US Annual Military Exercises

Since 2002, all three organs of the Indian and US armed forces have been holding series of joint military exercises, the most prominent among them being the annual Malabar joint naval exercise off the Indian coast since 2003[10] onwards, though it had been started in 1992 and suspended during 1998–2002. The format of the 'Malabar' joint naval exercise has changed, and Japan has joined India and the USA in it since 2015, thus making it a trilateral naval exercise. The 22nd edition of the Malabar naval exercise was held in June 2019.[11] The trilateral naval exercise is expected to include Australia as the fourth partner in light of ongoing cooperation under the Quad. The annual joint US-Indian military exercises, US arms sales to India and the nuclear deal signing in 2005 had caused anxiousness in both Pakistan and China. Earlier, China had pretended that India did not pose any challenge to it, but the developments over the last few years between India and China along their border do point out that the anxiety of China's President Xi Jinping has increased a lot because of the close Indo-US strategic partnership. Both Pakistan and China are concerned that the induction of advanced weapons systems into the region could disrupt the 'strategic balance'. The sale of US defence equipment and weapons systems worth US$18 billion to India during 2008–2020 has compelled both China and Pakistan to re-strategize their policies under the changed circumstances. China's Belt and Road Initiative (BRI) and China–Pakistan Economic Corridor (CPEC) are the outcomes of their re-strategizing with respect to India.

The NSSP, since its inception, has led to the consolidation of ties between the US and Indian militaries, as high-level visits of Indian and

---

[9] Available at http://www.state.gov/r/[a/prs/rs/2007 (accessed on 5 October 2020).

[10] Government of India, Ministry of Defence, *Annual Report 2005–06*, 3–12.

[11] *The Economic Times*, 8 June 2018.

US flag officers to each other's country has become a regular feature. Participation of officials under the IMET programme has been continuing regularly. The post-NSSP period also prepared the grounds for the beginning of sale of US defence equipment and weapons systems to India. There has been a significant increase in their military-to-military ties, and US arms sales to India has taken a higher profile. The first major US arms sale to India came in 2002, when the USA sold 12 AN-TPQ-37 Firefinder counterbattery radars worth US$190 million to the Indian army. Important beginnings were made in the direction of enhancing civilian nuclear technology cooperation. Besides military officials' visits and regular military exercises, grounds were prepared for enhancing civil nuclear cooperation for meeting India's energy security goals through the enactment of legislative frameworks. The US NRC Chairman Richard Meserve's visit to India in 2003 prepared the ground for the signing of the nuclear cooperation deal in 2005. The US Congress in 2002 itself was notified of another sale to India involving up to US$40 million's worth of aircraft and self-protecting systems to be mounted on Boeing 737s that carry the head of the Indian state.[12] The success of their strategic partnership led to US companies like Boeing International and Lockheed Martin Corporation winning contracts for the sale of fighter aircraft to India along with Russian, British and French companies. These companies have been participating in the annual air shows being held in Bangalore, India, regularly, and their presence has attracted much media attention about their superiority. Their interests in the mid-2000s helped Lockheed Martin recently enter into an agreement with BEL, India, in February 2020, for the supply and manufacture of F-21 multi-role fighter aircraft for the IAF. India has become the first country outside the NATO to receive such modern fighter aircraft from the USA.

Defence Ties under the Agreed Minutes on Defence Cooperation, 1995, 2005 and 2015

Another hallmark of the NSSP 2004 was the signing of the 'Agreed Minutes on Defence Cooperation' for 10 years during US Defense Secretary William J. Perry's visit to India on 12 January 1995. Perry's

---

[12] Kumar, *Indo-US Politico Strategic Relations*, 190–195.

visit was hailed as a 'milestone' and the 'beginning of a new era' in Indo-US bilateral relations. All earlier agreements, such as the 1985 MOU and General Kicklighter's proposal, were subsumed under the new agreement of 1995. Under the agreed minutes, cooperation expanded between the following: India's Ministry of Defence and its US counterpart; the Indian and US militaries; and the DRDO and the US defence, R&D and production sectors. Perry's initiative was successful primarily because it satisfied the concerns of both the civilian and military constituents of the two countries' defence establishments.[13] It laid important groundwork for further transfer of technology meant for defence projects. The most important feature of the 1995 agreement was the proposed periodic consultations between civilian officials of India and that of the USA and military officials from the two nations' respective defence ministries.[14]

Indo-US defence ties have expanded manifold as on date, with increased frequencies of bilateral exercises and the establishment of dialogue mechanisms like the DPG, Defence Joint Working Group (DJWG), Defence Procurement and Production Group (DPPG), Senior Technology Security Group (STSG), JTG, Military Cooperation Group (MCG) and service-to-service ESGs.[15] Their cooperation under the trilateral Malabar naval exercises has helped both immensely in improving coordination and interoperability in the Indo-Pacific region under the LEMOA and COMCASA agreements signed in 2016. The details are analysed in the subsequent sections.

US–Indian Counterterrorism Cooperation

Tackling of global terrorism has been a very important area in the Indo-US strategic partnership since November 2001, and leaders of both countries agreed that 'terrorism threatens not only the security of the United States and India, but also their efforts to build freedom, democracy and international security and stability around the

---

[13] Sidhu, *Enhancing Indo-US Strategic Cooperation*, 57.

[14] For details on the text of the Agreed Minutes of Defence Cooperation, see *USIS Press Release*, 12 January 1995.

[15] Government of India, *Brief on India–US Relations*.

world'.[16] In 2002, they launched the India-US Cyber Security Forum to safeguard critical infrastructure from cyberattacks. Later, the July 2005 'New Framework for the US-India Defence Relationship' listed 'defeating terrorism and violent religious extremism' as one of four key shared security interests, and it called for the bolstering of mutual defence capabilities required for such a goal.[17] Officials of both countries have been cooperating with each other on a regular basis for combatting terrorism. India has received significant US help whenever it has come under a terrorist attack, such as the July 2006 Bombay train bombings, 26 November 2008 Bombay terrorist attack and the Uri and Pathankot attacks in 2016. Both countries have also been working together on the implementation of UNSC Resolution 2396 for the naming and shaming of countries supporting terrorism on a worldwide basis.

Indo-US cooperation in counterterrorism stood institutionalized after the signing of the 'India-U.S. Counter-Terrorism Cooperation Initiative' in 2010, which comprises sharing, information exchange, operational cooperation, counterterrorism technology and equipment and capacity building. A Homeland Security Dialogue was established in November 2010[18] to further deepen operational cooperation, counterterrorism technology transfers and capacity building. The 16th meeting of the India-US JWG on Counter Terrorism was held in Washington D.C. on 29 March 2019.[19] Both countries have committed to maintain pressure on Pakistan to take appropriate actions against terrorist organizations operating from its soil.

THE NEXT STEPS IN STRATEGIC PARTNERSHIP, 2004, LEADING TO THE INDO-US NUCLEAR DEAL, 2005

The NSSP signed in September 2004 was also to facilitate the easing of export restrictions on India on dual-use technology goods and an

---

[16] Joint Statement of US–India on Terrorism, Bilateral Ties, US Department of State, *Washington File* (9 November 2001).

[17] Available at http://www.indianembassy.org/press-release/2005/June/31htm (accessed on 5 October 2020).

[18] Government of India, *Brief on India–US Relations*.

[19] *The Economic Times*, 30 March 2019.

increase in civilian nuclear and civilian space cooperation and missile defence. The ground prepared under the NSSP 2004 led to the signing of the historic nuclear deal, a strategic agreement having far-reaching consequences for India's energy security, during PM Manmohan Singh's summit-level meeting with President George W. Bush on 18 July 2005. The nuclear deal has been a major milestone in their relationship of almost 75 years. It ended the ban on India's nuclear trade with the rest of the world that had badly impinged on its civil and military nuclear programmes. It ensured the resumption of sale of nuclear reactors and EPR technologies, besides the sale of uranium, to India in the following years.

The Indo-US joint statement of 18 July 2005 provided the framework for cooperation in the field of civilian nuclear power, as the Bush administration promised to persuade the US Congress to make changes in its domestic legislation and to persuade the NSG to make suitable adjustments in its regulations, with matching actions by India in return. The deal recognized India as a 'responsible state with advanced nuclear technology' and resulted in a tacit US recognition of India's status as a de facto nuclear weapon state outside the NPT. It ensured US cooperation with India on civil nuclear energy issues on a long-term basis. Later, the Hyde Act, 2006 and the '123 Agreement' of August 2007 led to the modification of US laws, which enabled the resumption of nuclear cooperation between the two nations. The Hyde Act further facilitated the signing of the '123 Agreement' between them in 2008, named thus since it is section 123 of the US Atomic Energy Act, 1954 which allows for nuclear cooperation between the USA and any other nation. The '123 Agreement' laid out the main nature and structure of nuclear cooperation between the USA and India.[20] For understanding the nuances of the different stages of the nuclear agreement and their implications for India, one needs to revisit Chapter 3. This deal had significant implications for guaranteeing India's energy security as well as military security. Besides the detailed analysis in Chapters 3 and 4, a brief reference of the nuclear agreement is made here, as it was a major step in the direction of overall Indo-US strategic cooperation. The resumption of sale of uranium for India's

[20] The author acknowledges late Prof. Gurnam Singh's help, with whom he co-authored the article 'Dynamics of Indo-US Nuclear Deal and Its Strategic Implications', 43–70.

civil nuclear reactors would help India in saving its existing uranium stock for its military nuclear programme under a separation plan. The Indo-US nuclear agreement was meant to enable the transfer of EPR technologies through the seeking of waivers from all nuclear and missiles regimes so as not to jeopardize India's reprocessing rights of spent nuclear fuel for further extraction of plutonium from it. It was also meant to give a boost to India's three-stage nuclear programme, at the third stage of which thorium-based nuclear reactors were to be developed, which would help India in reducing its dependence on imported uranium and manufacturing reactors using thorium as the basic fuel.

Indo-US Civil Nuclear Agreement, 2008: Political Limitations

The nuclear deal of 2005, paving the way for the signing of the final nuclear agreement in 2008, led to the eruption of a political crisis in India in July 2008. The period of 2005–2008 had seen fears in India that the nuclear deal with the USA would not be favourable to India, likely affecting its sovereignty, and would lead to the Indian foreign policy being tied to that of the USA. Political parties in India raised a lot of hue and cry that the deal was going to affect India's strategic autonomy, as the USA was roping India into non-proliferation regimes in a covert manner and seeking the separation of the civil and military nuclear plants of India. The UPA-I government under PM Manmohan Singh denied all such charges vehemently on the floor of the Indian Parliament. The matter had become so political that it led to the withdrawal of support of Left parties from the UPA-I coalition government of PM Manmohan Singh in July 2008. The UPA-I government survived in office as another regional party, Samajwadi Party, decided to support the government on the nuclear agreement with the USA. The deal of 2005 would not have been formalized into the agreement of 2008 had PM Manmohan Singh not succeeded in pushing it through the Indian Parliament. The same was true on part of President Bush, who had to make a lot of effort in getting all the necessary legislations amended and compatible with meeting India's requirement of waivers from the IAEA, NSG, MTCR, Zangger Committee and Wassenaar

Arrangement for the resumption of nuclear trade as a non-signatory to the NPT and CTBT.

From the above, it is evident that at times, political parties in India may go to any extent and start fighting the government tooth and nail. This was manifested not only by the Left parties just before the final agreement signing in July 2008, but also when another opposition party, the BJP, forced PM Manmohan Singh's government in 2010 to enact the 'Civil Liability for Nuclear Damage Act 2010'. The BJP thus became responsible for the non-operationalization of the nuclear agreement over the next several years, as no sale of nuclear reactors by US companies could take place because of the penal provision of ₹5 billion on any operator in case of any nuclear accident, a sum that was too much for Indian private companies to bear. Their stand on the nuclear issue was influenced by pure politics. The Left parties in India were perturbed because they were faced with ideological constraints and would not have liked India to join the USA as its junior partner, especially against a country like China, through formalizing its strategic cooperation with the USA. According to them, India had to support China, along with other non-aligned nations, against the USA for a multipolar world. It can rightly be said that prospects of India's closer defence cooperation with the USA in the past or present have suffered because of the political matrix in the country. It is worth mentioning here that in the past, opposition parties in Parliament had not allowed PM Chandra Shekhar's government to allow the refuelling of US fighter aircraft, which were to accomplish their missions in Iraq during the Gulf crisis in 1991, on Indian soil.[21]

Because of these reasons, the UPA-I and UPA-II governments led by Manmohan Singh (2004–2014), never succeeded in having a very close defence cooperation with the USA and faced much difficulties over the finalization and signing of the LEMOA with the USA after the Indo-US nuclear agreement.

It was being apprehended that India would be becoming a second-grade partner of the USA. The people and media in India turned critical

---

[21] Kumar, *Indo-US Politico Strategic Relations*, 190–195.

when India voted against Iran in a USA-supported IAEA resolution on 27 November 2009, later leading to the imposition of sanctions against Iran. Besides the media, opposition groups accused GOI that it was under US pressure that India had delayed the finalization of the Iran–Pakistan–India pipeline, which was later abandoned. They also alleged that India would become a host to the US navy in the latter's military misadventures in West Asia and elsewhere. They concluded that a deeper engagement with the USA would lead to India buying US arms, particularly expensive aircraft and missiles, draining its foreign reserves. It showed that any Indo-US strategic cooperation remained vulnerable to politics of the country too. Despite all political oppositions, their strategic cooperation has reached its peak after the arrival of PM Narendra Modi's government in May 2014, which is a single-party majority government, unlike the coalition government of PM Manmohan Singh. The Modi government has taken many hard decisions in the country's interests, especially in building stronger ties with the USA.

The China Factor in Indo-US Strategic Cooperation in the 21st Century

Issues such as nuclear order, energy security, peace and stability in the Indo-Pacific region and global balance of power are supposed to shape the dynamics of the India–USA–China triangular relationship. According to an expert, 'strained US-China relations were to make India the pivotal power in the US-China-India triangle but tense India-China relations were to put the US in a pivotal position', thereby underlining the crucial roles of the USA, China and India in the emerging configuration of the balance of power in the 21st century.[22] India's relationship with China has seen significant improvement in recent years, despite the emergence of frequent tensions along their border. India is also continuing its strategic cooperation with China. It was because of the continuous improvement in India's relations with China that China remained India's largest trading partner until 2017, when the USA replaced it.

---

[22] Pant, ed., *Indian Foreign Policy in a Unipolar World*, 15.

A narrative has been developed that China's rise in the South Asian region has prompted the USA to seek a strategic relationship with India. 'The United States is trying to cement its relationship with the world's largest democracy, in order to counterbalance China', Ferguson stated. The Bush (Jr.) administration was 'hoping that latching onto India as the rising star of Asia could help them handle China', Sokolski opined. Despite the ongoing narrative, it can authoritatively be said that over a period of time, China has consistently proved to be an important actor of the South Asian security architecture. Of late, many official reports in India have suggested the rising threat from China to India's security. India prevailed over the USA in telling the latter that one of the reasons that compelled it to acquire nuclear weapons in the late 1990s was the China factor.[23] In recent years, Indian policymakers have unleashed a series of initiatives, with the China factor figuring in their annual defence budgets, to acquire military capacity to engage simultaneously with Pakistan and China in a two-front war. Many believe that India should 'create precisely the kind of dilemmas for China that Beijing has created for it'.[24]

A lot has been written analysing the China factor as central to future Indo-US strategic understanding. It is apprehended in India that China, under President Xi Jinping, has been making extra efforts in improving its relations with Pakistan, Myanmar, Bangladesh, Nepal, Sri Lanka and the Maldives, along with growing its military and economic presence in the Indo-Pacific region in the 21st-century world order. Therefore, the USA would want India[25] to play the role of a counterweight in the coming years, keeping the strategic compulsions of India in mind. This positions the USA–India and China–India relationships in the centre of a serious debate. Malik adds that the traditional Sino-Indian geopolitical rivalry has acquired a maritime dimension. Since 2011–2012, the USA, along with Australia and Japan, in view of the expanding threats of China in the Asia-Pacific and Indian Ocean regions, has started using the term 'Indo-Pacific',

---

[23] Muhammad, *Indo-US Civilian Nuclear Cooperation Agreement*.

[24] Ibid.

[25] Malik, 'India and China', 163–192.

denoting the two ocean geographies and the adjoining maritime areas. It is in this context that Indo-US cooperation in terms of 'Indo-Pacific' strategy has become all-important.

China's pursuance of an assertive and aggressive policy towards its neighbours proves that Beijing is laying the groundwork for its naval presence along maritime choke points in the South China Sea (SCS), the Straits of Malacca, the Indian Ocean and the Straits of Hormuz in the Persian Gulf through the acquisition of or access to the naval bases of countries situated in the Indian Ocean and Pacific regions for protecting its long-term economic and security interests. China's BRI is also aimed at serving such goals and objectives. For its part, India has countered the Chinese efforts by promoting defence and maritime cooperation with several countries in the Indian Ocean region and ASEAN countries, besides the USA, Japan, Australia, Iran, Oman and Israel. The Indo-US strategic cooperation in the Malabar series of joint naval exercises and under Quad are new forms of 'Indo-Pacific' cooperation.

As part of its 'Look East'/'Act East' strategy, India has concluded over a dozen defence cooperation agreements over the last decade, and the Indian Navy has been holding joint naval exercises with East and Southeast Asian countries to signal to the Chinese navy that its future presence will not go unchallenged.[26] A US expert has been categorical in saying that exploitation of the Chinese military threat helps India to create an illusion in the West, especially in the USA, that if helped in its pursuit of becoming a great regional/global power, India could in fact become a counterweight to China.[27] One may disagree with such a straightjacket formulation, as the USA also has its own obligations to defend the interests of its allies such as Taiwan, South Korea, Japan and ASEAN countries. It is the convergence of Indian and US strategic interests arising out of the deteriorating security situation, on account of China's behaviour, in the Indo-Pacific region that has formed the basis for closer cooperation between the two countries. India has consistently tried to allay apprehensions that it might become a willing

---

[26] Ibid., 181.

[27] Tellis, *US–India Atomic Energy Cooperation*, 7.

partner to the US policy of containment of China under the pretext that it is bound by the policy of maintaining 'strategic autonomy' in its foreign and security policies. Notwithstanding the 'strategic autonomy' position of India, the Quad—USA, Japan, Australia and India—has become a reality in 2020. It has become one of the most important bases for the ongoing Indo-Pacific cooperation in light of the emerging China threat on account of China's ventures in the Indian Ocean region and the BRI-led initiative CPEC getting operationalized throughout South Asia.

India has been making it very clear right from the beginning that the Quad is not directed towards any third country. Both India and China have made serious efforts to mend their relationship in recent years, and there has been a remarkable improvement in the Sino-Indian relationship. Their bilateral trade touched the mark of US$40 billion in the year 2006–2007, and it reached up to US$76 billion in 2017 and US$109 billion in 2020. China remained the top trading partner of India between 2014 and 2017. It was only in 2018–2019 that the USA[28] replaced China as the top trading partner of India. Even as on date in 2020, China is the second largest trading partner of India, following the USA. India's PM has been holding a summit-level meeting with China every year. The two have been cooperating under several multilateral bodies, such as BRICS, BASIC and SCO, since 2017. The limited cooperation of China was important in the mobilization of a waiver for India on the part of the 45 NSG members, as a requirement under the Indo-US nuclear agreement of 2008, and the making of necessary changes in the NSG guidelines. It is noteworthy that the same China has been opposing India's membership of the NSG for the past several years. At times, it also appears that the growing economic relationship between China and India is so critical that India's interests in China cannot be threatened or replaced by any agreement with the USA. Over the last decade,[29] the emergence of a close politico-strategic cooperation between India and the USA has made China pursue its policies in the South Asian region aggressively.

---

[28] *The Economic Times*, 23 February 2020.

[29] Kumar, 'Emerging Indo-US Strategic Partnership and the China Factor'.

Cooperation and competition continue among the three key players, India, China and the USA.

Spurt in Indo-US Defence Deals (2010–2020)

India has acquired P8I Submarine Hunter aircraft worth US$2.1 billion and C-17 Globemaster III aircraft worth US$5.8 billion from the USA.[30] It recently flew a C-17 Globemaster sold to it by the USA to the Leh–Ladakh region, very close to the LAC, which was described as a game changer by the IAF chief in the backdrop of the People's Liberation Army's (PLA) incursions near the LAC in April–May 2013.[31] India signed nuclear agreements with Russia, France, Canada, South Korea and Japan, besides the USA, laying emphasis on maintaining its policy of 'strategic autonomy' in its foreign and security affairs. India, in the last few years, has also imported weapons and aircraft from Russia, France, Sweden and Israel as well. It has become one of the largest importers of arms[32] in the world in recent years. Its missile development and space programmes are moving ahead satisfactorily. India also has aircraft carriers, and a few more are being developed indigenously.

In recent years, Indo-US relations have expanded and developed into what is now a strategic partnership in the contemporary era. A significant facet of this relationship is evident in their close bilateral defence ties that have made all US governments agree to sell sophisticated arms and military equipment to the Indian armed forces. The closer defence cooperation involving the sale of hi-tech arms and equipment to India also suits US companies in capturing India's defence market and replacing Russia as the largest supplier of military hardware to India. Things are likely to turn around for US companies if they take advantage of the Indian government's decision to raise the limit of FDI in the defence sector to 49 per cent. A large number of US companies can now play a very vital role in the modernization

[30] Singh, 'India and the Market of War'.

[31] *The Hindustan Times*, 23 September 2013, 11.

[32] SIPRI Yearbook 2011.

of India's defence sector, which has been occurring at a very slow pace. If these projections turn into reality at the ground level, the USA might take the position of the former USSR in building India's defence capabilities, thereby taking the Indo-US strategic partnership to a newer height.

US defence companies such as Lockheed Martin, Boeing, Raytheon and Sikorsky have emerged as the largest US companies to sell aircraft, including the C-17 and C-130J transport aircraft and Apache and Chinook helicopters, to India. The defence trade between the USA and India during 2010–2020 has reached up to US$18 billion. As India stands designated as the major defence partner of the USA, it is likely to receive US technologies pertaining to intelligence, surveillance and reconnaissance, fifth-generation fighter aircraft's co-development and joint production, the Future Vertical Lift plan and advanced-technology GCVs. On a number of occasions, top officials of the USA have expressed the sentiment of their government to help India in overcoming its defence and security concerns by enabling it to produce things jointly with the USA. India received four out of 11 CH-47F (I) Chinook and eight out of 22 Apache military helicopters from the US company Boeing in 2019. This deal of military helicopters was worth US$3 billion and signed on 28 September 2015. It is pertinent to mention here that given the superiority of the Chinook and Apache helicopters, India made use of both military helicopters in lifting heavy material and men near the LAC in Ladakh, where Indian forces were involved with the Chinese PLA in skirmishes, in March–April 2020.

Signing of the COMCASA and LEMOA and the Commencement of the '2+2 Dialogue'

In the 21st century world order, India's relationship with the USA on defence and strategic issues has been reinforced. This is reflected in the defence relationship between the USA and India, which has reached a new height with the signing of the '2+2 dialogue'. The expanded nature of the defence relationship has resulted in a new format, since 2018, for cooperation between the foreign and defence ministers/secretaries of the two countries—the '2+2 dialogue'—where intense discussions are held and decisions are expedited on a priority basis. These discussions involve areas like water resource management, peacekeeping in the Indo-Pacific region, launch of the Coalition for Disaster Resilient Infrastructure (CDRI), Space Situational Awareness (SSA) and a host of other issues. The first '2+2 dialogue' in New Delhi in 2018 resulted in India and the USA signing a third foundational agreement—the COMCASA—for enabling very close cooperation between their defence forces. The COMCASA enables the two nations' air forces to exchange information and have greater access to each other's facilities and advanced defence systems. It allows Indian forces to make use of US-origin platforms. This agreement followed other important agreements that the two countries had signed—the LEMOA in 2016 and the General Security of Military Information Agreement (GSOMIA) in 2002—as part of the operationalization of defence agreements reached under NSSP 2004 and the minutes agreement in 2005 and 2015, respectively. Both these agreements allow the two counties' armed forces to make use of each other's facilities under interoperability norms and gain access to advanced communication, reconnaissance and refuelling infrastructure at greater ease. These are the agreements that will facilitate closer cooperation on the part of the two counties' armed forces, including all three organs, whenever they are to conduct joint operations or hold joint exercises in any part of the world. They expose the members to each other's war doctrines and technologies. Another benefit of the agreements is that India stands designated as a Major Defence Partner of the USA since 2016. It is noteworthy that the credit for the Indo-US defence and strategic cooperation is given to PM Modi, as it was his government that opened the final doors for the signing of such agreements as the COMCASA and LEMOA. As discussed earlier, the governments of the past had been reluctant to have the COMCASA and LEMOA agreements finalized with the USA. This issue had been hanging between the USA and India for more than a decade and a half. To remind the reader, India's government was compelled to stop the refuelling of US aircraft at the Bombay airport in 1991 because of the stiff political opposition to closer defence cooperation with the USA. Given the 1991 episode, the signing of all the interoperability agreements prove that the two countries have moved far ahead, to a point where no reversal can be visualized anymore.

STRATEGIC PARTNERSHIP ON A HIGH TRAJECTORY UNDER PRIME MINISTER MODI (2014–2020)

PM Modi's visit to the USA in 2014 led India and the USA to declare themselves as the 'closest partners' and renewed for 10 more years the 2005 New Framework for the US-India Defense Relationship. As on date, the two are under obligation to continue privileged military-to-military cooperation with each other. India also expects from the USA that their cooperation will lead to India gaining membership in the UNSC. The USA will continue to work with other countries for admitting India into the NSG. On the USA's initiative, India is now a member of the MTCR, the Wassenaar Arrangement and the Australia Group. PM Modi's first visit to the USA in 2014 underlined the positives in the Indo-US relationship: increase in mutual trade from US$100 billion to US$500 billion and the signing of an MOU of US$1 billion between the Exim Bank and the Insurance Regulatory and Development Authority (IRDA) to bolster India's move towards becoming a low-carbon economy.[33] After the nuclear agreement of 2008, more than 50 bilateral dialogue mechanisms have been instituted by the two governments. The deeper nature of their cooperation can be gauged from the fact that the dialogue mechanisms cover the following subjects: commerce,[34] defence and strategic cooperation, clean energy and issues of climate change, trade and economy, education and agriculture, science and technology and development, besides innovation and health. The visits of high-ranking officials from either country have been continuing on a regular basis for sustaining these bilateral dialogue mechanisms. The reader is advised to visit the United States Information Service's (USIS) official website on a regular basis for factual information on all such visits and details of their outcomes.[35] Given the success of deeper Indo-US strategic cooperation, it can be affirmed that their engagements have yielded good results, guaranteeing peace and stability and shaping a security architecture consistent with international laws and regulations in the

---

[33] Prasannan, 'Trip', 45.

[34] Government of India, *Brief on India-US Relations*.

[35] Ibid.

Indo-Pacific region and finding solutions to issues bothering Asian and global politics, under PM Modi in the contemporary era. Both the countries have shown immense maturity to make sure that differences do not overshadow their achievements so far, such as India's security concerns after the withdrawal of the US forces from Afghanistan in aftermath of recent US peace deal with the Taliban group, deterioration in US–Pakistan relations and receding US war threats against Iran, US–China trade war, China–Pakistan collusion, China's BRI and CPEC flagship programmes, Indo-US strategic cooperation would warrant reducing China's domination in the region by ensuring US presence in the region.

India–China–USA Competition in the South China Sea and East China Sea Regions

In recent years, the SCS and East China Sea (ECS) regions have emerged as a flashpoint between India, China and the USA, demanding greater Indo-US strategic cooperation under their Indo-Pacific strategy. China's conduct in these seas has been completely against the established norms and practices. It has simply been disregarding the UN Convention on the Law of the Sea (UNCLOS) norms for the settlement of its long-running maritime boundary disputes with a number of its neighbours, such as the Philippines, Vietnam, Taiwan, Japan, Malaysia and Indonesia. China has been claiming complete sovereignty over these regions by taking refuge in historical facts like 'nine-dash lines' and by creating of artificial islands, thereby denying its neighbours control over their territory and sovereign rights over their resources beneath water by bullying them. It has recently completely rejected the verdict pronounced by the Permanent Court of Arbitration, Hague, in favour of the Philippines over the Spratly Islands dispute, thereby raising concerns for many other countries of the region. China has increased its presence in the Indian Ocean region, stating that the 'Indian Ocean' does not belong to India, while forgetting that the SCS and ECS do not belong to China. India is a strong supporter of the idea of freedom of navigation in international waters and the right of passage in high seas under the UNCLOS. It has been of the view that all countries must exercise restraint and resolve bilateral issues diplomatically, according to principles of international law and without recourse to the use or threat of use of force.[36] It is in this context that India has entered into several agreements with the USA to cope up with the emerging maritime threats from China. Of late, there has been greater realization on the USA's part that India can play an important role in its 'Indo-Pacific' policy.

It is estimated that global trade worth US$5 billion passes through the SCS every year, including 50 per cent of India's trade with the ASEAN and the East Asian countries. Thus, India is opposed to the idea of the SCS being dominated by any one power like China, which would have a detrimental impact on its trade with these countries. India has been raising concerns regarding China's behaviour in the SCS and ECS regions with many countries of the world, including the USA and Japan. India had received US support on the issue of China's assertiveness in the SCS and ECS regions when President Obama, during his visit to India in January 2015 had stated that the Asia-Pacific region consisting of the SCS and ECS remained an area where India and the USA could cooperate. This expression of their coopera-tion with regard to the China issue has been institutionalized under their Indo-Pacific cooperation in the recent era. The present situation between India and China along the LAC since March–April 2020 may compel India to join the USA, Japan and Australia in strengthening the existing level of defence and strategic cooperation in the overall Indo-Pacific region on a long-term basis. The rationale underlying such cooperation is that no one power is in a position to stop China from pursuing aggressive policies towards its neighbours in and around the Indo-Pacific region. India has been careful to avoid spoiling its relationship with China, its next-door neighbour and trading partner. But the recent developments in the post-COVID-19 world order have exposed the limitations of such a reconciling stance towards China. It is a little early to say how things will shape up between India and China, on the one hand, and between the USA and China, on the other hand. PM Modi, over the last few years, has met the Chinese presi-dent several times: during President Xi Jinping's visit to Ahmedabad,

---

[36] Government of India, Ministry of Defence, *Annual Report 2014–15*, 3.

India, in September–October 2014 and Chennai, India, in October 2019; during his meeting with the Chinese leader in Wuhan in 2017; and during SCO, BRICS, UN and G-20 summit-level meetings held periodically. Still, the two sides need to work very closely to resist the aggressive policies of China in the region.

The New India–USA Partnership in the Indo-Pacific Region

There has been an important change in US policy towards the Asia-Pacific/Indo-Pacific in recent years. This is evident in the USA's new approach to Asia, released as part of its new defence strategy that articulates a policy aimed at containing China and making Asia a central US preoccupation.[37] The USA was allegedly being blamed by many countries of Southeast Asia for neglecting the Asia-Pacific/Indo-Pacific region because of its preoccupation with several wars in West Asia and the Middle East. The USA, in the post-9/11 era, has been busy in Iraq War, Afghanistan War, Syrian civil war, Libyan Civil War, Egyptian civil war, its support for Ukraine against Russia and its differences with North Korea and Iran. All these resulted in its decreased presence in the Asia-Pacific region, which was exploited by China in increasing its influence in the region. However, with the announcement of the 'Asia Pivot' policy by President Obama and the 'Indo-Pacific' strategy by President Trump, it has once again been trying to recover its ground vis-à-vis China in the region.

A study by an US think tank[38] points that US strategy should be designed to raise the costs of Chinese use of force and to check Chinese assertiveness at the expense of regional stability and US interests. For India, it would make sense to avoid getting caught in trap of USA–China–Japan rivalry. It also needs to continue rapprochement with China while at the same time pursuing a policy of military deterrence towards China. In this context, the USA and India signed a 'US-India Joint Strategic Vision for the Asia-Pacific and Indian Ocean Region'

37 Obama, 'Remarks by the President on the Defense Strategic Review'.
38 Perlez, 'US Unveils Military Boost in Asia'.

in 2015,[39] which sought 'a closer partnership' to promote 'peace, prosperity and stability' in the Indo-Pacific region, including a joint endeavour to boost regional economic integration, connectivity and regional security. Today, India is closely working with like-minded countries of the Indo-Pacific region, in the Arabian Sea and in Africa for ensuring a regional rule-based order that promotes transparency, respect for sovereignty and international law, stability and free and fair trade. The role of the USA in this region has been traditional one, and hence, there remains a larger scope for the Indo-US relationship to reflect a real convergence of strategic interests in the Indo-Pacific region too.[40]

The closer Indo-US cooperation under the 'Indo-Pacific' strategy has opened the doors for India, a 'major defence partner of the USA', for intense defence trade and technology cooperation with it. Their Defence Technology and Trade Initiative (DTTI) provides a bilateral platform for defence trade and technology sharing on a fast-track basis. US companies have an opportunity to participate in PM Modi's 'Make in India' initiative involving a US$150 billion defence modernization plan by focusing on co-production and co-development in hi-tech defence, missile and space projects.[41] In respect of maritime freedom and security, it is important that the USA and India act as 'anchors of stability' in the Indo-Pacific. They can also join each other in the co-production of fifth-generation fighter aircraft, nuclear submarines and aircraft carriers. It is going to be a win-win situation for both the largest democracies of the world.

The Quad Initiative

After a gap of several years, a new initiative involving the USA, Japan, Australia and India has started. India has been the latest entrant into this previously trilateral arrangement for taking care of the security scenario

[39] Available at file:///C:/Users/Vashu/Downloads/ORF-Heritage-Hudson.pdf (accessed on 1 July 2020).

[40] Ibid.

[41] Ibid.

in the Indo-Pacific region. There are different views regarding the Quad being a security alliance of member countries to counter China's threat in the region. It is also aimed at helping countries in coordinating regional economic and development assistance. China has led the narrative that the Quad is nothing more than a containment network against it. The Quad group has its origin in the 'Tsunami Core Group' that had come into being on the day of Tsunami in 2004.[42] Since then, it has undergone several transformations, and today, it has stabilized as a quadrilateral initiative of like-minded countries in the region. It is also seen as an enlarged version of the Malabar 2007 naval exercises involving the navies of all major countries of the region except China. Since there remains a lack of specificity about the Quad's purpose and objectives, it is difficult for the author to analyse it. It is still in the stage of evolution. It will take more time for one to arrive upon a conclusion that the Quad has the potential of becoming the Asian NATO.

China's One Belt One Road/Belt and Road Initiative

Chinese President Xi Jinping launched an ambitious flagship programme in 2013, OBOR, also known as the BRI. It is being seen as a revival of China's traditional 'Silk Route', over which trade from China to Europe via the present Central Asia used to take place before China came under the colonial rule of Japan and other Western powers. It is estimated that the BRI involves an expenditure of around US$1 trillion over the next decade or so. China through 'BRI' has plans of increasing its connectivity with the rest of the world through new land and sea routes in order to push its goods into markets of Europe, Africa and Latin America. These two different routes ultimately connect China with Europe, Africa and Southeast Asia.[43] The BRI also involves two additional projects within it, the CPEC and the Bangladesh–China–India–Myanmar (BCIM) corridor. It is the CPEC against which India has serious reservations, as it proposes to pass through India's sovereign territory under the occupation of Pakistan, known as Gilgit

---

[42] Available at https://www.csis.org/analysis/defining-diamond-past-present-and-future-quadrilateral-security-dialogue (accessed on 1 July 2020).

[43] Leer, 'China's New Silk Route'.

and Baltistan. It is on this ground that India has kept itself away from all summit-level meetings held since 2016 for discussing the BRI, in which more than 60 countries have been participating as partners. The USA has not been very supportive of China's BRI project, as it sees it as an attempt by China to establish its hegemony worldwide. China has been blamed for trapping poor countries by giving them loans for the completion of various costly infrastructure projects and, in the case of non-repayment of the loans, taking over their land and sea ports under its own control and turning them into army and naval bases in the name of ensuring the security of prominent sea routes for its trade with the rest of the world.[44] The entire project is full of contradictions. The issue that has raised India's concerns in the present era is China's policy of surrounding India from all sides by entering into agreements with smaller South Asian countries and roping them into its BRI/CPEC project. All such projects have economic connotations, but they have serious security implications for a country like India. For example, the CPEC begins from China's Xinjiang region, passes through Pakistan-occupied Kashmir (POK), enters Pakistan and moves from north to south, terminating at Gwadar Port in Baluchistan.

India has been raising serious concerns regarding China's biggest ever project worth more than US$60 billion 'China Pakistan Economic Corridor' (CPEC) being undertaken as part of its OBOR/BRI Grand Strategy as it is likely to pass through POK's Gilgit and Baltistan region of Pakistan which is under dispute with India. The Indian government's views were made explicit through PM Narendra Modi's speech from the ramparts of the Red Fort on 15 August 2016, when he said that POK, Gilgit and Baltistan were part of India. India has serious objections to the CPEC project as it considers Gilgit-Baltistan to be its sovereign territory. The area has assumed more significance after the abrogation of Article 370, which ended the special status of the earlier state of Jammu and Kashmir on 5 August 2019. India has officially boycotted all meetings on the BRI despite the fact that China is not happy with India as it has been objecting to the project from several platforms at the international level.

---

[44] Jin, 'Can China Keep India Silent Over the South China Sea'.

It has been found that in order to 'protect' sea ports, such as the Gwadar Port in Pakistan and Hambantota Port in Sri Lanka, Chinese submarines have been docking at these ports, thereby seriously raising security threats for India in the Arabian Sea and Indian Ocean regions. China is also aggressively entering into the Bay of Bengal region because of its increased trade with Myanmar and Bangladesh, which again poses a serious security threat to India's maritime security in the Andaman and Nicobar Islands. The USA is of the view that in order to turn the BRI project into a reality, China has been trying to dominate in the SCS and ECS regions and has adopted an aggressive posture towards its neighbours, including naval powers like the US Navy in the region. The US vision of the Indo-Pacific Economic Corridor[45] supplements India's Act East policy, and Indo-US cooperation in physical and soft infrastructure can link cross-border transport corridors; help create regional energy connections; and facilitate people-to-people interactions. Further, the USA can nurture burgeoning regional partnerships between Japan, South Korea, Australia and India, as these countries work towards building a consultative and collective Asian framework.

Hence, Indo-US strategic cooperation under the Indo-Pacific strategy has assumed more importance as on date. The recent stalemate between India and China along the LAC in March–April 2020 has a CPEC angle, as China does not want the presence of the Indian army close to its CPEC route, which is expected pass through an area close to the LAC. The Indo-US partnership has an important role to play in this respect.

CONCLUSION

In essence, over the last decade and a half, the Indo-US strategic partnership has enabled India to a fairly large extent in positioning itself at the international level to assume greater responsibilities. India's stature stands enhanced as on date. The country has increased its footprints on all important global platforms. This has led to India's new-found

---

[45] Available at file:///C:/Users/Vashu/Downloads/ORF-Heritage-Hudson.pdf (accessed on 1 July 2020).

confidence in various spheres, including the military and economy, such that today no major international issue can be concluded without its participation. The signing of a defence framework agreement, US affirmations to help India become a 'global superpower', the working out of a deal for civilian nuclear transfer—all these events have triggered a new shift in India's policy from non-alignment to strategic alignment with a country like the USA. India in the 21st century has been developing an approach towards the USA that would enable their growing economic–scientific–technological relationship and enhance India's military capabilities, which would help the country blunt Chinese assertiveness along and beyond its borders. PM Narendra Modi's six visits to Washington D.C. have contributed immensely to the consolidation of their relationship. After President Clinton's visit in 2000, all successive US presidents, including President Trump in February 2020, have visited India, which speaks volumes about their new strategic partnership.

Concurrent with the diplomatic thaw over the last decade, China has facilitated India's membership to the SCO, but continues to oppose India's entry into the NSG. China and India have been competing with each other over the development of infrastructure in areas close to their borders. The two countries' armed forces had very close encounters in areas close to the Indian side of the LAC in Ladakh because of PLA's incursion in those areas in March–April 2013. It must be mentioned here that after the PLA's incursion at Depsang Valley in the summer of 2013 and later at Doklam in Bhutan in June–August 2017, once again, serious skirmishes between India and China in Galwan Valley and Pangong Tso near the LAC began in March–April 2020. This posturing of China close to the LAC points out that the China factor will continue to provide rationale for the continuance of closer Indo-US strategic partnership on a long-term basis. Even on China's recent skirmishes with India, the USA has stood by the latter. It has been maintaining closer contacts with the Indian government at the highest level. The recent tensions with China on LAC have increased the relevance of cooperation with USA on long term basis. India's defence deals with the USA and other countries are largely attributed to China's assertiveness and aggressiveness towards its neighbour in the West,

India, and towards ASEAN and other countries in the SCS, ECS and Yellow Sea regions in recent years. Going by the discussions so far, it would not be an exaggeration to mention here that the China threat has emerged as the number one threat to India in recent years, which will continue to provide it grounds for seeking closer defence and strategic cooperation with the USA in the years to come. Till things stabilize, India and the USA will continue to work together to blunt China's policy of assertiveness in the Asia-Pacific/Indo-Pacific region, either at the Quad level, involving closer strategic–military cooperation among the four powers, the USA, India, Japan and Australia, or at the bilateral NSSP level. All these strategies and counter-strategies stand institutionalized in their strategic partnership.

The Road Map Ahead

Indo-US Relations at 75 and Beyond

India's relations with the USA have been marked by difficulties throughout the period under study except the last three decades. One of the hallmarks of their relations has been that at no point of time did they break completely. India and the USA being the two largest democracies of the world, their national interests have been basic to the structure and functioning of their respective foreign policies. In the last 75 years, they have moved from the average to the peak. In the past decades, they have clashed over a number of issues having international as well as regional significance. The nature of the world order in the shadows of the Cold War remained largely responsible for the eruption of their frequent misunderstandings, miscalculations and missed opportunities. The end of the Cold War and beginning of the new millennium provided them grounds for compensating for the losses of the past decades.

Barring the 1962 India–China war, there was hardly any occasion in the past when both countries remained on the same page. The 1971 India–Pakistan war made things much more complex because of the dismemberment of Pakistan, a US ally, and the Indo-Soviet Treaty of Peace, Friendship and Cooperation, leaving very little scope for the two to share anything substantive till the end of the Cold War and collapse of the former USSR. Throughout the Cold War period, for the USA, relations with India were guided by its global policies, and occasionally by regional policies, and rarely from the point of view of bilateralism. India, on its part, resented that the USA had subordinated bilateral relations and interests to regional, extra-regional and global considerations. Being a developing country, India found it difficult to attract the attention of US policymakers towards itself. The non-visit of any US president to India between 1979 and 1999 proved that India was off the radar of the USA.

India, being known for drawing inspiration from its past civilizations and glories, felt that it had not received sufficient recognition of its position and importance from the USA. The USA, on most occasions, had tried to downgrade and denigrate India, remaining very harsh on India's policy of non-alignment. It did not miss any opportunity to malign India for leaning towards the USSR as a non-aligned country. India vehemently resisted all US moves to equate it with its neighbour Pakistan, which sees India as a historical enemy. Within the country, the number of supporters favouring the idea of correcting its past historical mistakes regarding Pakistan has risen considerably in the 21st century, and they want India to follow a muscular policy towards its neighbour. No doubt, the role of Pakistan always remained a central element of Indo-US Cold War relations. It could never be bypassed in determining the cordiality of their relations. Any success in terms of stronger Indo-US relations depended upon India developing the skill and technique to keep them immune from US-Pak relations, rarely possible in international relations based upon principles of realism.

It was only towards the end of the Cold War period that Indo-US bilateral relations began to witness prospects for improvement. Indira Gandhi's 1982 visit to the USA and Rajiv Gandhi's visit in 1985 marked new milestones in Indo-US relations. Their signing of an MOU in 1985 ushered in a new phase of cooperation. The USA agreed to export dual-use technology to India for the first time. This also marked a new phase of increased understanding between the two countries in the field of defence and strategic cooperation. A large number of top military officials visited each other's country, and such visits gave a boost to Indo-US relations. It is noteworthy that the consolidation of their relations in the 21st century is largely attributed to the groundwork prepared through the famous 1985 MOU. It has taken the two countries almost 35 years to realize the goals and objectives visualized in 1980s to their fullest extent in 2020.

During the 1980s, Indo-US relations generally witnessed an upswing. This was partly because of a perceptible change in the

USA's attitude towards India in terms of its recognition of the latter as a major power in the South Asian region. The changes during the mid-1980s were guided to a great extent by the USA's desire to accommodate India's interests more than it had ever done in the past. It was willing to accommodate India's interests because it saw that the country could be a regional power and contribute to the world's stability by playing an important role globally as well as working for stability in the region. The consistent policies of India's government in the last few decades have enabled it to emerge as a major power and attain the ability to command respect and goodwill. They have allowed it to participate in international platforms as a powerful and responsible nation contributing significantly to peace and security at the global level. The leadership of both the sides must be given credit for having shown an enormous amount of patience and pragmatism in nurturing the idea of developing complementarities in their overall politico-strategic relations in the 21st century.

Intermittently in the early and mid-1990s, issues of arms transfer, nuclear non-proliferation, human rights, terrorism, trade and commerce made for areas of divergences between the two countries. The USA's policy on the issue of Kashmir, especially during the initial years of the Clinton administration, also cast a serious shadow over their relations. It was inclined to involve the third party, 'the people of Kashmir', in Indo-Pak bilateral talks on the future of the region, which did not fit in with India's stance on Kashmir—that it was a bilateral matter between India and Pakistan as per the Shimla Agreement of 1972. The US administration went ahead and tried to connect the issue with a possible Indo-Pak nuclear war and human rights violations in Kashmir in the 1990s. All these developments affected India's relations with the USA throughout the 1990s. The latter had been exerting immense pressure on it to sign the NPT and adhere to MTCR regulations, even though India was not party to it. The concern over nuclear proliferation was also used by the US administration to slow down the process of its ongoing cooperation with Indian defence establishments on the transfer of dual-use technologies. This largely hampered the course of Indo-US relations, which had witnessed a significant improvement during the Rajiv–Reagan era. Once again, the USA's global policies took the centre stage rather than any genuine desire on the part of its administration to give importance to its relations with India.

The nuclear proliferation issue throughout the period of study remained a bone of contention between the two countries, with a major impact on their bilateral relations in terms of political, economic and technological dimensions. However, their relations reached its peak once the USA offered a nuclear deal to India in 2005 and the two formalized the Indo-US Civil Nuclear Agreement in 2008. Since then, neither country has looked back. It has proved to be a landmark agreement responsible for bringing a historical transformation in 75 years of Indo-US politico-strategic relations.

It has been brought out in the present work that India was not going to bow down under any kind of bilateral or international pressure. The country had always been in favour of disarmament, but reports of any kind of external pressure or discrimination had been sufficient for its people to put pressure on their government to not succumb to any kind of external pressure on their core national interests. It was evident that the nuclear issue, which had remained an important one between India and the USA, had links with domestic politics too. India's position was not merely an idealistic position but was rooted in its national interests. With a declared nuclear state to its north, an undeclared nuclear state to its west and vessels carrying nuclear weapons sailing in the Indian Ocean, it was difficult for India to give up its nuclear option or accept any USA-imposed restraint on it, unless there was genuine acceptance of the goal of global nuclear disarmament and concrete movement towards it in a step-by-step manner as part of a well-defined nuclear disarmament process.

The Talbott–Singh 'Indo-US dialogue' facilitated the resumption of Indo-US ties and President Clinton's visit to India in March 2000, leading to a complete turnaround in Indo-US relations. India's newfound confidence and diplomatic victory made all the important leaders of the world visit the country and help end its seclusion since the May 1998 nuclear explosions that had led to the imposition of sanctions on it by many countries. They prepared sufficient grounds for getting Indo-US relations institutionalized during President Bush's (Jr.) tenure in many ways. NSSP 2004 and the enhanced level of military cooperation between the two countries were very significant. The rapprochement process continued during President Bush's (Jr.) second term in the US president's office. The visit of US State Secretary Condoleezza Rice to India in March 2005 definitely indicated that both countries were keen to maintain the momentum of their strategic partnership that had been formalized post the 9/11 terrorist attack on the World Trade Center.

President Bush (Jr.) initiated the famous NSSP with India in 2004, and one of the cornerstones of the NSSP had been the nuclear deal of 2005, which later became the Indo-US Civil Nuclear Agreement of 2008. Since then, neither country has looked back. It has been an extraordinary achievement of successive Indian governments' diplomacy that since 2000, every single US president has visited India, including President Trump in February 2020. All these US presidents took steps as if they were competing among themselves to help India become a powerful nation. The visit of President Obama to a school-cum-college in Mumbai, PM Modi's visit to the USA and his address to the Indian diaspora in New York and Houston in 2019 and President Trump's visit to Ahmedabad, India, in February 2020 generated so much euphoria that every millennial in India and the USA would remember the golden period of Indo-US bilateral relations for next several decades to come.

Ultimately, it was the triumph of the Indian diplomacy in remaining completely committed to nuclear non-proliferation, its willingness to work bilaterally and multilaterally to achieve the objective of nuclear disarmament, which enabled it to sign the nuclear agreement with the USA in 2008. The agreement was a milestone for their future relations, as it solely facilitated India's entry into international nuclear and missiles regimes, such as the IAEA, London Group, Australia Group, NSG, MTCR, Zangger Committee and Wassenaar Arrangement, after it received necessary waivers for the resumption of nuclear trade and transfer of technology as a non-signatory to the NPT. Sufficient grounds were covered by India and the USA for writing a new history close to the completion of 75 years of their bilateral relationship. India's nuclear policy and its efforts over the past seven decades have finally helped it attain a great-power status at the global level.

They have helped it realize its development-cum-security goals and be part of global high table and made it capable of following an independent policy in terms of its own national interests.

With the passage of time and the changed international order, the USA's readiness to acknowledge India's regional interests paved the way for India's willingness to take into account US strategic concerns with regard to South Asia and adjoining areas. The USA expected that India, soothed by US technological support for its defence and other industries, would adopt a more constructive approach than it had in the past towards US strategic interests in the Indian Ocean and the Persian Gulf. The signing of the nuclear cooperation agreement with the USA in 2008 led to a spurt in Indo-US technological cooperation and rise in their collaboration in defence projects that had been languishing in the past because of clashes of their politico-strategic interests. Technological cooperation as part of overall strategic cooperation, which had started on a sound footing in 1985 and later developed a snag due to US global objectives of nuclear non-proliferation clashing with India's regional security concerns during the 1990s, picked up once again after the nuclear agreement. India signed an agreement with the IAEA, became a member of the MTCR and other groups and received a waiver from the NSG and other nuclear regimes after amendments in the US NNPA 1978. Following the historic 2008 agreement, US help opened the doors for India receiving key dual-use technologies for all held up national flagship programmes. The longest prevailing nuclear issue as bone of contention in Indo-US relations had ended. A new era had begun for their politico-strategic relations.

The nuclear agreement of 2008 gave a huge boost to India's future energy security policy, and it also helped the UPA government retain its position at the centre in 2009, with Manmohan Singh becoming PM for the second time. One of the high points of Indo-US cooperation in the 21st century has been their seeking of peace and security in the Indo-Pacific region, earlier the Asia-Pacific region. Another pillar of their cooperation has been defence and counterterrorism cooperation. A very important area that received President Trump's and his predecessor's attention was military hardware and transfer of key technologies to India. The decision of the Trump administration to sell Sea Guardian UAVs to India was remarkable, as India became the first non-NATO country to receive the transfer. As on date, India and the USA have complete understanding on how to end nuclear and missile proliferation to Iran, Pakistan and North Korea by China.

India and the USA are expected to find more paths for extending their defence and security cooperation to guarantee that a stable power structure prevails in Asia. Areas such as joint peacekeeping missions, in which India has a lot of expertise, maritime interdiction as Indian Navy is a 'Blue-water' navy and security-cooperation in the Indian Ocean and IOC littoral region, for guaranteeing 365 x 24 peaceful trade from the Persian Gulf to the Straits of Malacca, where US maritime power and diplomacy may bring added advantage for the Indian Navy in ensuring complete security of the Indo-Pacific region without posing a danger to the littoral regions. It is the time to ensure fast-track approach towards India which has opened up to defence cooperation with the USA despite diversification approach and is eager to expedite significant defence purchases from the USA in the light of fast-changing circum-stances in its neighbourhood with China, success will depend upon the US administration's ability to sell certain fifth-generation defence technologies to India and by contributing in its 'Make-in-India' by undertaking joint production of key military hardware components.

India's relationship with the USA on defence and strategic issues in the 21st century has been reinforced. A complete structural transfor-mation is underway in their defence relationship, which has risen to a new height with the initiation of the '2 + 2 dialogue'. This present format of forever 'two plus two dialogue' involving biennial meeting between their defence and diplomatic secretaries/ministers accompa-nied with their officials, India and the USA has accomplished a third foundational agreement to encourage closer defence cooperation. India and the USA signed the long-awaited COMCASA recently. This new arrangement with US will facilitate India's access to advanced US defence systems and empower it to ideally use its current US origin platforms. Before signing the COMCASA, India and the USA, under PM Modi and President Trump, respectively, had signed two other foundational agreements: the LEMOA in 2016 and the GSOMIA way back in 2002. The significance of the COMCASA can be gauged from the fact that besides interoperability, it will throw open the chance of Indian armed force units accessing a protected Common Tactical Picture. This would mean that Indian Navy and IAF surveillance aircraft and fighters can receive information from the USA and other friendly partners during exercises or joint military operations. In addition, another feat that has been achieved in 2016 is that India stands designated as a Major Defence Partner of the USA. Further, the new arrangement under the COMCASA opens up the chance of India bringing in US frameworks unrestricted by potential constraints on guidance, communication and sensor technologies. Both these agreements with the USA will ensure sharing of information, learning of each other's military techniques and interoperability of each other's armed forces' platforms in hours of emergency. It is noteworthy that it was the Modi government that got open the final doors for the signing of the LEMOA and COMCASA. Earlier governments could not mobilize enough political support for signing the agreements having far-reaching consequences. This issue of the LEMOA and COMCASA had been pending between the USA and India for more than one and a half decade. The agreements will help India in sharing communication platforms when it comes to coordinating with the navy and/or air force of the USA or its NATO allies such as France, Japan, Australia and others.

PM Narendra Modi and President Donald J. Trump during their first meeting in June 2017 expressed their determination to carry forward the momentum gained since the nuclear agreement in 2008. Both leaders have promised to keep working to develop closer defence and security cooperation under the US recognition of India as a Major Defence Partner. The joint statement issued after their meeting highlighted the continuance of the cooperation achieved between them on advanced defence equipment and technology at the same level as that of the cooperation between the USA and its closest partners and allies. In the bilateral Strategic Energy Partnership meeting in April 2018, India agreed to import crude oil and liquefied natural gas (LNG) from the USA in order to maintain the supply of crude oil that had been affected after the imposition of US sanctions against Iran. The two countries took their military cooperation to another level by holding the first Indo-US tri-service military exercise and expanding their existing military exercises. Overall, much has been achieved between them as on date. The need is for them to continue maintaining the same level of understanding in future too. It is expected that institutionalization of the different aspects of their relationship will enable the cooperation to continue without being affected by smaller pins and pricks that are likely to emerge at any time in the future between the two vibrant democracies under people's pressure. Exceptional commitment towards each other is needed in the coming years as well.

Indo-US counterterrorism cooperation has helped the two countries work in tandem and avoid unnecessary embarrassment inside the UNSC. An important understanding was evident in the aftermath of the Pulwama attack leading to the killing of 44 security personnel, prompting the designation of JeM chief Masood Azhar as a global terrorist under UNSC Resolution 1267. It was a matter of satisfaction for Indian diplomats when Pakistan was put on the grey list of the Financial Action Task Force. The USA-led war against terrorism has spread across the world. India and the USA are today among the principal targets of terrorism in the world. Though some success has been accomplished with the decimation of the Taliban and al-Qaeda bases in Afghanistan and Iraq, there remain colossal tasks ahead. In all such endeavours, the USA and India have common interests. Their counterterrorism cooperation has been remarkable all these years. The launch of the first ever US-India Counterterrorism Designations Dialogue has been a very important outcome of their closer cooperation, as it has helped India in getting international pressure exerted against Pakistan, which has continued to pose a serious threat to India's unity and territorial integrity. Countering religious fundamentalism and drug trafficking in South Asia, Central Asia and the Caucasus would assist them in keeping global terrorism, of which both nations have been victims, under control. Both countries have a common interest in the restoration of peace and stability in Afghanistan, despite some reservations on the part of India because of the USA's 'peace agreement' with Taliban forces. The USA has acknowledged India's good work in education, health infrastructure, vocational training and small industries for the people of Afghanistan despite Pakistan's objection in recent months. Both ought to sustain similar cooperation in future too, as it is a matter involving a country sharing India's border.

A very important area that has assumed importance and needs continuous cooperation between the two countries in times to come is the Indo-Pacific region. President Obama had initiated the Pivot to Asia policy that emphasized India as a key balancer to restrain the assertive and aggressive rise of China. On the part of policymakers in both countries, a multi-pronged approach is needed for the sustenance of defence and strategic cooperation in the Indo-Pacific region to counter China in the SCS, ECS and Indian Ocean. The USA has considered India to be an inevitable part of the Indo-Pacific narrative under the incipient Quad involving the USA, Australia, Japan and India. The two countries need to consolidate their cooperation through augmentation of their resources and manpower in light of another emerging threat on account of China's flagship BRI under President Xi Jinping. India needs to change its approach against the backdrop of the current global political and economic scenario to have more say in global administration. As mentioned before, maritime security has become a territory of long-term geopolitical cooperation between India and the USA under the new nomenclature, 'the Indo-Pacific'. The triggers are the significant presence of the Chinese naval force in the Indian Ocean and adjoining areas and China's quest for maritime stations and bases in the Indian Ocean, close to Indian and US bases, besides its conflicts in the SCS. The USA has renamed its Pacific Command as the Indo-Pacific Command. It is imperative for India to continue cooperation with the USA for maintaining peace and security in the entire region on a long-term basis.

The achievement of the Indian diaspora, especially in information technology (IT), and the high cooperation of Indians and Indian-Americans in Silicon Valley and various US high-technology sectors have helped enormously in the consolidation and sustenance of multidimensional cooperation between the two countries. The USA has realized that India, which is the fifth largest economy and is likely to have the third highest GDP in the next 10 years, has the potential of having the second largest GDP after China by 2050. Thus, there remain immense possibilities for US companies to tap into India's gigantic market and talented human capital and continue to act as an adhesive to solid Indo-US ties in the future. The disenchantment of China in the post-COVID-19 period and the ongoing USA–China trade war has thrown up a huge opportunity for US companies to shift their operations to India and formulate a new road map ahead. If this were to turn into a reality in the next few years, then neither country has to worry about some of the trade-related irritants in recent years, arising from President Donald Trump's America First policy in the economic dimension. There has been some restlessness in India since the Trump administration chose to end the Generalized System of Preferences (GSP) meant for India in June 2019. It has already been visualized that Indo-US annual trade is likely to reach up to $550 billion in the next few years' time. At the time of concluding this work, the author has the feeling that this goal is going to be realised sooner than projected, because of the backlash India–China trade is going to witness in the aftermath of the Galwan Valley skirmishes along the LAC in the post-COVID-19 scenario.

At the global level, the USA has supported India's membership in the UNSC, NSG, IAEA, MTCR and other multilateral organizations in the 21st century. Today, their cooperation under Quad and the Indo-Pacific strategy have become very important for both countries, who have common concerns arising on account of the assertive policies of China in the Indian Ocean, SCS, ECS and Yellow Sea regions. Both countries have been sharing common concerns over China's ambitious BRI, a worldwide connectivity project through which China plans to establish direct connectivity running through Europe to Africa through road and sea routes. President Trump has been very supportive of PM Modi's policies and used many euphoric phrases in his meetings with the Indian leader, providing reasons to expect that the US administration would continue its policies towards India even if a new president takes over.

So far, the Trump administration has not been harsh with India and allowed US defence and energy exports to India to continue. Indo-US relations under PM Modi and President Trump have been witnessing their best phase in the history of their diplomatic relationship of 75 years. India has the potential to offer US companies a very important alternative to China, and the USA has been supportive of policies and matching actions that would aid the expansion of their economic and trade links in general, and in the post-COVID-19 scenario in particular. It is important to mention here that US companies have shown heavy interest in being part of several programmes launched by the Modi government, such as Smart Cities Mission, Skill India, Swachh Bharat Mission, Make in India, Atmanirbhar Bharat, Digital India and several others. The unexpectedly prolonged trade war between the USA and China and the emergence of the COVID-19 pandemic and India–China LAC border crises may expedite the shifting of the base of many US companies from China to India, thereby further consolidating Indo-US relations on a permanent basis. This would help India in realizing its pending task of becoming part of the developed world soon. The China factor in the post-COVID-19 era will further transform Indo-US relations.

India's defence ties with the USA, as stated earlier, will keep extending through institutional plans under the COMCASA and LEMOA and other factors like the Industrial Security Annex, STA-1, India's Major Defence Partner status, the Basic Exchange and Cooperation Agreement (BECA), which is underway, and the DTTI. India needs to shed its inhibitions, and it is expected that the present setback from China has the potential to compel it to take a fresh look at the USA without seeing it as a compromise to its 'strategic autonomy' policy in the post-COVID-19 scenario. India has achieved a lot through making the USA change its approach towards Pakistan, Afghanistan, Iran and West Asia.

Needless to say, a new situation has arisen in the world today on account of COVID-19. A global war against COVID-19 is on. The entire world is experiencing lockdowns. Till date, more than 2 lakh people have died across the world due to the disease. The G-7 countries, including the USA, have been the worst sufferers. The USA has become the country with the largest number of COVID-19 casualties—more than 30,000 till date. Among the G-20 nations, India and China have been the worst sufferers. China has been the worst sufferer, as it is reported that the pandemic originated from Wuhan. India is going to see a rise in COVID-19 cases, with the number of patients having reached 1 million and number of deaths rising up to 10,000 by the end of June 2020. The current situation has thrown up a new opportunity for India and the USA to work together in the post-COVID-19 world order.

A new world order is likely to come into being as the world continues to grapple with the situation towards the end of 2020. The world stands divided today in pinpointing countries or international bodies such as the WHO and UN as responsible for not having taken adequate precautionary steps to check the spread of the COVID-19 pandemic across the world. There has been a small gesture on the part of India through its sending the much-needed medicine HCQ (hydroxychloroquine) to the USA and 55 other countries of the world. It has established India's position at the centre stage even during the pandemic, because the whole world is glued to India. It is anxious to know the way India has handled the COVID-19 scenario by preventing the death of a large chunk of its population despite being the second largest populated country in the world. On balance, Indo-US relations have improved much in the 21st century and are expected to be sustained under the changing circumstances. Notwithstanding episodes of cooperation, political and strategic factors continue to remain significant in shaping them. The world's two largest democracies are expected to continue to harness the synergies pooled over the last 75 years of their bilateral relationship. Their bilateral relations in areas covering defence, energy security, space and high-technology exchange and economic cooperation are likely to flourish in future too. The leadership in either country has shown willingness to go the additional mile to sustain the gained momentum in their cherished relationship.

BIBLIOGRAPHY

PRIMARY SOURCES

Adeoba, Adentunji. *Technology Transfer and Joint Ventures: The Nigerian Experience* (UNCTAD/ITP/TECHNOLOGY/9). New York, NY: United Nations, 1990.

Alam, Mohammed B. *Clinton's India Policy: Avoidable Miscalculations*, 17. New Delhi: Third Concept, December 1993.

Armacost, Michel H. 'South-Asia and the US: An Evolving Partnership.' *Department of State Bulletin* (July 1987): 75–79.

Bhartiya Janata Party National Executive. *Foreign Policy-National Security and UPA's Disastrous Governance*. New Delhi: Bhartiya Janata Party, 2008.

Biswal, Nisha Desai. Assistant Secretary, Bureau of South and Central Asian Affairs, *Re-energizing U.S.–India Ties, Testimony, Senate Foreign Relations Committee*. Subcommittee on Near Eastern & South & Central Asian Affairs (Washington, 16 July 2014). www.usagov.org.

Bose, T. C. 'The United States and South Asia: The Nuclear Proliferation Dimension.' *Strategic Analysis* XVI, no. 12 (March 1994): 1604.

Buckley, James L. 'Arms Transfers and the National Interest'. *Department of State Bulletin*. Washington, DC: GPO, 1981.

C.R.S. Report. *US Nuclear Cooperation with India: Issues for Congress*. 12 January 2006. https://fas.org/crs/nukePDF (accessed on 25 September 2020).

C.R.S. Report. *US Nuclear Cooperation with India: Issues for Congress*, 12 January 2006. https://fas.org/crs/nukePDF.

Carnegie Endowment for International Peace Report. Washington, DC: 1988–2016.

Chadha Government of India, Ministry of Defence. *DRDO Major Projects, Standing Committee on Defence (95–96) 5th Report, 10th Lok Sabha* (New Delhi, August 1995), paras. 4.22 and 4.23.

Chadha, K. D. 'Time for Introspection: The Stakes in the DRDO's Light Combat Aircraft are Far Too High.' *Hindustan Times*, 14 April 1991.

Chaudhri, Parmit Pal. 'American Indian Century.' *The Hindustan Times* (New Delhi), 7 April 2005.

Chengappa, Raj. 'Nuclear Dilemma.' *India Today* (New Delhi), 30 April 1994, p. 42.

CISIS. *Indo-US Relations: A Report Prepared.* New Delhi, 2003–2004.

Cohen, Stephen P. *India: Emerging Power.* New Delhi: OUP, 2001.

Cohen, Stephen. *Deal Gone Too Far.* https://www.orfonline.org/2006/03 (accessed on 25 September 2020).

Cohen, Stephen. *Deal Gone Too Far.* November 2005. www.orfonline.com.

Commission on Industrial Competitiveness. *U.S. President's Commission on Industrial Competitiveness, Report: Global Compton, The New Reality,* vol. I. Washington, DC: Commission on Industrial Competitiveness, 1985.

Conference on Disarmament. *Nuclear Disarmament* (Working Paper No. CD/1816). Geneva: Conference on Disarmament, 2007.

Congressional Quarterly Inc. *Congressional Records.* Washington, DC: Congressional Quarterly Inc., 1984–2016.

Crabb Jr, C. V. *The Doctrine of American Foreign Policy: Their Meaning, Role and Future,* 144. London: LSU Press, 1982.

Cronin, Richard P. 'Policy Alert: The Rajiv Gandhi Visit: Issues in U.S.-India Relations'. *Congressional Research Service* (Working Paper No. 85–838F). Washington, DC: Congressional Research Service, 1985.

Dean, John Gunther. *Indo-US Relations: Fulfilling the Promise.* New Delhi: USIS, 1987.

Department of State Bulletin. Washington, DC: 1983–2015.

Department of State. *American Foreign Policy: Current Documents.* Washington, DC: Bureau of Public Affairs, 1985–2015.

Dulles, John Foster. 'The Cost of Peace'. *US Department of State Bulletin* 34 (18 June 1956).

Dutt, V. P. *Foreign Policy of India.* New Delhi: Deep and Deep Publications, 1989.

Encyclopedia of Social Sciences. New York, NY, 1968.

Federal Register. *22 Code of Federal Regulations,* Part 121, in *Federal Register* 49: 236 (6 December 1984): 47686–9.

Fisher, David. *Towards 1995: The Prospects for Ending the Proliferation of Nuclear Weapons,* 5. Brookfield: UNIDIR, 1993.

Frontline. 'Cover Story.' 24 March 2006. https://frontline.thehindu.com/magazine/issue/vol23-05/ (accessed on 25 September 2020).

Gandhi, Rajiv. *Selected Speeches and Writings, 1984–85,* vol. I. New Delhi: Publication Division, Ministry of Information and Broadcasting, Government of India, 1985.

———. *Selected Speeches and Writings, 1986,* vol. II. New Delhi: Publication Division, Ministry of Information and Broadcasting, Government of India, 1986.

———. *Selected Speeches and Writings, 1987,* vol. III. New Delhi: Publication Division, Ministry of Information and Broadcasting, Government of India, 1987.

———. *Selected Speeches and Writings, 1988,* vol. IV. New Delhi: Publication Division, Ministry of Information and Broadcasting, Government of India, 1988.

———. *A World Free of Nuclear Weapons: An Action Plan* (Address to the Third Special Session on Disarmament of U.N. General Assembly, 9 June 1988). New Delhi: Government of India, 1988.

Gandhi, Rajiv. *Selected Speeches and Writings, 1989*, vol. V. New Delhi: Publication Division, Ministry of Information and Broadcasting, Government of India, 1989.

Goheen, Robert F. 'Indo-US Relations: Nuclear Proliferation and Technology Transfer.' In *Bridging the Non-Proliferation Divide: The United States and India*, edited by Francine R. Frankel, 3–4. New Delhi: Konark Publications, 1995.

Gopalakrishnan, A. A Nuclear Regulator Without Teeth. *The Hindu* (New Delhi, 16 September 2011). http://www.tribuneindia.com/2011/20110619/main1.htm (accessed on 19 June 2011).

Government of India, Ministry of Defence. *Annual Report*. New Delhi: Government of India, 1984–2018.

Government of India, Ministry of External Affairs. *Annual Report*, 1967–1968, p. 11.

———. *Annual Report*, 1971–1972, p. 75.

———. *Brief on India-US Relations*. http://www.mea.gov.in/Ind...PDF.

———. *Foreign Affairs Record* xxxiii, no. 10 (21 October 1987).

———. *Foreign Affairs Record* (New Delhi), vol. 33, no. 5 (1987): 339.

———. *Annual Report*. New Delhi: Government of India, 1984–2018.

Government of India. *A strategy for the Growth of Electrical Energy in India*. http://www.dae.gov.in/publ/doc10/index.htm.

———. *Economic Survey 2011–12*, 260–1. http://indiabudget.nic.in.

———. *Economic Survey 2012–13*, 231–2. http://indiabudget.nic.in.

———. *Economic Survey, 2013–14*. http://indiabudget.nic.in.

———. *India 1984—A Reference Annual*. New Delhi: Government of India Publications Division, 1984.

———. *Import Certificates Procedure Under the Indo-U.S. Memorandum of Understanding on Technology Transfer*, 2. New Delhi: Government of India, 1985.

———. 'Text of Prime Minister Rajiv Gandhi's Statement at the White House, after lunch with President Ronald Reagan on 20 October 1987'. *Foreign Affairs Record* 33, no. 5 (1987).

———. *Foreign Affairs Record*. New Delhi: Government of India, 1986–2018.

———. 'Text of Mexico Declaration' in *Foreign Affairs Record* 32, no. 8 (1986). New Delhi: Government of India, 1986.

———. *Lok Sabha Debates*. New Delhi: Government of India, 1984–2016.

———. *Joint Statement on India-USA Civil Nuclear Cooperation*. New Delhi: 2005. http://dae.nic.in/?q=node/61 (accessed on 1 October 2020).

———. *National Report to the Convention on Nuclear Safety*. New Delhi: GOI, 2007.

Gupta, Amit. 'Determining India's Force Structure and Military Doctrine.' *Asian Survey* XXXV, no. 5 (May 1995): 448.

Gupta, Shekhar. 'India–Pakistan: War Games.' *India Today* (New Delhi), 28 February 1990.

Guy Hope, A. *America and Swaraj: The US Role in India's Independence*. Washington, DC: Public Affairs Press, 1968.

Hibbs, Mark. *The Future of the Nuclear Suppliers Group*. Washington, DC: C.E.I., 2011.

Hobbs, David, 'The Impact of Technology Control Regimes'. In *Arms and Technology Transfers: Security and Economic Considerations Among Importing and Exporting States*, edited by Sverre Lodgaard and Robert L. Pfaltzgraff, Jr. *UNIDIR/95/22*. New York, NY, and Geneva: United Nations, 1995.

Hyde Act, 2006. http://www.gpo.gov/fdsys/pkg/BILLS-109hr5682enr/pdf/BILLS-109hr5682enr.pdf.

IAEA. *IAEA Board Approves India Safeguards Agreement*. Vienna: IAEA, 2008. http://www.iaea.org/newscenter/news/2009/indiaagreement.html (accessed on 1 October 2020).

———. *India Signs Convention of Supplementary for Compensation for Nuclear Damage*. Vienna: IAEA, 2010. http://www.iaea.org/newscenter/news/2010/indiaconvention.html (accessed on 1 October 2020.

IDSA Task Force Report. *Development of Nuclear Energy Sector in India*. New Delhi: Institute for Defence Studies and Analyses, 2010.

Ikle, Fred. 'Under Secretary of Defence for Policy.' *The Washington Post*, 4 May 1985.

Inderfurth, Karl F., and S. Amer Latif. 'U.S.–India Military Engagement: Steady as She Goes.' A CSIS Report Rollout Event (13 June 2012). www.csis.org/program/wadhanichair.

Jain, S. K. 'Nuclear Power in India—The Fourth Revolution.' (Chairman and Managing Director, Nuclear Power Corporation of India Limited and Bharatiya Nabhikiya Vidyut Nigam, India). *An International Journal of Nuclear Power* 18, nos. 2–3 (2004): 17.

Jegathesan, J. *Factors Affecting Access to Technology Through Joint Ventures* (UNCTAD/ITP/TECHNOLOGY/9). New York, NY: United Nations, 1990.

Jervis, Robert. 'Co-operation Under the Security Dilemma.' *World Politics* 30, no. 2 (1978): 167–214.

Jetly, Nancy. 'South Asia in Post-Cold-War Period.' In *India's Foreign Policy: Challenges and Prospects*, edited by Nancy Jetly, 190–2. New Delhi: Vikas Publishing House, 1999.

Jin, Wang. 'Can China Keep India Silent Over the South China Sea.' *The Diplomat*, 17 August 2016.

Kamath, P. M. 'Security Considerations in Indo-US Relations: 1965–1990.' In *Four Decades of Indo-US Relations: A Commemorative Retrospective*, edited by A. P. Rana, 127. New Delhi: Har-Anand and the US Educational Foundation in India, 1994.

Kaul, T. N. *The Kissinger Years: Indo-American Relations*, 37. New Delhi: Arnold-Heinemann, 1980.

Kaushik, Devendra. *Soviet Relations with India and Pakistan*. Delhi: Vikas Publications, 1971.

Kavic, Lorne. *India's Quest for Security: Defence Policies 1947–65*, 198–200. Berkeley, CA: University of California Press, 1967.

Kerr, Paul K. *U.S. Nuclear Cooperation with India: Issues for the Congress* (CRS Report No. RL33016). Washington, DC: USCRS, 2012. https://www.fas.org/sgp/crs/nuke/RL33016.pdf (accessed on 1 October 2020).

Kissinger, Henry. *White House Years.* Boston, MA: Little Brown & Co., 1979.

Kochhar, Chanda. 'A Spring in the Economy's Step.' *The Hindustan Times* (Jalandhar), 1 March 2015, p. 12.

Krishnaswamy, Sridhar. 'Armitage's Visit Reflect Warm Ties, Says Boucher.' *The Hindu,* 16 July 2004. http://www.hindu.com/2004/07/16stor ies/2004071604471604471100.htm.

Kumar, Dinesh. *Defence in Indo-US Relations.* IDSA Occasional Paper Series. New Delhi: IDSA, August 1997.

Kumar, Rajesh. 'Emerging Indo-US Strategic Partnership and the China Factor.' *Punjab Journal of Politics* xxxii–xxxiii, no. 1 (2008–2009).

———. 'PM Modi Government's Diplomacy for India's Nuclear Energy Security: Continuity and Changes.' *World Focus* (August 2014).

———. 'South Asia and Future of the Nuclear Non-Proliferation Regime in the 21st Century.' *South Asian Affairs* 3, nos. 1 & 2 (2009).

———. *Indo-U. S. Politico Strategic Relations.* New Delhi: Independent Pub, 2007. ISBN:81-85359-38-5.

———. *Indo-US Politico Strategic Relations,* 190–95. New Delhi: Independent Publishing Co., 2007.

Kumar, Rajesh and Gurnam Singh, 'Dynamics of Indo-US Nuclear Deal and Its Strategic Implications.' *Punjab Journal of Politics* 34, nos. 1–2 (2010): 43–70.

Kumar, Satish. Ed. 'India and the World: Foreign Policy Trends.' In *Yearbook on India's Foreign Policy,* edited by Satish Kumar, 11. New Delhi, 1988.

Limyae, S. P. *US–Indian Relations: The Pursuit of Accommodation.* Boulder, CO: Westview Press, 1993.

Lok Sabha Debates. Series 10, vol. XXVIII, no. 1, Session 9 (New Delhi, 21 February 1994): cc. 417–9.

———. Series 10, vol. XXX, no. 29, Session 10 (New Delhi, 2 May 1994): c. 429.

———. Series 8, Session 10, vol. 38, no. 39 (New Delhi, 25 April 1988): cc. 319 and 330–31.

———. Series 8, vol. III, no. 13 (New Delhi, 27 March 1985): cc. 97–98.

———. Series 8, vol. VIII, no.13 (New Delhi, 14 August 1985): cc. 121–22.

———. Series 10, vol. XXXV, no. 23, Session 13 (New Delhi, 25 August 1994): cc. 385–6.

———. Series 7, vol. 2, no. 7, Session 11 (New Delhi, 24 February 1983): c. 56.

———. Series 7, vol. XLIV, no. 10, Session 14 (New Delhi, 6 March 1984): cc. 374–5.

———. Series 7, vol. XLIV, no. 6, Session 14 (New Delhi, 1 March 1984): cc. 207–208.

———. Series 7, vol. XLV, no. 11, Session 14 (New Delhi, 7 March 1984): cc. 375–6

———. Series 7, vol. XLV, no. 20, Session 14 (New Delhi, 21 March 1984): cc. 419–22.

———. Series 7, vol. XLVI, no. 27, Session 14 (New Delhi, 30 March 1984): cc. 395–6.

Lok Sabha Debates. Series 8, vol. 4, no. 19, Session 2 (New Delhi, 9 April 1985): cc. 296–7.

———. Series 8, vol. 4, no. 23, Session 2 (New Delhi, 15 April 1985): cc. 390–6.

———.. Series 8, vol. 4, no. 26, Session 2 (New Delhi, 18 April 1985): cc. 343–6.

———. Series 8, vol. 7, no. 26, Session 3 (New Delhi, 29 July 1985): cc. 354 and 356.

———. Series 8, vol. III, no. 20 (New Delhi, 10 April 1985): c. 267.

———. vol. III, no. 19 (New Delhi, 9 April 1990): c. 590.

———. vol. VI, no. 43 (New Delhi, 17 May 1990): c. 537.

———. vol. VIII, no. 50 (New Delhi, 10 April 1990): c. 483.

———. vol. XIV, no. 2 (New Delhi, 22 February 1991): cc. 464–590.

———. vol. XXI, no. 33 (New Delhi, 27 April 1993): cc. 346–53.

Mahapatra, Chintamani. 'US Policy Towards Nuclear Issues in South Asia.' *Strategic Analysis* XVI, no. 5 (August 1993): 526–7.

Malik, Mohan. 'India and China: As China Rises, India Stirs.' In *Indian Foreign Policy in a Unipolar World*, edited by Harsh V. Pant, 163–92. New Delhi: Routledge, 2009.

Mallick, P. K. *2+2 Dialogue and Indo-US Relations.* New Delhi: V.I.F., 2018.

Malviya, Goopal Ji. 'An American Approach to India's Kashmir.' *Strategic Analysis* XVII, no. 5 (August 1994).

Maynes, Charles William. 'America Without the Cold-War.' *Foreign Policy* Spring (1990): 3–25.

Mohan, R. C. 'N-Deal: Now Focus on IAEA Safeguards.' *Indian Express* (New Delhi), 25 December 2005.

Muhammad, Adil Sultan. *Indo–US Civilian Nuclear Cooperation Agreement: Implications on South Asian Security Environment.* Washington, DC: Henry L. Stimson Center, July 2006.

Nayar, Baldev Raj. 'Regional Power in a Multi Polar World.' In *India a Rising Middle Power*, edited by John W. Mellor, 147–72. New Delhi: Routledge, 1981.

———. *Superpower Dominance and Military Aid: A Study of Military Aid to Pakistan.* New Delhi: Manohar Publications, 1991.

Nehru, Jawaharlal. 'Apsara.' In *Jawaharlal Nehru's Speeches*, vol. 3 (March 1953 to August 1957). Delhi: Publications Division of the Government of India, 1958.

———. *Letters to the Chief Ministers*, vol. 3, p. 442, Letter of 15 November 1953.

———. *Speeches, September 1946–May 1949*, vol. 1. Delhi: Government of India, Publications Division, 1949.

———. *India's Foreign Policy: Selected Speeches (September 1946–April 1961).* New Delhi: Government of India, Publications Division, 1963.

NPCIL. *Plants in Operation.* http://www.npcil.nic.in/main/AllProjectOperationDisplay. aspx.

Obama, Barack. 'Remarks by the President on the Defense Strategic Review.' *The White House*, Office of the Press Secretary, 5 January 2012.

Ohajunwa, Emeka. *India-US Security Relations: 1947–1990*, 66. Delhi: Chanakya Publications, 1992.

Pande, Savita. 'US Non-Proliferation Policy Failures.' *Strategic Analysis* XII, no. 7 (October 1988): 749.

Perlez, Jane. 'US Unveils Military Boost in Asia.' *The Hindu* (New Delhi), 3 June 2012.

Planning Commission, Government of India. *Tenth Five Year Plan*, Chapter 7.3, Sect. 2. http://planningcommission.nic.in/plans/planrel/fiveyr/welcome.html (accessed on 15 June 2007).

Prasannan, R. 'Trip, Trap, Triumph.' *The Week*, 12 October 2014, p. 45.

Raja Mohan, C. 'N-Deal: Now Focus on IAEA Safeguards.' *Indian Express* (New Delhi), 25 December 2005.

———. *The Shaping of India's New Foreign Policy: Crossing the Rubicon*. New Delhi: Penguin Publishers, 2003.

Rajya Sabha Debates. vol. 170, no. 26 (New Delhi, 2 May 1994): cc. 300–302.

———. vol. 170, no. 27 (New Delhi, 3 May 1994): c. 254.

Ramachandran, R. 'Hurdles Ahead.' *Frontline*, 20 February 2015, pp. 10–11.

Raphel, Robin. 'United States Policy Toward South-Asia'. *U.S. Department of State Dispatch* 6, no. 13 (27 March 1995).

Rasgotra, Maharaj Krishna. 'America Needles in Kashmir Again.' *The Hindustan Times* (New Delhi), 2 June 1993.

Richard, Cronin P. *The United States, Pakistan and the Soviet Threat to Southern Asia: Options for Congress* (Report no. 85192 F). Washington, DC: Library of Congressional Research Service, September 1985.

Secretary Christopher. 'America's Commitment to Human Rights.' *US Department of State Dispatch* 5, no. 6 (7 February 1994): 53.

Senate Governmental Affairs Committee. *To Examine Nuclear, Biological and Chemical Weapons Threats of the 1990s*. Washington, DC: Senate Governmental Affairs Committee, 1993.

Singh, Jaswant. *A Call to Honour*. New Delhi: Rupa Co., 2006.

Singh, Manmohan. *Prime Minister's Address to the Nation*. New Delhi: Government of India, 2004. http://pmindia.gov.in/speech-details.php?nodeid=1 (accessed on 1 October 2020).

———. *Prime Minister's Statement to the Media at the Joint Press Conference with the U.S. President*. New Delhi: Government of India: 2010. http://pmindia.gov.in/speech-details.php?nodeid=950 (accessed on 1 October 2020).

Singh, Rahul. 'India and the Market of War.' *The Hindustan Times* (Jalandhar), 5 February 2012.

Singh, Swarn. 'US Nuclear Non-Proliferation Policy: The Clinton Doctrine.' *Strategic Analysis* XVI, no. 6 (August 1993): 533.

SIPRI Yearbook 2011. *Armaments, Disarmament and International Security*. Oxford University Press. www.sipri.org.com.

Smith, Chris. *India's Ad Hoc Arsenal: Direction or Drift in Defence Policy?* Sweden: SIPRI, Oxford University Press, 1994.

Talbott, Strobe. *Engaging India: Diplomacy, Democracy, and the Bomb*. New Delhi: Penguin, 2004.

Talbott, Strobe. *Engaging India: Diplomacy, Democracy, and the Bomb*. New Delhi: Penguin, 2004.

Tellis, Ashley. *US-India Atomic Energy Cooperation: Strategic and Nonproliferation Implications*. Prepared Testimony to the Senate Foreign Relations Committee (26 April 2006), p. 7.

The Economic Times. 'Indo-US Nuclear Deal: India Gets NSG Waiver.' 6 September 2008.

The White House. *President's Statement on Strategic Partnership with India*. Washington, DC: The White House, 2004. http://georgebush-whitehouse. archives.gov/news/releases/2004/01/20040112-1.html (accessed on 1 October 2020).

Thomas, Caroline. *In Search of Security: The Third World in International Relations*, 1. Boulder, CO: Wheatsheaf Books, 1987.

Thornton, Thomas Perry. 'US Role in South-Asia.' In *Asian Security: Old Paradigms*, edited by Jasjit Singh, 159. New Delhi: Lancer Publishers, 1991.

U.S. Department of Defence. *The Technology Security Programme, A Report to the 99th Congress, Second Session*. Washington: U.S. Government Printing Office, 1989.

U.S. Department of State. 'U.S.–India Energy and Climate Cooperation.' *Diplomacy in Action* (31 July 2014).

———. *Remarks by President Bush in Signing of H. R. 5682-The US India Peaceful Atomic Energy Cooperation Act*. Washington, DC: U.S. Department of State, 2006. http://2001-2009.state.gov/p/sca/rls/2006/77928.htm.

———. *Security and Arms Control: The Search for a More Stable Peace* (Report Prepared for the Bureau of Public Affairs). Washington, DC: GPO, 1983.

Under Secretary of State, Armacost, Michel. *South-Asia and US Foreign Policy*. Speech given at World Affairs Council, (Philadelphia), 12 December 1984, in USIS, *Backgrounder* (New Delhi, 12 December 1984).

United States Information Service (USIS). *The Fact Sheet*. 11 November 2004. http:/newdelhi.usembassy.gov/wwwhpr11604a.html.

———. *Factsheet*. New Delhi: United States Information Service, 1990–2015a.

———. *Official Text*. New Delhi: United States Information Service, 1990–2015b.

———. *Backgrounder*. New Delhi: USIS, 1990–2016a.

———. *Wireless File*. New Delhi: USIS, 1990–2016b.

———. *Text of Prime Minister P. V. Narsimhan Rao's Speech*. New Delhi: USIS, 1994.

US Department of Commerce. *Overview of the Export Administration Program*. Washington, DC: Department of Commerce, undated.

van der Leer, Yeroen. *China's New Silk Route: The Long and Winding Road*. February 2016, www.pwc.com/gmc.

Vardarajan, Sidharth. 'The Nuclear Deal and "Minimum Deterrence".' *The Hindu* (New Delhi), 10 July 2006.

———. 'The Nuclear Deal and "Minimum Deterrence".' *The Hindu* (New Delhi), 10 July 2006.

Venkatramani, M. S. 'An Elusive Military Relationship.' *Frontline* (Chennai) (April 9, 1999), pp. 67–68.

Victor, Cecil. *India: The Security Dilemma*. New Delhi: Patriot Publishers, 1990.

Wienberger, Casper W. *The Technology Transfer Control Programs: A Report to the 98th Congress, Second Session*. Washington, DC: U.S. Department of Defense, February 1984.

Woolsey, Jammes. *Director of CIA's Testimony Before the Senate Governmental Affairs Committee on 24 February 1993* (Text in the Mimeographed Publication *Wireless File*). New Delhi: USIS, 1993.

World Nuclear Association. *Nuclear Power in India* (March 2010). http://www.world-nuclear.org/info/inf53.html.

———. *Nuclear Power in India*, 6–7. London: World Nuclear Association, December 2009. http://www.world-nuclear.org/info/inf53.html.

———. *Nuclear Power in India*. London: World Nuclear Association, March 2020. http://www.world-nuclear.org/information-library/country-profiles/countries-g-n/india.aspx.

———. *Nuclear Power in India*. London: World Nuclear Association, 2020. http://www.world-nuclear.org/information-library/country-profiles/countries-g-n/india.aspx (accessed on 1 October 2020).

Zuberi, Matin. *The Nuclear Deal: India Can't be Coerced*. 9 November 2005. https://www.orfonline.com.

SECONDARY SOURCES

Books

Appadorai, A., and M. S. Rajan. *India's Foreign Policy and Relations*. New Delhi: South-Asian Publishers Pvt. Ltd., 1988.

Ayoob, Mohammed. *The Third World Security Predicament: State Making, Regional Conflict, and the International System*. Boulder, London: Lynne Publishers, 1996.

Babbage, Ross, and Sandy Gordon. *India's Strategic Future*. Oxford: Macmillan Academic& Professional Ltd., 1992.

Bajpai, U. S. *India's Security: The Politico-Strategic Environment*. New Delhi: Lancer Publishers, 1982.

Bajpai, Kanti, and Amitabh Mattoo, eds. *Engaged Democracies: India–US Relations in the 21st Century*. New Delhi: Har Anand Publishers, 2000.

Bajpai, Kanti P., P. R. Chari, Pervaiz Iqbal Cheema, Stephen P. Cohen, and Sumit Ganguly. *Brasstacks and Beyond: Perception and Management Crisis in South Asia*. New Delhi: Manohar Publishers, 1995.

Bandopadhyaya, J. *The Making of India's Foreign Policy: Determinants, Institutions, Processes and Personalities*. New Delhi: Oxford University Press, 1984.

Basu, P. *The Press and Foreign Policy of India*. New Delhi: Lancers, 2003.

Baylis, J. Smith, and P. S. Owens. *The Globalization of World Politics: An Introduction to International Relations*. New Delhi: Oxford University Press, 2014.

Beaton, Leonard. *The Reform of Power: A Proposal for an International Security System*. London: Chatto & Windus, 1972.

Bertsch, Gary K., Seema Gahlaut, and Anupam Srivastava, eds. *Engaging India: US Strategic Relations with the World's Largest Democracy*. New York, NY: Routledge, 1999.

Bhambhari, C. P. *The Foreign Policy of India*. New Delhi: Sterling, 1987.

Bindra, S. S. *Indo-Pak Relations*. New Delhi: Deep & Deep Publications, 1984.

Brands, William J. *India, Pakistan and the Great Powers*. New York, NY: Praeger, 1977.

Brands, H. W. *India and the United States: The Cold War Peace*. Boston, MA: Twayne Publishers, 1994.

Brines, Russel. *The Indo-Pakistani Conflict*. London: Pall Mall Press, 1968.

Burrows, William E., and Robert Winderm. *Critical Mass: The Dangerous Race for Super Weapons in a Fragmenting World*. New York, NY: Simon & Schuster, 1994.

Buzan, Barry. *People, States and Fear: The National Security Problem in the International Relations*. New Delhi: Wheatsheaf Books, 1987.

Buzan, Barry, and Gowher Rizvi, eds. *South-Asian Insecurity and the Great Powers*. London: Macmillan, 1986.

Cameron, F. 'India and the EU: A Long Road Ahead'. In *Indian Foreign Policy in a Unipolar World*, edited by H. V. Pant, 209–227. New Delhi: Routledge, 2009.

Chari, P. R. *Indo-Pak Nuclear Standoff: The Role of the US*. New Delhi: Manohar Publications, 1995.

Chatterjee, A. *International Relations Today*. New Delhi: Dorling Kindersley, 2010.

Chaulia, S. *Modi Doctrine: The Foreign Policy of India's Prime Minister*. New Delhi: Bloomsbury India, 2016.

Chellaney, Brahma. *Nuclear Proliferation: The U.S.-Indian Conflict*. New Delhi: Orient Longman Ltd., 1993.

———. *Regional Security and the Diffusion of Advanced Weapons and Technologies to India, Pakistan and China*. New Delhi: Centre for Policy Research, 1994.

Chopra, Ashwani Kumar. *India's Policy on Disarmament*. New Delhi: ABC Publishers, 1984.

Chopra, Surendra, ed. *Studies in India's Foreign Policy*. Amritsar: Guru Nanak Dev University Press, 1983.

Chopra, Pran. *The Crisis of Foreign Policy: Perspective and Issues*. New Delhi: Wheeler Publishing, 1993.

Chopra, V. D. *Pentagon's Shadow Over India*. New Delhi: Patriot Publishers, 1985.

Clinton, Bill, and Al Gore. *Putting People First: How We Can All Change America*. New York, NY: Praeger, 1992.

Cohen, Stephen P., and Richard L. Park. *India: An Emergent Power?* New York, NY: Crane Russak, 1978.

Cohen, Stephen P., ed. *The Security of South-Asia: American and Indian Perspectives*. New Delhi: Vistaar Publishers, 1988.

———. *Nuclear Proliferation in South-Asia: The Prospects for Arms Control*. Boulder, CO: West View Press, 1991.

Cortright, David, and Amitabh Mattoo, eds. *India and the Bomb: Public Opinion and Nuclear Options*. Notre Dame: University of Notre Dame Press, 1996.

Crunden, Robert M., Manoj Joshi, and R. V. R. Chandrasekhar Rao. *New Perspectives on America and South Asia*. Delhi: Chanakya Publications, 1984.

Damodaran, A. K., and U. S. Bajpai. *India's Foreign Policy: The Indira Gandhi Years*. New Delhi: Radiant Publishers, 1990.

De, P., and K. Iyengar. *Developing Economic Corridors in South Asia*. New Delhi: Asian Development Bank, 2014.

Desai, M. 'India and China: An Essay in Comparative Political Economy'. In *India's and China's Recent Experience with Reform and Growth*, edited by W. Tseng and D. Cowen, 1–22. London: Palgrave Macmillan, 2005.

Devotta, N. 'When Individuals, States, and Systems Collide India's Foreign Policy Towards Sri Lanka'. In *India's Foreign Policy Retrospect and Prospect*, edited by Sumit Ganguly. New Delhi: Oxford, 2016.

Dhar, Panalal. *India and Her Neighbours and Foreign Policy*. New Delhi: Deep & Deep Publications, 1991.

Dixit, J. N. *My South Block Years: Memoirs of a Foreign Secretary*. New Delhi: UBS Publishers, 1996.

———. *Across Borders: Fifty Years of India's Foreign Policy*. New Delhi: Thomson Press, 1998.

———. *Indian Foreign Service: History and Challenge*. New Delhi: Konark, 2005.

Dutt, V. P. *India's Foreign Policy*. New Delhi: Vikas Publishers, 1989.

———. *India and the World*. New Delhi: Sanchar Publications, 1990.

———. *India's Foreign Policy in Changing World*. New Delhi: Vikas Publishing House, 1999.

———. *India's Foreign Policy Since Independence*. New Delhi: National Book Trust of India, 2015.

Dyke, Vernon Van. *International Politics*. New York, NY: Appleton-Century Crofts, 1957.

Elleman, B., S. Kotkin, and C. Schofield. *Beijing's Power and China's Borders: Twenty Neighbours in Asia*. New York, NY: Routledge, 2014.

Frankel, Francine R., ed. *Bridging the Non-Proliferation Divide: The United States and India*. New Delhi: Konark Publishers, 1995.

Fukuyama, F. *Nation-Building: Beyond Afghanistan and Iraq*. Baltimore, MD: JHU Press, 2006.

Ganguly, Sumit. *The Origins of War in South Asia: The India–Pakistan Conflicts Since 1947*. Boulder, CO: West View Press, 1993.

Glazer, Sulochana R., and Nathan Glazer, eds. *Conflicting Images: India and The United States*. Riverdale Park, MD: Riverdale Co. Publishing, 1989.

Gopal, Servepalli, ed. *Jawaharlal Nehru: An Anthology*. Delhi: Oxford University Press, 1980.

Gordon, Sandy. *India's Rise to Power in the Twentieth Century and Beyond*. London: Macmillan, 1995.

Gould, Harold A., and Sumit Ganguly, eds. *The Hope and the Reality: U.S.-Indian Relations from Roosevelt to Reagan*. Boulder, CO: Westview Press, 1992.

Gross, Feliks. *Foreign Policy Analysis*. New York, NY: Praeger Publishers, 1954.

Grover, Varinder, ed. *International Relations and Foreign Policy of India*, vol. VII, USA and Foreign Policy of India. New Delhi: Deep & Deep Publications, 1992.

Guha, R. *India After Gandhi: The History of the World's Largest Democracy*. New Delhi: Pan Macmillan India, 2017.

Haftendorn, Helga, and Jakob Schissler. *The Reagan Administration: A Reconstruction of American Strength*. New York, NY: de Gruyter, 1988.

Harrison, Selig S., and Geoffrey Kemp. *India and America After the Cold War*. Washington, DC: Carnegie Endowment for International Peace, 1993.

Hasiao, Gene T., and Michael Witunski, eds. *Sino-American Normalization and Its Policy Implications*. New York, NY: Praeger & Southern Illinois University, 1983.

Healy, Katheen. *Rajiv Gandhi: The Years of Power*. New Delhi: Vikas Publishing House, 1989.

Hyman, A. *Afghanistan Under Soviet Domination, 1964–91*. London: Springer, 2016.

Holsti, K. J. *International Politics: A Framework for Analysis*. New Delhi: Prentice Hall of India, 1995.

Jacobson, Harold K. *Networks of Interdependence: International Organizations and the Global Political System*. New York, NY: Alfred A. Knopf, 1979.

Jain, B. M. *India and the United States, 1961–63*. Delhi: Radiant Publishers, 1987a.

———. *South-Asia: India and the United States*. Jaipur: RBSA Publishers, 1987b.

———. *Reflections on India's Foreign Policy*. Jaipur: RBSA Publishers, 1989.

———, ed. *International System and Great Power Relationship*. Jaipur: INA Shree Publishers, 1998.

———. *India-US Relations in the Age of Uncertainty*. New Delhi: Routledge India, 2016.

Jetly, Nancy, ed. *India's Foreign Policy: Challenges and Prospects*. New Delhi: Vikas Publishing House, 1999.

Kamath, P. M., ed. *Indo–US Relations: Dynamics of Change*. New Delhi: South-Asian Publishers, 1987.

Kapur, Ashok. *India's Nuclear Option: Atomic Diplomacy Decision Making*. New York, NY: Praeger, 1979.

———. *The South Asian Nuclear Non-Proliferation Debate: Issues, Interests and Strategies of Change* (Project Report No. PR-642). Ontario: Directorate of Strategic Analysis, 1993.

Kapur, K. D. *Nuclear Non-Proliferation Diplomacy: Nuclear Power Programme in the Third World*. New Delhi: Lancer Books, 1993.

Kapur, Harish. *India's Foreign Policy: Shadows and Substance (1947–94)*. New Delhi: SAGE Publications, 1994.

Karat, P. *Subordinate Ally: The Nuclear Deal and India–US Strategic Relations*. New Delhi: Left Word, 2007.

Kashyap, Subhash. *National Policy Studies*. New Delhi: Lok Sabha Secretariat and Tata McGraw Hills, 1990.

Kaul, T. N. *Ambassadors Need Not Lie*. New Delhi: Lancer International, 1988.

Kaul, B. M. *India and the Super Powers*. New Delhi: Pulse Publishers, 1989.

Kaushik, Surendranath, Rajan Mohan, and Ramakant, eds. *India and the South Asia*. New Delhi: South Asian Publishers, 1987.

Keohane, Robert O., and Joseph S. Nye. *Power and Independence*. Boston, MA: Little, Brown, 1977.

Kheli Tahir, Shirin R. *India, Pakistan and the U.S.: Breaking with the Past*. New York, NY: Council on Foreign Relations, 1997.

Kirk, J. A. 'The Evolution of India's Nuclear Policies'. In *India's Foreign Policy Retrospect and Prospect*, edited by S. Ganguly. New Delhi: Oxford, 2016.

Krishnan, Unni T. V. *The Unfriendly Friends: India and America*. New Delhi: I.B.C. Publishers, 1974.

Kumar, Mahender. *Theoretical Aspects of International Politics*. Agra: Shivlal Agarwal Co., 1984.

Kumar, Rajesh. 'Nuclear Disaster and Sustainability of Indian Agriculture'. In *Disaster Risk Management in Agriculture*, edited by Huong Ha, R. S. Fernando, and Sanjeev Kumar Mahajan. New York, NY: Business Expert Press, 2019.

Kumar, Rajesh. 'Mainstreaming Nuclear Disaster Risk Reduction in India'. In *Disaster Risk Reduction: Community Resilience and Responses*, edited by Bhupinder Zutshi and Ahmad Akbaruddin. Gateway East: Palgrave Macmillan, Springer Nature Co., 2019.

Kumar, Satish, ed. *Yearbook on India's Foreign Policy, 1985–1993*. New Delhi: SAGE Publications, 1987–1993.

Kumaraswamy, P. R. *India's Israel Policy*. New York, NY: Columbian University Paper, 2010.

Kux, Dennis. *Estranged Democracies: India and the United States, 1941–91*. New Delhi: SAGE Publications, 1993.

Lerche, Charles O. Jr., and Abdul A Said. *Concepts of International Politics*. Englewood Cliffs, NJ: Prentice-Hall, 1963.

Limyae, S. P. *U.S.-Indian Relations: The Pursuit of Accommodation*. Boulder, CO: Westview Press, 1993.

Lippman, Walter. *United States Foreign Policy: Shield the Republic*. Boston, MA: Little, Brown, 1943.

Kathpalia, P. N. *National Security Perspectives*. New Delhi: Lancer International, 1986.

Mahapatra, Chintamani. *Indo-U.S. Relations into the 21st Century*. New Delhi: Knowledge World, 1999.

Malhotra, I. 'Introduction'. In *Shedding Shibboleths: India's Evolving Strategic Outlook*, edited by K. Subrahmanyam. New Delhi: Wordsmiths, 2005.

Malone, D. M. *Does the Elephant Dance? Contemporary Indian Foreign Policy*. New York, NY: Oxford University Press, 2011.

Malone, M. *The Oxford Handbook of Indian Foreign Policy*. New Delhi: Oxford University Press, 2016.

Mansingh, Lalit, ed. *India's Foreign Policy: Agenda for the 21st Century*, vols. I & II. New Delhi: Konark Publishers and Foreign Services Institute, 1997.

Mansingh, Surjit S. *India's Search for Power: Indira Gandhi's Foreign Policy, 1966–82*. New Delhi: SAGE Publications, 1984.

Mellor, John W., ed. *India: A Rising Middle Power*. New Delhi: Select Service Syndicate, 1981.

Menon, Shivshankar. *Choices: Inside the Making of India's Foreign Policy*. London: Penguin, 2018.

Menon, V. P. *The Story of the Integration of the Indian States*. Bombay: Orient Longmans Ltd., 1961.

Mohite, Dilip H. *Indo–US Relations: Issues in Conflict and Cooperation*. New Delhi: South-Asian Publishers, 1995.

Moshaver, Ziba. *Nuclear Weapons Proliferation in the Indian Subcontinent*. London: Macmillan, 1991.

Nair, Vijai K. *NPT Extension Conference: Validity and Efficacy of Nuclear Weapon States Initiatives*. New Delhi: Forum for Strategic and Security Studies, 1994.

Narayanan, K. R. *India and America: Essay in Understanding*. New Delhi: Dialogue Publishers, 1984.

Nath, D. J. *Indian Foreign Service: History and Challenge*. Delhi: Konark Publishers, 2005.

Nayar, Baldev Raj. *American Geo-politics and India*. New Delhi: Manohar Book, 1976.

Nehru, J. *The Discovery of India*. New Delhi: Penguin India, 2008.

Nixon, Richard. *The Memoirs of Richard Nixon*. London: OUP, 1978.

Nugent, Nicholas. *Rajiv Gandhi: Son of a Dynasty*. London: BBC Books, 1990.

Nye, J. *Soft Power: The Means to Success in World Politics*. New York, NY: Public Affairs, 2004.

Ollapally, D. M. 'India and Russia Renewing the Relationship'. In *Indian Foreign Policy in a Unipolar World*, edited by H. V. Pant. New Delhi: Routledge, 2009.

Ollapally, Deepa, and S. Rajagopal. *Nuclear Cooperation: Challenges and Cooperation*. Bangalore: National Institute of Advanced Studies, 1997.

Palmer, Norman D. *The United States and India: The Dimensions of Influence*. New York, NY: Praeger, 1984.

Pande, Savita. *Pakistan's Nuclear Policy*. New Delhi: B. R. Publishing, 1991.

Pant, H. V. *Contemporary Debates in Indian Foreign and Security Policy: India Negotiates Its Rise in The International System*. London: Springer, 2008.

Pant, H. V. *Indian Foreign Policy in a Unipolar World*. New Delhi: Routledge India, 2012.

Pant, H. V. 'India–Japan Relations a Slow, But Steady, Transformation'. In *India's Foreign Policy*, edited by Sumit Ganguly. New Delhi: OUP, 2016.

Pant, H. V. *Indian Foreign Policy: An Overview*. New Delhi: Strategic Books, 2016.

Paranjpe, Srikant. *U.S. Non-Proliferation Policy in Action: South Asia*. New Delhi: Sterling Publishers, 1987.

Pathak, K. K. *Nuclear Policy of India: A Third World Perspective*. New Delhi: Geetanjali Publishers, 1980.

Perkovich, George. *India's Nuclear Bomb: The Impact on Global Proliferation*. New Delhi: Oxford University Press, 2000.

Pierre, Andrew J. *The Global Politics of Arms Sales*. Princeton, NJ: Princeton University Press, 1982.

Poulose, T. T., ed. *Perspectives of India's Nuclear Policy*. New Delhi: Young Asian Publishers, 1978.

———. *The CTBT and the Rise of Nuclear Nationalism in India*. New Delhi: Lancer Books, 1996.

Prasad, Bimal, ed. *India's Foreign Policy: Studies in Continuity and Change*. New Delhi: Vikas Publishing House, 1979.

Rana, A. P., ed. *Four Decades of Indo–US Relations: A Commemorative Retrospective*. New Delhi: Har Anand Publications, 1994.

Rasgotra, M. K., V. D. Chopra, and K. P. Misra. *India's Foreign Policy in the 1990s*. New Delhi: Patriot Publishers, 1996.

Rao, K. R. *India, US and Pakistan: A Triangular Relationship*. Bombay: Himalayan Publishing House, 1985.

Rose, Leo E., and Eric Gonsalves, ed. *Toward a New World Order: Adjusting India-U.S. Relations*. Berkeley, CA: University of California, 1992.

Rose, Leo E., and Noor A. Hussain, ed. *United States–Pakistan Forum: Relations with the Major Powers*. Lahore: Vanguard Books, 1987.

Rosenau, James N. 'National Interest'. In *International Encyclopedia of Social Sciences*, edited by David L. Sills. New York, NY: Macmillan, 1968.

Rosenau, James N., Thompson Gavin Boyd, and W. Kenneth, ed. *World Politics: An Introduction*. London: OUP, 1976.

Rudolph, Llyod, and Susanne, eds. *The Regional Imperative: US Foreign Policy Towards South Asian States*. Atlantic Highlands, NJ: Atlantic Highlands, 1981.

Schaffer, Howard B. *Chester Bowles: New Dealer in the Cold War*. New Delhi: Prentice Hall of India, 1994.

Signer, H. W., ed. *Technology Transfer by Multinational*. New Delhi: Ashish Publishing House, 1988.

Singh, A. K. *Impact of American Aid on Indian Economy*. Bombay: Vora & Co., 1973.

Singh, Jasjit, ed. *India and Pakistan: The Crisis of Relationship*. New Delhi: Lancer International, 1990.

———. *Asian Security: Old Paradigms and New Challenges*. New Delhi: Lancer International & IDSA, 1991.

———. *Indo–US Relations in a Changing World*. New Delhi: Lancer International, and IDSA, 1992.

———. *The Roads Ahead: Indo-U.S. Strategic Dialogue*. New Delhi: Lancer Publishers and IDSA, 1994.

———. *Asian Security in the 21st Century*. New Delhi: Knowledge World & IDSA, 1999.

———. *Nuclear India*. New Delhi: Knowledge World & IDSA, 1999.

Singh, Jaswant. *Defending India*. Bangalore: Macmillan Press, 1999.

Sinha, A. *Indian Foreign Policy: Challenges and Opportunities*. New Delhi: Academic Foundation, 2007.

Smith, Chris. *India's Ad-hoc Arsenal*. Sweden: SIPRI, Oxford University Press, 1994.

Spector, Leonard S. *Nuclear Proliferation Today: The Spread of Nuclear Weapons.* New York, NY: Vintage Books, 1984.

———. *The Undeclared Bomb.* Cambridge: Ballinger, 1988.

Subrahmanyan, K., ed. *India and the Nuclear Challenge.* New Delhi: Lancer International & IDSA, 1986.

———. *Security in a Changing World.* New Delhi: B. R. Publishing, 1990.

Sultan, Tanvir. *Indo-US Relations: A Study of Foreign Policies.* New Delhi: Deep & Deep Publications, 1983.

Tharoor, S. *The Paradoxical Prime Minister.* New Delhi: Aleph Book Company, 2018.

Thomas, Raju G. C. *The Great Power Triangle and Asian Security.* Lexington, KY: Lexington Books, 1983.

———, ed. *Perspectives on Kashmir: The Roots of Conflict in South Asia.* Boulder: West View Press, 1992.

Timothy, George, ed. *Security in Southern-Asia 2: India and the Great Powers.* Aldershot: Gower Publishers Co., 1984.

Tiwari, S. C. *Indo-US Relations 1947–76.* New Delhi: Radiant Publishers, 1977.

United States Information Service. *India and The United States* (Reprints). New Delhi: USIS, 1987.

Vinod, M. J. *United States Foreign Policy Towards India: A Diagnosis of the American Approach.* New Delhi: Lancer Books, 1991.

Yadava, Leela. *US–Pakistan Relations.* Kurukshetra: Kurukshetra University Press, 1979.

Articles

Aneja, Atul. 'Limits to Defence Ties'. *The Hindu*, 9 August 1995.

Arnett, Eric. 'Military Technology: The Case of India'. *SIPRI Yearbook*, 343–67. Stockholm: SIPRI, Oxford University Press, 1994.

Bajpai, K. Shanker. 'India in 1991: New Beginnings'. *Asian Survey* XXXII, no. 2 (1992): 215.

Ballard, Steward J. 'Technology Transfer Negotiations: Indocentric Perceptions'. *Strategic Analysis* XVI, no. 5 (1993): 609–20.

Beyer, Lisa. 'The Rush to India: A Once Disdainful Giant is Attracting Foreign Investments as Never Before'. *Times Chicago* 133, no. 24 (1989): 64–65.

Bhattacharya, S. S. 'Indian Ocean: Towards a Zone of Peace'. *Strategic Analysis* XIII, no. VIII (1990): 933.

Bhullar, Pritam. 'Defense Ties with United States of America'. *Tribune*, 21 September 1995.

Boltersdorf, Jorg. 'The Reagan Administration's Policy on Technology Controls: The Conflict of Economic Interests and Security Principles'. In *The Reagan Administration: A Reconstruction of American Strength*, edited by Helga Haftendorn and Jakob Schissler, 159–75. New York, NY: Walter De Gruyter, 1988.

Bose, Tarun C. 'Indo-US Security Relations, 1965–1990'. In *Four Decades Indo-US Relations: A Commemorative Retrospective*, edited by A. P. Rana, 108–109. New Delhi: Har Anand Publications, 1994.

———. 'Nuclear Proliferation: A Case Study of Pakistan'. *Punjab Journal of Politics* VII, no. I (2009): 34.

Caputo, John A. *The Indo-Soviet Relationship and How It Affects US Military Assistance to India*. Unpublished Paper Submitted to the National War College, National Defense University, Washington, February 1987, p. 19 cited in S. P. Limyae, *US-Indian Relations: The Pursuit of Accommodation*, 182. Boulder, CO: Westview Press, 1993.

Chakrapani, R. 'US Offers Help to Modernize Defense'. *The Hindu*, 9 March 1985.

Chakravarty, Nikhil. 'Indo-US Perspective: A Historical View'. *Man & Development* VII, no. 3 (1985): 61.

Chanda, Nayan. 'A Thaw with Washington'. *Far Eastern Economic Review* (1984): 21.

———. 'Hi-Tech Diplomacy: U.S. Technology Sales to India and China to Reap Political Gains'. *Far Eastern Economic Review* 131, no. 8 (1986): 36–37.

Chaudhary, Rahul Roy. 'India's Security Policy'. *Strategic Analysis* XIX, no. 2 (1996): 183–94.

Cheema, S. A. 'India–Iran Relations: Progress, Challenges and Prospects'. *India Quarterly: A Journal of International Affairs* (2016).

Chellaney, Brahma. 'Non-Proliferation: An Indian Critique of U.S. Exports Controls'. *ORBIS* (Summer 1994): 441.

———. 'The Implications of Wassenaar Group'. In *Nuclear Cooperation: Challenges and Cooperation*, edited by Deepa Ollapally and S. Rajagopal, 183–94. Bangalore: National Institute of Advanced Studies, 1997.

Cheriyan, J. 'From Non-alignment to Strategic Partnership'. *Frontline* 34, no. 17 (2017): 90–95. https://www.google.com/amp/s/frontline.thehindu.com/cover-story/from-nonalignment-to-strategic-partnership/article9820890.ece/amp/ (accessed on 1 October 2020).

Chidambram, R., and V. Ashok. 'Embargo Regimes and Impact'. In *Nuclear Cooperation: Challenges and Cooperation*, edited by Deepa Ollapally and S. Rajagopal, 61–76. Bangalore: National Institute of Advanced Studies, 1997.

Clark, William Jr. *India and the United States: Closer Together in a Shrinking World*. New Delhi: United States Information Service, 1982.

Clausen, Peter A. 'Non-proliferation Illusions: Tarapur in Retrospect'. *ORBIS* (Fall 1983): 744–45.

Cohen, Stephen P. 'South Asia and United States Military Policy'. In *The Regional Imperative: US Foreign Policy Towards South Asian States*, edited by Llyod and Susanne Rudolph, 113. Atlantic Highlands, NJ: Atlantic Highlands, 1981.

———. 'U.S.-Pakistan Security Relations'. In *United States-Pakistan Relations*, edited by Leo E. Rose and Noor A. Hussain, 25. Berkeley, CA: Institute of East Asian Studies, 1985.

———. 'The Reagan Administration and India'. In *The Hope and the Reality: U.S.-Indian Relations from Roosevelt to Reagan*, edited by Harold A. Gould and Sumit Ganguly, 139–53. Boulder, CO: Westview Press, 1992.

Cohen, Stephen P. 'Nuclear Neighbours'. In *Nuclear Proliferation in South-Asia: The Prospects for Arms Control*, edited by Stephen Cohen, 1–22. Boulder, CO: West View Press, 1991.

Deva, Yashwant. 'Dual Use Information Technology Criticalities and Denial'. In *Technical Brochure, Info-Tech96*, 133–37. New Delhi: G S Army HQs, 1996.

Dhar, M. K. 'The Human Rights Clash in Geneva'. *The Hindustan Times*, 19 February 1994.

———. 'Perry's Visit Marks a New Era in Indo-US Relations'. *The Hindustan Times*, 16 January 1995.

Dhume, S. 'India Is Falling behind China in an Asian Arms Race'. *Wall Street Journal*, 7 February 2019. https://www.wsj.com/articles/india-%20is-falling-behind-china-in-an-asian-arms-race-11549583595 (accessed on 1 October 2020).

Diamond, Larry. 'Promoting Democracy'. *Foreign Policy*, no. 87 (1992): 26–27.

Dixit, Abha. 'India, Pakistan and the Great Powers'. In *India and Pakistan: The Crisis of Relationship*, edited by Jasjit Singh, 16–49. New Delhi: Lancer International, 1990.

Dixit, J. N. 'Clinton's Presidency: A Mid-Term Appraisal'. *Indian Express*, 7 March 1995.

———. 'India's Security Concerns and Their Impact'. In *India's Foreign Policy: Agenda for the 21st Century*, edited by Lalit Mansingh, vols. I & II. New Delhi: Konark Publishers and Foreign Services Institute, 1997.

Dua, H. K. 'Kashmir: Dangerous Curves Ahead'. *The Hindustan Times*, 1 October 1993.

FE Online. 'PM Modi's Maldives Visit: Maritime Security in Indian Ocean and Development Initiatives to be Focus'. *The Financial Express*, 7 June 2019. https://www.financialexpress.com/india-news/pm-modis-maldives-visit-maritime-security-in-indian-ocean-and-development-initiatives-to-be-focus/1600768/ (accessed on 1 October 2020).

Fifield, Russel H. 'The Introductory Course in International Relations'. *American Political Science Review* (1948): 1190.

Fontaine, R. 'U.S.-India Relations: The Trump Administration's Foreign Policy Bright Spot'. *War on The Rocks*, 24 January 2019. https://warontherocks.com/2019/01/u-s-india-relations-the-trump-administrations-foreign-policy-bright-spot/ (accessed on 1 October 2020).

Freeman, Charles W. 'The Process of Rapprochement: Achievements and Problems'. In *Sino-American Normalization and Its Policy Implications*, edited by Gene T. Hasiao and Michael Witunski, 1–27. New York, NY: Praeger & Southern Illinois University, 1983.

Ganguly, Sumit. 'Avoiding War in Kashmir'. *Foreign Affairs* 89, no. 5 (1990–1991): 67–73.

Ganguly, Sumit. 'Security Issues in South Asia: A Framework for Conflict Resolution'. In *The Roads Ahead: Indo-U.S. Strategic Dialogue*, edited by Jasjit Singh, 23. New Delhi: Lancer Publishers, 1994.

Goel, R. P. 'Propelling a "Cryo"'. *Hindustan Times*, 14 March 1994.

Gopalan, Sita. 'Indo-US Relations: Cause for Optimism'. *Strategic Analysis* 15, no. 5 (1992): 365–77.

Hagerty, Davin T. 'Nuclear Deterrence in South-Asia: The 1990 Indo-Pakistani Crisis'. *International Security* 20, no. 3 (1995–1996): 79–114.

Hagerty, Davin T. 'South-Asia's Nuclear Balance'. *Current History* 95, no. 600 (1996): 79–114.

Harrison, Selig S. 'India, Pakistan and the US: Case History of a Mistake'. *The New Republic* 141, nos. 6–7 (1959): 10.

Hazari, K. K. 'National Security: Future Threat & Challenges'. *AGNI* 2, no. 1 (1996): 1–16.

Hersh, Semour M. 'On the Nuclear Edge'. *New Yorker* (1993): 56–73.

Iyengar, R. 'The US and India are Heading for a Showdown on Trade'. *CNN*, 13 February 2019. https://www.google.co.in/amp/s/amp.cnn.com/cnn/2019/02/13/economy/wilbur-ross-india-us-trade/index.html (accessed on 1 October 2020).

Jagmohan. 'Kashmir: Illusion and Reality'. *The Hindustan Times*, 7 September 1994.

Jain, B. M. 'Indo-US Relations: Prisoners of Strategic Compulsions'. In *International System and Great Power Relationship*, edited by B. M. Jain, 121–44. Jaipur: INA Shree Publishers, 1998.

Jaishankar, D. *Survey of India's Strategic Community*. The Brookings Institution, 1 March 2019. https://www.brookings.edu/research/%20introduction-survey-of-indias-strategic-community/ (accessed on 1 October 2020).

Jame's Defense Weekly. 'LCA Programme Talks Set as USA and India Move Closer'. *Jame's Defense Weekly* 6, no. 8 (1986): 1089.

Jha, N. K. 'Reviving U.S.-India Relationship in Changing International Order'. *Asian Survey* XXXIV, no. 12 (1994a): 1035–1046.

———. 'India and the United States: Pursuits and Limits of Accommodation'. *Strategic Analysis* XVII, no. 1 (1994b): 89–107.

Joseph, J. 'What is the Doklam Issue All About?' *The Hindu*, 27 January 2018. https://www.google.com/amp/s/www.thehindu.com/news/national/what-is-the-doklam-issue-all-about/article22536937.ece/amp/ (accessed on 1 October 2020).

Joshi, Manoj. 'Dousing the Fire? Indian Missile Programme and the United States' Non-Proliferation Policy'. *Strategic Analysis* XVII, no. 5 (1994): 567.

Joshi, Manoj. 'Prithvi May have been Deployed'. *The Times of India*, 22 June 1994.

Kamath, P. M. 'The End of the Cold War: Implications for Indian and American Relations'. *India Quarterly A Journal of International Affairs* (January–June 1993): 63.

Karnad, Bharat. 'LCA Venture Expensive: US Expert'. *The Hindustan Times*, 24 February 1986.

Katju, V. 'India's New Foreign Secretary Has Inherited a Structural Imbalance He Needs to Fix'. *The Wire*, 2018. https://thewire.in/diplomacy/virtual-foreign-policy-advisor-pm-jaishankar-left-enough-time-mea-tasks (accessed on 1 October 2020).

Katyal, K. K. 'Indo-US Defence Relations'. *The Hindu*, 30 March 1992.

Kaushik, Brij Mohan. 'India's Nuclear Policy'. *International Studies* 17, nos. 3–4 (1992): 23–24.

Kumar, Rajesh. 'U.S. and South Asia in the New Millennium'. *Pakistan Horizon* 53, no. 1 (2000): 43.

———. 'Indo-US Strategic Partnership on High Trajectory'. *World Focus* XXXV, no. 12 (2014): 134–41.

———. 'Indo-U.S. Energy Cooperation Under Modi Government'. *World Focus* 36, no. 5 (2015): 74–78.

———. 'Indo-U.S. Strategic Partnership: Road Map Ahead Under Donald Trump'. *World Focus* 37, no. 12 (2016): 53–60.

———. 'Revisiting Indo-U.S. Nuclear Agreement of 2008 Under Prime Minister Modi and President Trump'. *World Focus* 38, no. 468 (2018): 62–70.

———. 'India's Foreign Policy Under PM Modi 2.0: Continuity and Change'. *World Focus* 39, no. 480 (2019): 69–76.

Kumar, Satish. 'Limits of Indo-US Cooperation'. *The Tribune*, 18 September 1986.

Kumar, Sumita. 'The Human Rights Issue in Pakistan's Kashmir Stratagem'. *Strategic Analysis* XVII, no. 107 (1994).

Litwak, Robert. 'The Soviet Union in India's Security Perspectives'. In *Security in Southern-Asia 2: India and the Great Powers*, edited by Timothy George, 127. Aldershot: Gower Publishers Co., 1984.

Mahapatra, Chintamani. 'Looking Indo-US Relations in a Changing World'. *Strategic Analysis* XIV, no. 4 (1991): 381–95.

———. 'Indo-US Defence Cooperation'. *Strategic Analysis* XIV, no. 8 (1991): 656–79.

———. 'Indo-US Dialogue'. *Strategic Analysis* XV, no. 2 (1992): 113–23.

———. 'Cryogenic Technology Deal: American Pressure Tactic'. *Strategic Analysis* (1992): 312–13.

———. 'New Trends in Indo-American Relations'. *Strategic Analysis* XVII, no. 11 (1995): 1533–47.

Majumdar, Madhumita. 'The Vexed Issue of Human Rights'. *The Hindustan Times*, 20 April 1994.

Mansingh, Surjit S. 'Rajiv Gandhi and Indo-US Relations'. *Mainstream* XXIV, nos. 9 & 10 (1985): 49–52.

Mansingh, Surjit S. 'New Directions in Indo-US Relations'. In *Yearbook of India's Foreign Policy, 1985–1986*, edited by Satish Kumar, 185–165. New Delhi: SAGE Publications, 1987.

MEA. *EU-India Agenda for Action-2020, Brussels*. New Delhi: Government of India, 2016.

———. *India-China Relations* (January 2016). https://www.mea.gov.in/Portal/ForeignRelation/China_Jan_2016.pdf (accessed on 1 October 2020).

———. *India Bangladesh Relations* (September 2017). https://www.mea.gov.in/Portal/ForeignRelation/Bangladesh (accessed on 1 October 2020).

MEA. *India–Nepal Relations* (November 2017). https://www.mea.gov.in/Portal/ ForeignRelation/Nepal_November_2017_new.pdf (accessed on 1 October 2020).

———. *India-Sri Lanka Relations* (November 2017). https://www.mea.gov.in/ Portal/ForeignRelation/Sri_Lanka__NEW.pdf (accessed on 1 October 2020).

Mellor, John W., and Philip O. Oldenberg. 'India and the United States'. In *India a Rising Middle Power*, edited by John W. Mellor, 5. New Delhi: Select Service Syndicate, 1981.

Menon, N. C. 'US Proposes to Improve Defence Ties with India'. *The Hindustan Times*, 11 November 1994.

Menon, R. 'A Mismatch of Nuclear Doctrines'. *The Hindu*, 2014. https://www. google.com/amp/s/www.thehindu.com/opinion/op-ed/a-mismatch-of-nuclear-doctrines/article5602609.ece/amp/ (accessed on 1 October 2020).

Merrill, Dennis. 'The Political Economy of Foreign Aid: The Case of India, 1947–63'. In *Four Decades of Indo-US Relations: A Commemorative Retrospective*, edited by A. P. Rana, 222–23. New Delhi: Har Anand Publications, 1994.

Mir, S. A. 'India Iran Relations During UPA 1st and 2nd Mutual Cooperation, Constraints and Challenges'. *International Journal of Research* (2016): 195–200.

Mistry, D. 'Diplomacy, Domestic Politics and the US-India Nuclear Agreement'. *Asian Survey* 46, no. 5 (2006): 678–98.

Mohan, Raja C. 'Non-Proliferation, Disarmament and the Security Link'. In *Nuclear Cooperation: Challenges and Cooperation*, edited by Deepa Ollapally and S. Rajagopal, 13–20. Bangalore: National Institute of Advanced Studies, 1997.

Mohan, Raja C. 'India's Relations with the Great Powers: Need for Reorientation'. In *Asian Security in the 21st Century*, edited by Jasjit Singh, 79–95. New Delhi: Knowledge World & IDSA, 1999.

Mukherjee, A. 'The Evolution of India's Israel Policy: Continuity, Change, and Compromise Since 1922'. *Israel Affairs* (2017): 990–92.

Mukherjee, Dilip, 'U.S. Weaponry for India'. *Asian Survey* XXVII, no. 6 (1987): 595–614.

Muni, S. D. 'Indo-US Relations: The Pakistan Factor'. *Man & Development* VII, no. 3 (1985): 9–27.

———. 'Global Developments: Implications for South-Asia'. In *India and Pakistan: The Crisis of Relationship*, edited by Jasjit Singh, 1–15. New Delhi: Lancer International and IDSA, 1990.

———. 'India and the Post-Cold War World'. *Asian Survey* XXXI, no. 9 (1991): 862–74.

———. 'India and Its Neighbours: Persisting Dilemma and New Opportunities'. *International Studies* 30, no. 2 (1993): 189.

Nair, Vijay K. 'The Nuclear Policy: The Regional Options'. *The Hindustan Times*, 20 December 1992.

Nayaar, Baldev Raj. 'Regional Power in a Multi Polar World'. In *India: A Rising Middle Power*, edited by John W. Mellor, 149. New Delhi: Select Service Syndicate, 1981.

New York Times. 'US to Sell High-Tech Equipment for Arms Upgrading Plan'. *New York Times*, 1 October 1986, p. A15.

Noorani, A. G. 'Indo-US Nuclear Relations'. *Asian Survey* 21, no. 4 (April 1981): 399–416.

Panda, A. 'What the Recently Concluded US-India COMCASA Means'. *The Diplomat*, 9 September 2018. https://thediplomat.com/2018/09/what-the-recently-concluded-us-india-comcasa-means/ (accessed on 1 October 2020).

Pande, Savita. 'Approach to Nuclear Issue'. *Strategic Analysis* XVI, no. 8 (1993): 1009–1022.

———. 'CTBT and NPT: A Study in Linkages'. *Strategic Analysis* XVII, no. 9 (1994): 1067–85.

———. 'CTBT and India'. *Strategic Analysis* XIX, no. 2 (1996): 157–81.

Pasricha, P. M. 'Military Balance Between India and Pakistan'. In *Studies in Indo-Pakistan Relations*, edited by V. D. Chopra and P. N. Haskar. New Delhi: Patriot Publishers, 1984.

PTI Report. 'Air Forces of the US and India to Hold Joint Exercise "Cope India 2019"'. *The Economic Times*, 29 November 2018. https://www.google.co.in/amp/s/m.economictimes.com/news/defence/air-forces-of-the-us-and-india-to-hold-joint-exercise-cope-india-2019/amp_articleshow/66868769.cms (accessed on 1 October 2020).

Raj, Ashok. 'US Hi-Tech Diplomacy and The Indian Super Computer Deal'. *Strategic Analysis* 12, no. 6 (1987): 735–57.

Raja, Mohan, C. 'Raja Mandala: India's China Reset and BRI'. *Indian Express*, 2018. https://www.google.com/amp/s/indianexpress.com/article/opinion/columns/india-china-foreign-policy-trade-relations-xi-jinping-narendra-modi-doklam-5130866/lite/ (accessed on 1 October 2020).

Ray, A. K. 'Time to Shed Diplomacy by Harangue'. *The Hindustan Times*, 12 February 1995.

Rehman, A., and Sunil Sondhi. 'United States India Co-operation in S&T'. In *Four Decades of Indo-U.S. Relations: A Commemorative Retrospective*, edited by A P Rana, 283–96. New Delhi: Har Anand Publications, 1994.

Rose, Leo E. 'India's Regional Policy: Non-Military Dimensions'. In *The Security of South-Asia: American and Indian Perspectives*, edited by Stephen P. Cohen. New Delhi: Vistaar Publishers, 1988.

Santhanam, K., and Jasjit Singh. 'Confidence Restoring Measures for Indo-US Commerce in Controlled Commodities'. In *Bridging the Non-Proliferation Divide: The United States and India*, edited by Francine R. Frankel, 319–33. New Delhi: Konark Publishers, 1995.

Sathe, Vasant. 'PM releases "India to be a Global Power"', 2008. https://archivepmo.nic.in/drmanmohansingh/speech-details.php?nodeid=636 (accessed on 1 October 2020).

Shah, Prakash. 'Nuclear Non-Proliferation Implications and the NPT Review: An Indian Perspective'. *Strategic Analysis* XVI, no. 2 (1993): 137–46.

Sharma, Ritu. 'India's Autonomy and American Foreign Assistance: Politics of Uneven Equation'. *Strategic Analysis* 14, no. 7 (1991): 825–38.

Shingal, H. N. 'Kashmir: Human Rights Trap'. *The Hindustan Times*, 25 April 1994.

Shrivastava, B. K. 'Prospects for Indo-US Relations'. In *Yearbook on India's Foreign Policy, 1990–91*, edited by Satish Kumar, 31–46. New Delhi: SAGE Publications, 1991.

Shrivastava, B. K. 'Indo-American Relations: Search for a New Equation'. *International Studies* 30, no. 2 (1993): 215–30.

Sibal, Kanwal. 'India: Seeking a Democratic and Non-Discriminatory, New World Order'. *Arms Control Today* (1993): 9–11.

Sidhu, Waheguru Pal Singh. 'Enhancing Indo-U.S. Strategic Cooperation'. *Adelphi Paper* 313, pp. 1–77. New York, NY: Oxford University Press, 1997.

Singh, Jasjit. 'Rocket Deal: After the Setback'. *The Hindustan Times*, 18 July 1993.

———. 'The Moscow Message'. *The Hindustan Times*, 23 January 1994.

———. 'Ballistic Missiles: Security Concerns'. *The Hindustan Times*, 25 August 1994.

Singh, K. Natwar. 'An Irritant: Clinton on Kashmir'. *The Hindustan Times*, 15 October 1993.

Singh, R. 'India Still Largest Arms Importer, Spent More than $100 B in Last 10 Years: SIPRI'. *The Hindustan Times*, 12 March 2018. https://www.google.co.in/amp/s/m.hindustantimes.com/india-news/india-still-largest-arms-importer-sipri/story-w7R3VCsWxuelz97N2OsOqI_amp.html (accessed on 1 October 2020).

Singh, Ravinder Pal. 'Effects of MTCR and Multilateral Politics of North South Technology Transfers'. *Strategic Analysis* (1992): 299–312.

Singh, Ravinder Pal. 'Politics of Technology Transfer and Industrial Development'. *Strategic Analysis* XVI, no. 5 (1993): 597–607.

Singh, S. Nihal. 'Can the US and India be Real Friends?' *Asian Survey* XXIII, no. I (1983): 1023.

Singh, S. K. 'Security Environment of Southern Asia'. *Strategic Analysis* XVII, no. 2 (May 1994): 175–85.

Sirohi, S. *Trump's Trade Mantra: Heads We Win, Tails You Lose*. Observer Research Foundation, 7 March 2019. https://www.orfonline.org/expert-speak/india-and-major-powers-united-states-of-america-54060/?amp (accessed on 1 October 2020).

Special Correspondent. 'India's Arms Imports from U.S. Up by 550%: Report'. *The Hindu*, 18 March 2018. https://www.google.com/amp/s/www.thehindu.com/news/national/indias-arms-imports-from-us-up-by-550-report/article23166097.ece/amp/ (accessed on 1 October 2020).

Sridharan, E. *Sino-India Relations Since 1949*. Research Gate, April 2017. https://www.researchgate.net/publication/316328574_Sino-India_Relations_since_1949 (accessed on 1 October 2020).

Subramaniam, R. R. 'Indo-US Security Relations During the Decade 1979–89'. *Strategic Analysis* XIV, no. 1 (1990): 163–72.

———. 'Indo-US Security Relations During the Decade 1979–89'. In *Four Decades of Indo-US Relations: A Commemorative Retrospective*, edited by A. P. Rana, 140–149. New Delhi, Har Anand Publications, 1995.

Subramaniam, R. R. 'South Asian Security: The China, Pakistan, India Tangle'. *Strategic Analysis* XII, no. 7 (1988): 735–44.

Subrahmanian, K. K. 'Technology Transfer: Critical Issues and Strategy Options-A Review of Indian Situation'. In *Technology Transfer by Multi National*, edited by H. W. Signer, 308. New Delhi: SAGE Publications, 1988.

Subrahmanyam, K. 'Our Nuclear Predicament'. *Strategic Analysis* IX, no. 7 (1985): 647–668.

————. 'India's Security Environment'. *World Focus* 10, nos. 11–12 (1990): 21–23.

————. 'Nuclear Policy Perspective'. *World Focus* 12, nos. 11–12 (1991): 21–23.

Thakur, Ramesh. 'India and the United States: A Triumph of Hope over Experience'. *Asian Survey* XXXVI, no. 6 (1996): 574–91.

Thomas, Raju G. C. 'Prospects for Indo-US Security Ties'. *Orbis* (Summer 1983): 386.

————. 'U.S. Transfer of Dual-use-technologies to India'. *Asian Survey* XXX, no. 9 (1990): 825–45.

————. 'Reflections on the Kashmir Problem'. In *Perspectives on Kashmir: The Roots of Conflict in South Asia*, edited by Raju G. C. Thomas. Boulder, CO: West View Press, 1992.

Thornton, Thomas P. 'The United States and South Asia'. *Survival* 35, no. 2 (1993): 122.

US Department of Defence. *Enhancing Defence and Security Cooperation with India—Joint Report to Congress*. Arlington, VA: US Department of Defence, 2017. https://dod.defense.gov/Portals/1/Documents/pubs/NDAA-India-Joint-Report-FY-July-2017.pdf.

Vajpayee, A. B. 'India's Foreign Policy Today'. In *India's Foreign Policy: Studies in Continuity and Change*, edited by Bimal Prasad. New Delhi: Vikas Publishing Ltd., 1979.

Vas, Eric A. 'Pakistan's Security Future'. In *The Security of South-Asia: American and Indian Perspectives*, edited by Stephen P. Cohen. New Delhi: Vistaar Publishers, 1988.

Vinod, M. J. 'Idealism and Self Interest in Conflict: The Nuclear Issue in the US India Relations'. *The Indian Journal of Political Science* 53, no. 2 (1992): 222–29.

————. 'India–United States Relations in a Changing World: Challenges and Opportunities'. *Strategic Analysis* XX, no. 3 (1997): 439–49.

Wirsing, Robert. 'The Arms Race in South-Asia: Implications for the United States'. and 'India's Nuclear Space Programmes'. *World Politics* 38 (1986): 315–42.

Wortzel, Larry M. 'U.S. Technology Transfer Policies and the Modernization of China's Armed Forces'. *Asian Survey* XXVII, no. 6 (1987): 617–18.

Yadava, Leela. 'India's Reaction to US Military Aid to Pakistan'. In *Studies in India's Foreign Policy*, edited by Surendra Chopra. Amritsar: Guru Nanak Dev University, 1983.

Zuberi, H., and S. Kalyanaramnan. 'Science and Technology for Development: India's Space Programme'. *Strategic Analysis* XII, no. 11 (1995): 1431–36.

Newspapers

International Herald Tribune (Bangkok).
The Deccan Herald (Bangalore).
The Economic Times (New Delhi).
The Financial Express (New Delhi).
The Hindu (Chennai & New Delhi).
The Hindustan Times (New Delhi).
The Indian Express (Bangalore).
The New York Times.
The Print (Online)
The Statesman (New Delhi).
The Telegraph (Calcutta).
The Times of India (New Delhi).
The Tribune (Chandigarh).
The Washington Post.
The Wire (Online).

ABOUT THE AUTHOR

Rajesh Kumar is Associate Professor of Political Science and Chairperson at the School of Social Sciences in Guru Nanak Dev University, Amritsar, India. Dr Kumar's teaching and research interests are in the areas of international relations, Indian foreign policy and security affairs. He has published many articles in journals such as *World Focus*, *Pakistan Horizon*, *South Asian Affairs* and *Journal of Punjab Politics*, and he has also published the book *Indo-US Politico-Strategic Relations* (2007). He completed his MA and MPhil in political science from Guru Nanak Dev University, Amritsar. In 2000, he completed his PhD at the School of International Studies, Jawaharlal Nehru University, New Delhi. He is also an alumnus of the Regional Centre for Strategic Studies (RCSS), Sri Lanka. He is a member of the Network of Asia Pacific Schools and Institutes of Public Administration and Governance (NAPSIPAG), Jawaharlal Nehru University.

INDEX